AF607849

VALIDITY

British Council Monographs on Modern Language Testing

Series Editors: Barry O'Sullivan and Karen Dunn, both at the British Council

Founding Co-editor: Vivien Berry, British Council

This series – published in cooperation with the British Council – provides short books in the area of language testing. These titles are written by well known language testing scholars from across the world including members of the British Council's Assessment Research Group (ARG). The books offer both a theoretical and a practical perspective to language testing and assessment – proposing, where required, models of development, which are reflected in actual test tasks. They are unique in that they are authored by individuals with considerable academic, teaching and assessment experience, thus offering the reader a unique insight into the link between theory and practice in the area. In many cases, the books illustrate their approach with reference to actual test items, from the British Council's Aptis test service.

Published:

Assessing the language of young learners
Angela Hasselgreen and Gwendydd Caudwell

Rethinking the second language listening test: From theory to practice
John Field

Forthcoming:

Assessing reading
Tineke Brunfaut and Jamie Dunlea

Assessing second language writing: Current and future perspectives
Anthony Green and Kevin Rutherford

Assessing speaking: Current and future perspectives
Fumiyo Nakatsuhara and Vivien Berry

Comprehensibility in language testing
Parvaneh Tavakoli and Sheryl Cooke

Knowledge-based vocabulary lists
Norbert Schmitt, Karen Dunn, Barry O'Sullivan, Laurence Anthony and Benjamin Kremmel

Scoring second language spoken and written performance: issues, options and directions
Ute Knoch, Judith Fairbairn and Yan Jin

VALIDITY

Theoretical Development and Integrated Arguments

Micheline Chalhoub-Deville and Barry O'Sullivan

SHEFFIELD UK BRISTOL CT

Published by Equinox Publishing Ltd.

UK: Office 415, The Workstation, 15 Paternoster Row, Sheffield, South Yorkshire, S1 2BX
USA: ISD, 70 Enterprise Drive, Bristol, CT 06010

www.equinoxpub.com

First published 2020

British Library Cataloguing-in-Publication Data
A catalogue record for this book is available from the British Library.

ISBN-13 978 1 78179 989 5 (hardback)
978 1 78179 990 1 (paperback)
978 1 78179 991 8 (ePDF)

Library of Congress Cataloging-in-Publication Data
Names: Chalhoub-Deville, Micheline, author. | O'Sullivan, Barry, author.
Title: Validity : theoretical development and integrated arguments / Micheline Chalhoub-Deville, University of North Carolina at Greensboro, US, and Barry O'Sullivan, British Council, UK.
Description: Bristol : Equinox Publishing Ltd, 2020. | Series: British Council Monographs on Modern Language Testing | Includes bibliographical references and index. | Summary: "This monograph provides a historical overview of validity, targeting developments in both the UK and the US. It explores theoretical notions of validity as well as pragmatic validation practices and expands the arguments that need to be attended to document quality"-- Provided by publisher.
Identifiers: LCCN 2020003738 (print) | LCCN 2020003739 (ebook) | ISBN 9781781799895 (Hardback) | ISBN 9781781799901 (Paperback) | ISBN 9781781799918 (eBook)
Subjects: LCSH: Examinations--Validity.
Classification: LCC LB3060.7 .C42 2020 (print) | LCC LB3060.7 (ebook) | DDC 371.26--dc23
LC record available at https://lccn.loc.gov/2020003738
LC ebook record available at https://lccn.loc.gov/2020003739

Typeset by S.J.I. Services, New Delhi, India

DEDICATION

To Cyril Weir who had encouraged this project and had planned to serve as a reviewer.

ACKNOWLEDGEMENTS

Many thanks to Cathy Elder and Mike Kane for reviewing an earlier draft of this manuscript. Their insights and probing questions enriched the arguments. We are also grateful to Vivien Berry, Series Founding Co-Editor, whose critical editing helped unify voices (and spellings) and who offered suggestions for improvement. Finally, we would like to thank the editors at Equinox Publishing for copyediting. Any inaccuracies and/or errors that remain are, of course, the authors' responsibility.

We also would like to acknowledge the scholars whose work we built on in developing the ideas that drive this book. We trust the book will be of value to the field at large.

We are grateful to colleagues and students with whom we have interacted on issues of validity over the years. We have learned immensely from you all.

CONTENTS

LIST OF FIGURES

LIST OF TABLES

CHAPTER 1

INTRODUCTION

It is generally accepted by the global assessment community that validity plays a critical role in measurement practices, including language testing and assessment. Evidence for this eminence can be found in the central role occupied by validity chapters in major professional publications, e.g., the various editions of *Educational measurement* (Cureton, 1951; Cronbach, 1971; Messick, 1989; Kane, 2006) and the *Standards for educational and psychological testing* published by three major US organisations: American Educational Research Association (AERA), American Psychological Association (APA) and National Council on Measurement in Education (NCME) (APA, 1952, 1954; AERA & National Council on Measurement Used in Education, 1955; APA, AERA & NCME, 1966, 1974; AERA, APA & NCME, 1985, 1999, 2014). In foundational textbooks on language testing, validity also is prominently addressed, e.g., Alderson, Clapham & Wall (1995), Bachman (1990) and Weir (2005). Despite the central role validity plays in our thinking and practices, the conceptualisation of validity is far from established in the published literature (Newton & Shaw, 2014). The issues that have continued to be debated are of great importance to testing systems and warrant the present monograph.

Despite the historically established standing of validity in measurement at large, its theoretical scope as well as the practical role it plays in documenting quality of practices remain controversial. Embretson (2007: 449) states that '[v]alidity is a controversial concept in educational and psychological testing….' She adds that of the various types of validity evidence, construct validity is the 'most problematic' (Embretson, 2008). She speculates that the difficulties around construct validity could be 'because it involves theory and the relationship of data to theory' (Embretson, 2007: 9). This issue certainly resonates with language testing professionals who have long debated the attributes of the language construct that we measure and the lack of a coherent or strong theory of the language testing construct (Chapelle, Enright & Jamieson, 2010). This lack of a strong theory in language testing or in the broader social science, however, has not deterred researchers from positing construct validity as the anchor for all validity.

While construct validity is generally recognised as problematic, this 'most controversial type of validity became the sole type of validity in the revised *Standards*' (Embretson, 2007: 9). Following Messick's (1989) lead, the *Standards* (AERA, APA & NCME, 1999, 2014) have accorded construct validity a preeminent role. The *Standards* regard content, criterion, etc. as types of validity evidence, i.e., they are subsumed under construct validity. Such a portrayal has long been advocated by researchers such as Loevinger (1957). How validity is defined, Newton (2013) argues, is important because that dictates areas included/excluded in the validation plan, weight accorded to evidence type, approaches favoured for different purposes, among others. Given the state of affairs in validity and the continued contention about its delineation, it is appropriate and timely to articulate prevailing theories and engage in the current discussions.

Book background and audience

The idea for the present book emerged out of conversations we, the two authors, have had over the years while interacting at conferences and other professional meetings. Our conversations have shown us that our differences with regard to how we view validity and approach-related documentation is not simply a matter of personal opinion but comes from the traditions we have explicitly and implicitly embraced. Given our educational backgrounds and professional experiences, we are steeped in different traditions in terms of the scholarship of validity: the USA versus the UK. Chalhoub-Deville has received her higher education degrees and has worked as a faculty member in the USA. O'Sullivan has received his higher degrees and has been largely directing assessment operations in the UK. We have come to appreciate that the scholarship of validity as it has developed in the USA and in the UK has emphasised the importance of quality documentation for different activities/aspects of testing. For example, the UK validity tradition, on the one hand, has generally favoured test development and connections to the curriculum; the US validity tradition, on the other hand, has preferred technical, psychometric approaches to validity. These differences have been discussed by Spolsky (1995). While the USA and the UK traditions have continued to evolve, the divergent traditions remain entrenched. It is for this reason that we sought to collaborate on this book project. The journey to publish this book took several years. It was not easy for us to agree, given our perspectives, but ultimately, we are enriched by the experience. We trust that you will find the outcome of some use.

We are not aware of another book that provides comparative analysis of validity theory and or operations as they have taken place in the UK and the USA. Even the Spolsky (1995) volume dedicates only a small section to the topic. We therefore feel that this book will be of interest to a number of different audiences. While the most obvious of these will be language testing professionals on both sides of the Atlantic, we also hope that the book will be of value to test development boards, test publishers, technical advisory boards and related professionals in both the UK and USA. We also hope that it can initiate a discussion between language testing colleagues and educational measurement professionals around the world. In addition, educational measurement professionals theorising on validity might find the discussions included in this book to be of relevance to their thinking as they advance the knowledge base in the area, though we accept that this may be too ambitious an expectation. Finally, the committees responsible for the next edition of the *Standards* might find the comparative analysis and thoughts from the related discipline of language testing to be of use to their deliberations. We feel that those teaching courses on validity may assign sections of the book to their graduate students. In general, graduate students in the areas of educational measurement and language testing should also find the book to be of use to their professional development, contributing to their knowledge of the different perspectives that drive the understandings of validity that are explicated here.

An overview of the book

This monograph provides a historical overview of validity. It targets developments in both the United Kingdom (UK) and the United States of America (US). The monograph explores theoretical notions of validity as well as pragmatic validation practices, which necessitates expanding the arguments that need to be attended to in order to support claims of test quality. We need to consider, in addition to the psychometric evidence, which has continued to prevail especially in the US, other critical sources of quality evidence. We call attention to principled design and the evidence accumulated from various departments/groups involved in test design and development. We also promote the concept of impact by design, which places consequences at the top of the evidence chain to guide all testing efforts and quality documentation. We envision validity scholarship to attend to consequences at the individual, aggregate/group, and larger educational/organisational/societal levels. Concomitant with this attention to consequences are considerations of stakeholders and the tailoring of communication to engage intended groups. Such an approach yields a more convincing validity argument. The monograph ends by calling on professionals in the field to publish case studies which showcase localised validity arguments in practice. Local case studies represent critical endeavours to illustrate how evidence and arguments are pulled together to support the quality of a testing programme and all that it entails.

The monograph is organised in terms of the following six chapters:

CHAPTER 1 INTRODUCTION

We focus here on the background of validity as an area of scholarly activities. We also describe commonly referenced terms and ideas used with regard to validity.

CHAPTER 2 HISTORICAL OVERVIEW OF VALIDITY

In this chapter we provide a contrastive historical account of the validity and testing scholarship on each side of the Atlantic divide. The account highlights the divergent UK and USA perspectives and shows how the two traditions have continued to evolve.

CHAPTER 3 PRINCIPLED DESIGN, TEST DEVELOPMENT AND VALIDATION

We discuss in this chapter key models of validity that have been influential in shaping thinking and language testing operations. The analysis of these models takes into account their views on consequences and their role in validity research.

CHAPTER 4 VALIDITY AND CONSEQUENCES

In this chapter we urge researchers to consider broad – more than technical, e.g., differential test and item analysis – aspects of consequences in validity models. Given the limited state-of-knowledge in the field with regard to consequences, the undertaking, we contend, is massive. We present areas and issues to consider as researchers build their research programmes.

CHAPTER 5 AN INTEGRATED ARGUMENT-BASED APPROACH TO VALIDATION

We affirm in this chapter that the traditions represented in the USA and the UK are both critical to validity conceptualisation. We argue that these test development and measurement arguments, however, are not sufficient. Validity documentation should also consider arguments related to consequences and stakeholder engagement.

CHAPTER 6 CONCLUSION: VALIDATION, LOCALISATION AND CASE STUDIES

In this chapter we review the validity models that have guided the field and are discussed in the present book. We also build on expositions, e.g., validation in the context of higher-education admission testing and in reform-based educational accountability testing contexts, delineated in previous chapters to push for localised validity research that embraces an integration of the test development, the measurement, the theory of action and the communication engagement arguments.

The notion of validity

The scholarship on validity in the early part of its history was concerned with delineating types of validity along the lines of what appears above. Over time and in the US, two publications – the *Standards* and *Educational measurement* – have provided with their various editions a steady source of guidance on what validity theory and practice entail. These sources are routinely updated, every ten to twenty years. Chalhoub-Deville (2015 online and 2016: 5 in print) writes:

> An argument could be made that forward thinking validity conceptualizations are presented in the Educational Measurement editions. The chapters (as they have appeared in the various editions: Cureton, 1951; Cronbach, 1971; Messick, 1989; Kane, 2006) have been influential in advancing ideas that consider the educational and psychological knowledge base, psychometric developments, policy considerations, social values, and assessment practices. A more consensus-based approach to validity is embodied in the Standards for Educational and Psychological Testing (AERA, APA, and NCME, 1999). (Various editions of such guiding Standards have been published – 1954/1955, 1966, 1974, 1985, and 1999 [and 2014].) The Standards are published after extensive deliberations and a widely-sought vetting process.

> The Standards are endorsed by a variety of organizations, universities, and associations, including the International Language Testing Association. In short, Educational Measurement editions and the Standards are central to where thinking is in the professions at large, and the two sources, until recently, have grounded validity theory and practice in constructs and test scores.

By relying on the *Standards*, *Educational measurement* and other publications as sources of information, we offer a historical overview of how the concept of validity has evolved.

Basically, the first part of the 20th century witnessed a shift from '[a] test is valid for anything with which it correlates' (Guilford, 1946: 429) to a more encompassing representation that considers content and construct. The APA (1954) document, *Technical recommendations for psychological tests and diagnostic techniques* made official a validity definition that included content, predictive, concurrent and construct validity. In subsequent editions, the *Standards* represented predictive and concurrent as one category, which was labelled criterion validity. The three categories of validity: content, criterion and construct have been referred to as the holy trinity of validity and were intended to be made use of depending on the nature/purpose of the assessment. During this historical period, researchers and practitioners tended to align with a menu-style approach, which continues to be favoured by some today. For example, Lissitz & Samuelsen (2007a) argue for the demise of construct validity and the primacy of content validity.

More traditional sources of validity evidence have included content, criterion and construct. Table 1 includes definitional quotes that elaborate how the terms have generally been viewed, while Table 2 focuses on methodologies typically associated with these sources of evidence.

Increasingly, researchers working in the area of validity propose larger model structures, which encompass the types included in Tables 1 and 2, but that offer a coherent conceptual and practical structure, whether it is an evaluative judgement (Messick, 1989), a universal system (Embretson, 2008, 2009), an integrated argument (Kane, 2006), a socio-cognitive approach (Weir, 2005) or a justification system (Bachman & Palmer, 2010), among others. Before we delve into these works, we offer statements that represent elements of broad consensus and controversy.

Content	Criterion	Construct
'**content validity** A term used in the 1974 *Standards* to refer to a kind or aspect of validity that was "required when the test user wishes to estimate how an individual performs in the universe of situations the test is intended to represent" (p. 28). In the 1985 *Standards*, the term was changed to content-related evidence emphasising that it referred to one type of evidence within a unitary conception of validity. In the current *Standards*, this type of evidence is characterised as "evidence based on test content"' (AERA, APA & NCME, 1999: 174). 'content-related validity evidence: Evidence based on test content that supports the intended interpretation of test scores for a given purpose. Such evidence may address issues such as fidelity of test content to performance in the domain in question and the degree to which test content representatively samples a domain, such as a course curriculum or job' (AERA, APA & NCME, 2014: 218).	'**criterion validity** (or criterion-related validity) measures how well one measure predicts an outcome for another measure. A test has this type of validity if it is useful for predicting performance or behavior in another situation (past, present, or future). For example: A job applicant takes a performance test during the interview process. If this test accurately predicts how well the employee will perform on the job, the test is said to have criterion validity. A graduate student takes the GRE. The GRE has been shown as an effective tool (i.e., it has criterion validity) for predicting how well a student will perform in graduate studies.' http://www.statisticshowto.com/criterion-validity/ Concurrent: '…indicates the extent to which the test scores estimate an individual's present standing on the criterion' (Messick, 1989: 16). Predictive: '…indicates the extent to which an individual's future level on the criterion is predicted from prior test performance' (Messick, 1989: 16).	'**construct validity** A term used to indicate that the test scores are to be interpreted as indicating the test taker's standing on the psychological construct measured by the test. A construct is a theoretical variable inferred from multiple types of evidence, which might include the interrelations of the test scores with others variables, internal test structure, observations of response processes, as well as the content of the test. In the current standards, all test scores are viewed as measures of some construct, so the phrase is redundant with validity. The validity argument establishes the construct validity of a test' (AERA, APA & NCME, 1999: 174).

Table 1: Definitions of content, criterion and construct validity

Content	Criterion	Construct
'... is evaluated by showing how well the content of the test samples the class of situations or subject matter about which conclusions are drawn' (Messick, 1989: 16). Evidence collected includes: • Professional judgement • Analyses to document relevance to and representativeness of targeted domain • Think aloud protocols	'... is evaluated by comparing the test scores with one or more external variables considered to provide a direct measure of the characteristic or behavior in question' (Messick, 1989: 16). Concurrent: '... indicates the extent to which the test scores estimate an individual's present standing on the criterion' (Messick, 1989: 16). Predictive: '... indicates the extent to which an individual's future level on the criterion is predicted from prior test performance' (Messick, 1989: 16). Evidence collected includes: • Correlation and regression analyses • Standard setting and decision accuracy • Utility costs	'... is evaluated by investigating what qualities a test measures, that is the degree to which certain explanatory concepts or constructs account for performance on the test' (Messick, 1989: 16). Evidence collected includes: • Evaluation of theoretical structures underlying score interpretation and use • Factor analytic approaches • Clarity, coherence and completeness of interpretive strands

Table 2: Methodologies associated with content, criterion and construct validity

It is generally, though not universally, agreed upon that the broad features of validity include statements such as:

- Validity refers to the inferences drawn, not the instrument, though there have been some dissenting voices (see for example Borsboom, Mellenbergh & Van Heerden, 2004) who argue for a return to the acceptance that a test can be valid while rejecting the concept of validity in terms of test scores. While Borsboom et al. make some very sensible points around the importance of being able to demonstrate that a test functions as planned, their arguments essentially imply that the test is test-taker agnostic, and as such they are very much at odds with current thinking, in particular the socio-cognitive approach, see O'Sullivan & Weir (2002, 2011), Weir (2005) and O'Sullivan (2011, 2016).

- Validity is a unitary concept.
- Validity pertains to the interpretations and uses of scores.
- Validity is not an all-or-nothing but expressed in terms of degrees.
- Validity is specific to a particular purpose(s)/use(s).
- Validity research is an ongoing process.
- Validity offers a coherent plan of documentation.
- Validity depends on many different types of evidence.
- Validation involves professional judgement.

The features listed above are not intended to be exhaustive but meant to highlight some key elements, which have generally been prevalent in the measurement field and the language testing community. The present monograph will deal with these issues and point out where recent thinking is; how certain statements continue to be held, e.g., validity refers to inferences and not the instrument, whereas others are shifting, e.g., validity is a unitary concept or validation is ongoing. Some areas have historically been contested and remain hotly debated. The present monograph will delve into these controversial issues, which include:

- Validity is anchored in construct representation.
- Validity incorporates consequential evidence.

We make an argument that, moving forward, validity research cannot afford to continue to marginalise if not ignore the social aspects of a testing programme. Additionally, we make the case that language testing professionals cannot afford not to pay attention to constructs. These matters and related scholarship are explored in the various sections of the monograph. We begin by delineating the orientation of the two major testing cultures in the language testing field, i.e., the UK and US approaches to language testing and validity.

Validity in language testing: The UK and the US

It has been clear for some time that there emerged in the early years of the 20th century a clear divide in the approaches to language testing and validity that came to dominate the two major players in the field, namely the UK and the US. We can trace the beginning of the divide to a specific year, 1913. In that year, the committee of the Modern Language Association of Maryland decided to abandon the practice of the large-scale testing of spoken language due to the practical and logistical issues involved. This decision was taken despite the organisation's recognition of the importance of speaking as the primary focus of language development.

This decision should be viewed in light of a number of significant advances at around the same time period, such as:

- Pearson's chi-square test (1900) and Student's t-test (1908) in the UK,
- Tests of intelligence, such as that of Binet-Simon in France (1905),
- The creation, in the US, of the multiple-choice item, accredited to Kelly (1916) in his Kansas test of silent reading, and
- The development of standardised tests, again in the US, e.g., Hillegas' composition scale (1912) and the Courtis test battery (1914), which was to sell over 13 million tests in the first decade after its launch in 1914 (Johanningmeier & Richardson, 2008: 235) – all based on the pioneering work of Thorndike at Columbia University, New York.

It was the combination of all of these events, when coupled with the increasing demand for large-scale testing in the US, particularly in light of the war effort, that set the scene for the birth of the modern testing industry on that side of the Atlantic.

Meanwhile, in the UK, the University of Cambridge Local Examination Syndicate (UCLES – now Cambridge Assessment English but for the sake of brevity, in the remainder of this volume we will refer to the organisation in its various forms as simply Cambridge) launched their first English language proficiency examination in that same year (1913), the Cambridge Proficiency Examination (CPE). Unlike the tests that were emerging in the US at the time, this test took as its basis the language-for-communication model which formed the basis of the work of Sweet (1899) and placed emphasis on language production. In the chapter that follows, we will revisit the CPE as a starting point in understanding how the concept of validity was operationalised in UK examinations from this period.

While the CPE marks a clear starting point in the approach taken by UK-based test developers, in particular Cambridge, it is clear from the report of a government committee on the state of modern language testing in the UK (Committee GB, 1918) that much work was needed in the emerging field of language testing, particularly with regard to how, if at all, speaking was assessed. It seemed clear to this group that not enough was being done to ensure that tests reflected the reality of the classroom, where spoken communication was recognised as the main focus of language learning (see Weir, 2013: 260). Nevertheless, the report of the Committee GB highlights the feeling among UK education policymakers that despite the inherent difficulties, language tests should include a significant focus on production.

On reflection, it is interesting to note that the psychometric-oriented measurement approach, initiated in the UK, was essentially abandoned there in favour of the consideration of how the underlying trait, construct or ability as recognised in learning theories was reflected in the test. This was to remain the essential basis for almost all UK-inspired tests until today. Meanwhile, the emergence of the testing industry in the US saw the ascendancy of the measurement (or psychometric) approach, which continues to dominate the field in the US.

The outcome of these different reactions to a dilemma recognised on both sides of the Atlantic (how to assess productive language on a large scale) was to shape language test conceptualisation, development and validation for a century. In the following chapter we will explore how the two solutions led to two very different philosophical approaches to language testing and validity, dubbed 'the Atlantic divide' by O'Sullivan (2006).

In summary, this introduction has outlined the organisation for the book and introduced key terminology and concepts commonly observed in language testing and the measurement field. Chapter 2 provides a historical account of validity conceptualisation. This includes a discussion of some central models that have been published to guide validity research. Our discussion attempts to clarify the perspectives as they have existed in two geographic areas: the UK and the US. The perspectives discussed are quite divergent, having evolved in response to two very different learning and testing contexts. Chapter 3 moves to consider models and authors on both sides of the Atlantic who have explored validity in terms of test design and development. The chapter shows how ideas historically promoted in the UK are emerging as part of formal validity concepts in the US. Chapter 4 moves beyond the more technical, psychometric definition of consequences to accommodate a socially-grounded approach to validity. We propose an approach that considers consequences at the individual, group and societal/educational/larger structure levels, and targets stakeholders. Chapter 5 bridges the UK-US divide by integrating historical UK and US perspectives. The chapter details validity as an integration of four arguments that speak to various aspects of a large-scale testing programme operation. Chapter 6 concludes the book by calling attention to the importance of localisation in test validation and the need for case studies to illustrate practical endeavours to document quality evidence.

CHAPTER 2

HISTORICAL OVERVIEW OF VALIDITY

The UK approach

The scientific approach to measurement was first posited by Sir Francis Galton (see for example Galton 1879). Together with his associates (who included the eminent statistician Karl Pearson and the educational psychologist Cyril Burt) Galton set about creating the modern discipline of psychometrics. It is interesting to note that many of the statistical processes that came to define psychometrics emerged from this small group of academics, working mainly at the University of Cambridge in the UK and where the *Psychometric Laboratory*, the world's first, was set up in 1887. One exception is William Sealy Gosset, a graduate of the University of Oxford and friend (and occasional colleague) of Pearson. It was while working as a chemist at the Guinness brewery in Dublin that he published his original thesis on the t-statistic – he was forced to use the pseudonym *Student* as employees of the company were not allowed to publish. Student's t-statistic was originally intended to inform the quality assurance system of Guinness stout, but was to play an important part in the emerging psychometrics field, influencing, amongst others, R. A. Fisher (another Cambridge graduate). See Pearson's excellent 1939 article devoted to Gosset for a fuller discussion of his contribution to the field.

At approximately the same time as many of these events, F. Y. Edgeworth (1888, 1890) was beginning to explore the concept of reliability in terms of how student essay and examination writing was marked at the University of Cambridge. In this early work on marker reliability, Edgeworth demonstrated mathematically the extent of the difficulties inherent in human scoring.

The work of these individuals continues to play a significant role in both the research undertaken in SLA and Applied Linguistics, and in the whole approach to language (and other) testing across the world. However, it is even more interesting to understand that at this point in the history of language testing in the UK, all of this pioneering work was put to one side. The focus, instead, was to be on connecting language learning to language testing.

Cambridge and the link to learning

In 1913, Cambridge launched the Certificate of Proficiency in English (CPE). As Weir, Vidakovic & Galaczi (2013) have discussed in considerable detail, this test was explicitly located within the broad context of language learning, taking as its theoretical basis the work of Sweet (1899).

Henry Sweet (1845–1912) was an English phonetician and language scholar who was active in the latter part of the 19th century and the early years of the 20th century. Originally a specialist in German language, Sweet went on to write a number of particularly influential books on the teaching and learning of English. The most important of these was *The practical study of languages* (1899), a book he had worked on for over twenty years (Sweet, 1899: xiii) which outlined what he called his rationally progressive method. The approach to language learning he proposed is described in the book as follows:

> A good method must, before all, be comprehensive and eclectic. It must be based on a thorough knowledge of the science of language – phonetics, sound-notation, the grammatical structure of a variety of representative languages, and linguistic problems generally. In utilizing this knowledge it must be constantly guided by the psychological laws on which memory and the association of ideas depend (Sweet, 1899: 3).

He goes on to state that:

> The main axiom of living philology is that all study of language must be based on phonetics.
>
> Phonetics is the science of speech-sounds, or, from a practical point of view, the art of pronunciation. Phonetics is to the science of language generally what mathematics is to astronomy and the physical sciences. Without it, we can neither observe nor record the simplest phenomena of language. It is equally necessary in the theoretical and in the practical study of languages (1899: 4).

In addition, Sweet believed that:

> The second main axiom of living philology is that all study of language, whether theoretical or practical, ought to be based on the spoken language (1899: 50).

Howatt & Widdowson (1984: 202) describe Sweet's Practical Study as containing:

> a superbly sustained and coolly logical exploration of methodological principles and practices covering the five major areas of practical language learning: grammar, vocabulary, the study of texts, translation, and conversation. It is unsurpassed in the literature of linguistic pedagogy.

The focus on language production as the primary basis of language learning set Sweet aside as perhaps the most influential thinker on the topic of his day. His systematic analysis of the language saw him recognised as the founding father of applied linguistics and inspired the approach to assessment of language championed by the University of Cambridge. The five major areas identified by Howatt & Widdowson featured as the core elements of Cambridge's *Certificate of Proficiency in English* (CPE), which was launched in 1913 and was to go on to dominate thinking at Cambridge for over a century (Weir, 2003; Weir et al., 2013).

While theorists and practitioners in the US were engaged in building an increasingly abstract understanding of validity, typically from a psychometric perspective, little if any activity of a similar ilk was emerging in the UK. While we can infer, as Weir et al. (2013) have done, the underlying theory which supported the tests developed at Cambridge (with the active support of the British Council from 1941), no significant academic discipline around the area of language testing was to emerge until the mid 1970s.

Though there was no attempt by Cambridge in 1913 to consider the concept of the validity of the new CPE, it is clear that the organisation had understood the need to underpin the test with a plainly stated operational model of language ability. The validity of the test was presumed, we can only assume, at the time of its development to be supported by this explicit connection to Sweet's language-learning approach. That such a connection was recognised in the US as being necessary was confirmed from the US perspective by Prokosch (1922: 182) who pointed to the disjunction between the adoption of the Direct Approach in schools and

Stage	Period	Significant events	Impact on UK examinations
1. The beginning of theory	1870–1913	Direct Method – Berlitz Schools (1878) Reform Movement – Viëtor (1882); Passy (1899); Sweet (1899); Jespersen (1904)	CPE (1913) Hybrid – elements of Grammar Translation and Direct Method
2. Oral-Structural-Situational approaches	1921–c 1970	Oral Method – Palmer (1921) Structural Approach – Bloomfield (1926, 1933); Fries (1945) Situational Approach – Pittman (1963)	Lower Certificate (1939) Hybrid – elements of Direct Method and Structuralism [no translation]
3. Communicative approaches	c 1971–2000	Threshold Level – Van Ek (1975) Notional Syllabuses – Wilkins (1976) English for Specific Purposes – Munby (1978)	First Certificate in English (1975) Hybrid – elements of Direct Method, Structural Approach and Structuralism; reading and listening papers (also in CPE); speaking and writing papers include 'real' situations English Language Testing Service (1980) Hybrid – elements of Direct Method, ESP [discipline-focused papers] Test in English for Academic Purposes (1983; and 1999 as TEEP) Integrated Skills Later Cambridge Exams (PET, KET) – similar design
4. Socio-cognitive approaches	2000s	Initial call for a Socio-cognitive approach (O'Sullivan, 2000a) Weir (2005) seminal book O'Sullivan (2011, 2014, 2016) underlying theoretical model outlined	Retro-fitting of Cambridge Exams British Council ILA and Aptis tests China Standards of English

Table 3: Summary of significant influences on UK test development (based on Weir et al., 2013: 13–14)

colleges as compared to the continued reliance by the colleges on testing systems that were based on grammar-translation.

Weir et al. (2013) present an interesting overview of the degree to which Cambridge looked to the language classroom for inspiration when developing new examinations and when revising existing examinations. In Table 3 we have briefly summarised some of the main events that led to the development of the CPE and of the century that followed. In addition to the impact on Cambridge tests, we have included some additional examinations, such as the English Language Testing Service (ELTS – developed by the British Council) and the Test in English for Academic Purposes (TEAP – developed by Weir for the Associated Examining Board (AEB) and later revised by O'Sullivan under the new title *Test of English for Educational Purposes* at the University of Reading in 1999) as these were based on significant research into the language needs of prospective UK-bound students – see the account of the development of TEAP by Weir (1983) and for IELTS by Davies (2008) and Weir & O'Sullivan (2017). This table does not contain an exhaustive list of all UK tests developed in this period. In general, tests have not been included as their developers failed to adequately document their development and/or administration. The decision not to include tests reflects the findings of Alderson, Clapham & Wall (1995) who surveyed the major boards at that time and found either poor or no evidence of what had by then become accepted as appropriate professional practice.

Despite the fact that Weir et al. (2013) were able to construct a reasonable argument to support the inferring of an underlying construct for the Cambridge suite of examinations, it remains problematic that, at the time of the development of the tests, there does not appear to have been a clearly stated definition by the majority of the exam boards in the UK of an underlying validity model. The Cambridge approach over the years has been to look to the area of language teaching and learning and to ensure that there was always a clear link between the approach taken in their tests and the approaches current in the contemporary classroom. Weir et al. (2013: 424) see this approach as representing 'a strong commitment to the test task as the vehicle for measuring the underlying construct…' which they argue is 'a traditional strength of the British assessment system'. The traditional UK approach can therefore be best described as focusing on construct and content (i.e., the degree to which the underlying construct is represented in the test) rather than on how any resulting performance was evaluated – indeed, in their 2013 volume devoted to the history of the Cambridge approach, Weir et al. at no time refer to how test taker performance was assessed. We can surmise from the development by the British Council of a rudimentary rating scale (or rubric) in 1953 and its roll-out a year later that no such systematic approach to assessment was expected by Cambridge in their early examinations (see Weir & O'Sullivan, 2017).

In his internal Cambridge report of 1945, Roach discusses in considerable detail the issues around the standardisation of the delivery of oral examinations across a number of countries. His awareness of the likely threats to the reliability of such tests is remarkable in that they were written ten years before the Foreign Services Institute (FSI) tests and thirty years before mainstream language testing began to wrestle with the issues – indeed, the many theoretical and practical concerns expressed in his work are as relevant today as they were then. Examples of this include the conceptual problems around using reading aloud and dictation tasks as indicators of speaking ability – something which he roundly rejects, but something that is not uncommon in modern tests of speaking (pp. 39–40); the use of 'gramophone' recordings to standardise both within and across examiners – this is now regarded as essential practice but it was originally recommended by the British Council to the Joint Committee in 1942 (Weir & O'Sullivan, 2017); the use of double marking (p. 41); examiner training and accreditation; and the suggestion that '[D]efinition is needed of what the examiner should chiefly listen for…' (p. 42). These are just some of the issues touched upon in this far-reaching paper, which was reproduced as Appendix C in Weir et al. (2013).

It would appear that the UK approach to test development was, from an early stage, at least in the case of Cambridge and a small number of other tests, concerned with what we now see as the essential elements of validation – construct, content and, to a lesser extent, scoring. While the US tradition was to engage in a more formal theorising of validity and later validation, based on a primarily psycho-linguistic approach to the definition of language ability, little concern was demonstrated either in the UK language assessment literature or in language assessment practice with such theories, probably due to the more socio-linguistic oriented approach to language ability definition prevalent there. This is not to say that British scholars in the area of language testing were not working on validity-related ideas, or that they presented a unified approach to thinking in the area. In the 1960s, Alan Davies (1965) developed a very USA-inspired English Proficiency Test Battery (EPTB) for the British

Council. The EPTB was a multiple-choice based test of the receptive skills that was used by the British Council as a gatekeeping tool for individuals planning to enter the UK to study. It was eventually replaced (in 1979) by the more communicative-oriented English Language Testing Service (ELTS), developed in-house by Brendan Carrol and his team at the British Council (Weir & O'Sullivan, 2017). This was itself heavily criticised in the validation report carried out by Davies and his colleague Clive Criper (1988) and replaced with the International English Language Testing System (IELTS) in 1990. Davies was not a supporter of the communicative or specific-purpose testing movements (see, e.g., Davies, 1990); he represents a distinctive and consistent voice of dissention in the UK. Alderson's early work on English for Specific Purposes (ESP) testing (Alderson & Urquhart, 1985; Alderson, 1988, 2000a) and his highlighting of the washback effect that language tests have on teaching and learning (Wall & Alderson, 1993; Alderson & Hamp-Lyons, 1996) have contributed considerably to our knowledge and understanding of these areas. Similar arguments can be made for the work of people such as Clapham (e.g., 1996) and Hamp-Lyons, who in addition to her work with Alderson on washback, contributed immensely to our understanding of specific purpose testing (e.g., Hamp-Lyons, 1987) and second language writing (e.g., Hamp-Lyons & Mathias, 1984; Hamp-Lyons & Henning, 1991). In addition, Skehan's information-processing approach (e.g., Skehan, 1998, 2009; Skehan & Foster, 1997, 1999) has considerably enhanced our understanding of the complexities of task-based performance. While these scholars may not have written specifically on the theory of validity, their work has contributed significantly to our current understanding of the concept, particularly in the UK. The most obvious impact of this work has been on the conceptualisation of the socio-cognitive approach, which we turn to in the sub-section that follows.

The domination of assessment in the US by the measurement movement, which, as we saw above, had its birth in the UK, was at no time reflected in the UK – though the publication of Bachman et al.'s TOEFL/FCE comparability study in 1995 clearly had an impact on those managing the Cambridge suite of examinations. From that time, Cambridge focused much more on reliability estimates without really fully understanding the assumptions of the prevalent indices, or recognising their shortcomings in relation to breadth of construct definition or representation.

The first coherent and meaningful perspective on the test development process to be published in the UK can be found in the work of Weir

(1988; 1993; 2005). His earlier theoretical and practical contribution to the development of TEAP (1983) was to lay the foundations for current thinking on the theory and practice of test development in the UK and beyond.

Weir and the socio-cognitive approach

By the mid 1970s the British Council had begun to develop the English Language Testing Service (ELTS) development project. The project, led by Brendan Carroll, was supported by research into the language needs of overseas students in the UK, an early example of the process of needs analysis, which had emerged alongside the area of English for Specific Purposes (ESP) a few years earlier; see West (1994) for a historical overview of the origins and applications of needs analysis. The work in the area of communicative language learning of another British Council officer, John Munby, had influenced the ELTS development work in identifying and itemising the language needs of prospective students. Munby went on to publish his work in 1978, and it was this publication that was to influence the thinking of Cyril Weir in his complex and wide-reaching research which supported the development of the Test in English for Academic Purposes (TEAP), completed in 1983. Weir's work in the area of communicative language testing (Weir, 1990) marked the beginning of a new era of professionalism in the UK. Even in this early work, Weir was to begin the process of identifying criterial features of test task design that would later inform his ground-breaking work in the area of test validation.

In this early work, Weir (1990, 1993) focused on identifying the key performance parameters that guide test task design, referring to them at the time as *conditions*. He also considered, and it was here that the influence of Munby was most obvious, the language both of task input and expected output, which he referred to as *operations*. This approach to construct definition was, in many ways, typical of the UK tradition of test development, the understanding being that the *operations* reflected the underlying language to be elicited and assessed in the test task. By the end of the 1990s, Weir had begun to consider the cognitive aspects of language production in his work, and by 2002 was beginning to put together a set of frameworks for language validation in which he was to attempt to integrate both socio and cognitive elements into an essentially Messickian framework. O'Sullivan (2000a) had argued that such an approach was required for language test development, but it was

Weir (2005) who first formalised what has come to be called the *socio-cognitive approach* to test development and validation.

The original versions of the framework were outlined by O'Sullivan & Weir in an internal mimeo produced at the University of Surrey, Roehampton (O'Sullivan & Weir, 2002). The speaking framework, finalised following detailed discussion with O'Sullivan throughout 2000 and 2001, is reproduced here as Figure 1. With the addition of two additional interlocutor variables (number and gender) and the removal of the efficiency element, the framework remained essentially the same for his seminal publication (Weir, 2005).

Before moving on to describe the ways in which the socio-cognitive approach has been operationalised over the past two decades, it is worth pointing to at least one dissenting voice. Fulcher (2015: 117) dismissed the Weir (2005) frameworks as representing a technical approach to validity which harks back to a 'pre-Messick era of different "types" of validity.' He also felt that the categories were 'fairly traditional' and that they did 'not appear to add much to what had gone on before'. We agree that there is a danger of misinterpretation of the Weir approach due to his insistence on the use of the term *validity* for each of his five categories, see for example O'Sullivan's (2011) similar criticism. However, while the categories may appear traditional, Weir's (2005) discussion of how they interact and how they might be operationalised in a test development and validation process was clearly quite different to previous approaches. While there are clearly issues with the original Weir frameworks (see, e.g., O'Sullivan, 2011; O'Sullivan & Weir, 2011), the fact that they continue to form the basis of test development and validation projects across the globe suggests that Fulcher's dismissal of them as 'checklists' is, at best, off the mark.

Working with John Field (a specialist in the psychology of listening) and a succession of colleagues at Cambridge, Weir went on to produce or influence a series of books in which he refined his thinking on how cognition might be better represented in his frameworks (particularly for the receptive skills of reading and listening). These refined models were then applied to what amounted to a retrofitting of the Cambridge suite of English language proficiency examinations (Shaw & Weir, 2007; Khalifa & Weir, 2009; Taylor, 2011; Geranpayeh & Taylor, 2013). The work, which for the first time demanded of the developer that some significant focus on language cognition be undertaken when defining test constructs, was not always recognised across the profession (even in the UK) as

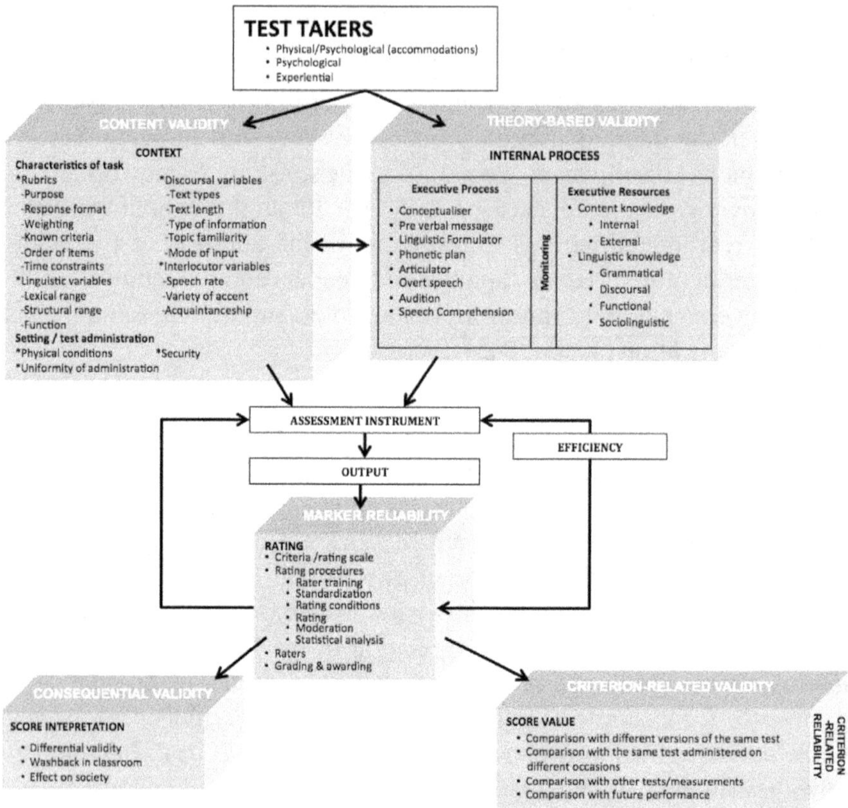

Figure 1: The speaking test validation framework (O'Sullivan and Weir, 2002)

being of practical value. It nevertheless came to influence test development there in the decades that followed – even if the focus on cognition over social context and communication went against the original conceptualisation of socio-cognitivism proposed by O'Sullivan (2000a).

By the end of the decade, the approach had been applied extensively by both Weir and O'Sullivan, in quite different ways. While the former was focusing on refining the theoretical aspects of the frameworks, the latter was exploring how they might be used in the test development process in a series of projects. Three of these are very briefly recounted below.

QALSPELL was a Council of Europe Leonardo da Vinci funded project designed to create a practical and localisable set of specifications for a test of English for specific purposes aimed at higher education institutions in the Baltic States. QALSPELL (2004) identified the lack of a solid theoretical approach in the literature to the development of test specifications – for example, Alderson et al. (1995) had listed a set of elements that a prospective developer might consider without a systematic process of identifying how each element might be addressed in a specification. A similar criticism can be made of other approaches to test specification (e.g., Bachman & Palmer, 1996; Davidson & Lynch, 2002; Fulcher & Davidson, 2007) where there is no consideration given to the necessity of a clear link between the specification approach recommended and validation – interestingly enough, the first recognition of the need for such a link was to come from the US in the work of Mislevy and others (Mislevy, Almond & Lukas, 2003; Mislevy & Haertel, 2006). The use of the nascent socio-cognitive frameworks to inform the general approach to assessment and in particular the test specification for QALSPELL acted to confirm the value of basing specifications on an operational validation model (which O'Sullivan had come to see the socio-cognitive approach as). It also suggested that the process of test validation starts right at the beginning of the development process and continues throughout that process.

In the EXAVER project (Abad et al., 2011), the approach was used to inform not one specification, but a series of three. This was because the proposed test series was to consist of three different examinations, each focusing on different levels of the Common European Framework of Reference for Languages (CEFR) – levels A2, B1 and B2. The approach taken was to create a single specification document in which the proposed papers could be viewed vertically (one test at a time) or horizontally (looking across tests to ensure that the degree of difficulty was systematically rising). A similar, if more ambitious, approach was taken with the development of a six-level series of course progress tests for the Zayed University preparatory English programme, in the United Arab Emirates (O'Sullivan, 2005).

It is important to note that the projects referred to here were all undertaken in cooperation with local teams. The fact that the approach was readily accepted by these teams suggested that it should be possible for people with relatively little assessment experience to construct tests that were sound both theoretically and operationally. This was because they had been encouraged to consider a comprehensive range of critical issues right from the beginning of the development process and had documented not only the obvious product (the test) but every decision that was made along the way. It was through this process of consideration and documentation that a coherent set of validation evidence was amassed. The fact that this could be achieved in all cases in a relatively short period of time by the project teams suggests that the whole conceptual approach is likely to be of practical value to test development teams across the world. It also implies that validation evidence should be accessible to a broader stakeholder community than is currently the case and that the concept of localisation might well be of major relevance in language (and other) test design and administration. This was to influence O'Sullivan's later thinking on the conceptualisation and operationalisation of localisation as a critical element of test validation (see O'Sullivan, 2019).

The whole experience suggests that the UK tradition of test development and validation is more likely to result in tests that are meaningful to key stakeholder groups as the way in which the *construct* is defined in as *direct* a manner as possible. The approach means that the test developer looks to language as it exists in real-life settings as the basis for understanding what learners can do, and then devises test tasks that give the learner an opportunity to demonstrate the particular skill or ability within this clearly defined context. Validity is demonstrated by showing that the test task has indeed resulted in the elicitation from successful learners of the expected language performance/task. We would therefore argue that validity, as it has come to be seen in the UK context, is participant-driven in that the key stakeholders are involved in the process of development and are recognised as having a significant input into the test.

As will become clear in the coming section, the way in which validity is conceptualised in the US is quite different from the situation in the UK. As we have seen in this section (and will return to later), the approach to construct definition taken by test developers in the UK has traditionally focused on performance, with tests and classrooms attempting to reflect what was referred to as the 'real world of language use'.

The traditional (since the early 20th century) approach taken to construct definition in the US, and the tests that resulted, was both less direct in focus and rejected the idea that it should be linked to the learning context. The psychometric-structuralist underpinning of educational measurement was given a modern theoretical support with the nomological network model described by Cronbach & Meehl (1955) – in which the construct is presented as a theoretical concept which is accessed indirectly through a set of test tasks/methods targeting traits. In this approach, which still dominates much of the US-inspired, measurement-driven language testing world, validity is then established by providing strong empirical support typically in the form of increasingly complex statistical analyses of test data which are designed to demonstrate significant links within the data to external evidence of the network elements. This representation of the construct (as understood by the *traditional* definition, as the 'ability or trait to be tested') has largely driven the US (and psychometric) approach to educational and psychological testing for over a century. In the next section, we detail the development of thinking in the US context.

The US approach

The present section provides a critical account of the validity scholarship as it has developed primarily in the US. The section is organised in terms of chronological periods that represent major shifts in thinking. We focus on publications as well as on scholars whose models have been influential and have shaped research, operations and publications widely. We also highlight language testing models that have provided a bridge between the measurement literature on validity and the language testing field at large.

Validity: Early development

From the late 19th century to the 1920s, the predominant approach to establishing validity was the content model – where test contents were expected to reflect particular language models or learning approaches. This situation held both in the US, certainly until the 1920s and beyond as a justification for selecting the appropriate criterion when performing correlation studies (Ebel, 1956; Ebel and Frisbie, 1991; Michael Kane, personal communication), and in the UK, where it continues to influence thinking, though not without its critics, see for example Fulcher (1999). In the late 1800s the correlation coefficient formula was developed by Pearson. This shaped thinking around the issue of validity. It was generally thought that a coefficient in the form of a robust correlation (e.g., correlations of test scores with teacher observations, grades and supervisor ratings) was sufficient validity evidence to support a test. Measurement professionals argued that a test is valid for anything with which it correlates (Thorndike, 1913; Kelley, 1927; Thurstone, 1932; Bingham, 1937; Guilford, 1946). The 1917 Army Alpha and Army Beta Tests, which sought to classify 1.5 million recruits, is a typical example of a testing programme of the era that used correlational predictive coefficients to support the quality of the measurements.

This view that validity is a correlation coefficient was later challenged. Several publications emerged (e.g., Pressey, 1920; Rulon, 1946; Jenkins, 1946) to point out problems associated with correlations as the basis for validity. These, now familiar, concerns included difficulty in identifying suitable criterion data and the classic dilemmas of why introduce a new measure if a strong correlation exists with an established criterion. Alternatively, if a weak correlation is found, it is not clear whether we should be concerned about issues with regard to the new test/instrument or the criterion. Also, test scores that correlate well with some criterion might also correlate with other variables, which weaken the value of correlational evidence provided. Correlational evidence basically offers weak grounds to address the question of *what does the test measure?* The lack of theoretical justification as well as the frequent difficulty of identifying an adequate criterion prompted measurement professionals to start thinking about expanding thinking about validity and its tools.

Dissatisfied with the limitations of correlational evidence to support the quality of their assessment practices, researchers sought other procedures to enhance the validity evidence. It is interesting to point out here that an argument has been made that the extensive use of correlational evidence supported the development of theoretical knowledge in a variety of disciplines and simultaneously highlighted shortcomings in correlational research. Strauss & Smith (2009: 5) write:

> In our view, the developing focus on theory was made possible, in part, by the substantive advances in clinical knowledge facilitated by the criterion-related validity approach. Perhaps ironically, the success of the criterion-related validity method led to its ultimate replacement with construct validity theory. The criterion approach led to significant advances in knowledge, which helped facilitate the development of integrative theories concerning cognition, personality, behavior, and psychopathology. But such theories could not be validated using the criterion approach; there was thus a need for advances in validation theory to make possible the emerging theoretical advances. This need was addressed by several construct validity authors in the middle of the 20th century (Campbell & Fiske 1959; Cronbach & Meehl 1955; Loevinger 1957).

In other words, correlation-based research enabled theoretical advances, which in turn, rendered the legitimacy of the narrowly-focused criterion documentation questionable. Researchers were prompted to expand their validity beyond correlational evidence.

The validity concept began to evolve from the 1920s and by the mid '50s included a trinitarian representation of criterion, content and construct. While criterion-related validity was accepted as the gold standard for validation (Cureton, 1951), rational examination of test content in terms of test purpose was also being considered and calls were made to address it in validity research, e.g., Rulon (1946). A formal emergence of validity evidence based on content could be observed in the first edition of *Educational measurement* where Cureton (1951) authored the chapter entitled 'Validity'. Cureton described the validity concept in terms of criterion-related relevance and reliability that strongly underscore the importance of a scientific approach to validity work. Cureton added that 'curricular relevance or content validity' is appropriate and subject matter experts (SMEs) can provide judgement to support/evaluate test content. SME judgement included evaluation of the 'fitness of items'. During this period, research also elaborated and gave prominence to construct validity conceptualisations. The APA document *Technical recommendations for psychological tests and diagnostic techniques* stated that construct is of interest when one 'wishes to infer the degree to which the individual possesses some trait or quality...presumed to be reflected in the test performance' (APA, 1954: 13).

Loevinger (1957) was an early proponent of construct-as-primary in validity conceptualisation. She offered a critique of criterion-related evidence as the basis for validity. She argued that 'Predictive and concurrent validities are…ad hoc.... Since ad hoc arguments are scientifically of minor importance, if not actually inadmissible, what is left, construct validity, is the whole of the subject from a systematic, scientific point of view' (Loevinger, 1957: 641). Cronbach (e.g., Cronbach & Meehl, 1955), perhaps, more than anyone else in modern times has shaped work around validity conceptualisation and pushed for a theory-based, construct validity research programme.

The Committee that developed the first set of testing standards in the US (Meehl & Challman, 1954) introduced of the concept of construct validity. The idea was elaborated by researchers such as Cronbach & Meehl (1955) who emphasised construct validity as a validation paradigm. They basically argue that construct validation is called upon in cases where tests are employed as measure of attributes/qualities which are not directly observable. In the area of personality testing, and as an example, for ego strength,

> there is no uniquely pertinent criterion to predict, nor is there domain of content to sample. Rather, there is a theory that sketches out the presumed nature of the trait. If the test score is a valid manifestation of ego strength, so conceived, its relations to other variables conform to the theoretical expectations (Cronbach, 1971: 322).

Cronbach & Meehl (1955) argued for the need to explicate the nature of the construct(s) that underpins any testing programme. A trait or construct is defined as a relatively stable set of characteristics, attributes or processes, which are consistently manifested despite variations in settings and conditions. They called for research programmes to investigate the implicit construct by documenting its stable attributes.

Cronbach & Meehl (1955) are credited with adopting the concept of a nomological network. The concept refers to a network of associations that attempts to render an implicit construct more explicit. Such a network can be described as an attempt to systematically deconstruct a trait or ability in order to locate a theoretical construct in a network of relationships (or theory) that implicitly defines the construct. The individual elements of this network could then be tested individually, and proficiency in the trait or ability reconstructed from the evidence gained in the test. More formally, a nomological network has been defined as elaboration of systems of laws and relationships that define a theory, intended to represent a construct (see Kane, 2006: 42). The process also entails the development of operations derived from theories and the detailing of hypotheses that connect theory and measurement. Validation is then the collection of relevant evidence that allows linkages among the various parts using test scores/observations.

> Cronbach and Meehl (1955) made it clear that the validation of an interpretation in terms of a theoretical construct would involve an extended effort, including the development of a theory, the development of measurement procedures thought to reflect (directly or indirectly) some of the constructs in the theory, the development of specific hypotheses based on the theory, and the testing of these hypotheses against observations (Kane, 2001: 323).

Cronbach & Meehl underscored the central role of theoretical representations of constructs and the importance of generating theory-based hypotheses, which are testable and falsifiable through the measures/instruments used to exemplify them. They asserted the need to present evidence in line with the proposed theory and nomological network that defines a given construct. As such, their understanding of construct differs from the traditional definition of construct = the trait or ability to be tested, as seen in the *Standards* (AERA, APA & MCNE, 2014). Cronbach calls the strong programme of construct validation 'a construction made explicit, a hypothesis deduced from it, and pointedly relevant evidence brought in' (1989: 162). The plausibility of the argument presented is judged in terms of the theory-driven tenets advanced. This line of thinking was exemplified operationally in the Campbell & Fiske (1959) multitrait-multimethod (MTMM) matrix.

In MTMM construct investigations, researchers documented convergent and discriminant evidence based on correlational patterns among traits/constructs and methods/tasks; convergent (convergence among features intended to measure similar constructs or traits) and discriminant (discrimination among features intended to measure dissimilar constructs or traits). More recently, sophisticated analyses such as structural equation modelling (Pitoniak, Sireci & Luecht, 2002) have also been employed in addition to MTMM for construct validation that systematically examines patterns of trait and method factors. Also, the *Standards* (1999) state: 'When a test provides more than one score, the distinctiveness of the separate scores should be demonstrated, and the interrelationships of those scores should be shown to be consistent with the construct(s) being assessed.' Several researchers have adopted the MTMM approach to articulate validation efforts for language testing systems. For example, Bachman's (1990) book, which has shaped thinking and practice in language testing, characterises the approach as follows: 'The classic approach to designing correlational studies for construct validation is the multitrait-multimethod (MTMM) matrix, described by Campbell and Fiske (1959)' (Bachman, 1990: 263).

Cronbach viewed validity as a unitary concept where 'all validation is one' (Cronbach, 1980: 99). Marching forward, Cronbach's work became instrumental in shaping major thinking on validity, e.g., as seen in the conceptualisations of validity by Messick (1989) and Kane (2006). Messick (1989) anchored all evidence in construct validity. It is interesting that these two types of validity, content and construct, more than others, have continued to be defined and redefined in recent years. This debate, Sireci (2009) reasons, can perhaps be explained in terms of disciplinary focus.

Professionals interested in educational matters and learning have sought to connect tests to learning materials (textbooks, syllabi and *Standards*), whereas professional test developers and theorists such as those in psychology have had to develop the unobservable systems of attributes that they sought to explain and test.

Alignment with content versus construct is strongly featured in language testing. This divide, it can be argued, resembles the differing interests in and approaches to validity on the two sides of the Atlantic Ocean. For example, professionals in the UK have historically advanced content as the anchor to their validity research programmes. This allowed testing programmes to be strongly connected to a curriculum of learning. Those in the US have generally favoured more proficiency tests, i.e., independent of any given textbook, method or curriculum, and so have tended to favour other aspects of validity such as criterion – concurrent and/or predictive. Increasingly, and for most testing programmes around the world, we observe a convergence towards validity research anchored in construct thinking, though how that construct is defined and its validity demonstrated remains quite divisive.

A unified model of construct validity: Messick

The later part of the 20th century basically moved the conversation to issues of construct validity. Whereas APA, AERA, NCME (1966 and 1974) *Standards* presented a trinitarian conceptualisation of validity in terms of criterion-related (concurrent and predictive), content and construct categories, the 1977 *Standards* presented validity as a unitary concept. The 1977 *Standards* also promoted the idea that construct validity is preeminent. The 1985 *Standards* more explicitly described validity as a unitary concept and promoted validity as documentation of score-based inferences. This conceptualisation of a unitary concept, anchored in construct validity can be attributed to the influential writings of Messick, as presented in the seminal 1989 chapter in *Educational measurement*. This point has been made by numerous researchers such as Sireci at the 2009 MARCES conference at the University of Maryland, College Park. (An aside: it is interesting to note that the 1985 *Standards* introduce for the first time a chapter dedicated to testing of Linguistic Minorities.)

Messick's often cited definition of validity is as follows: Validity is an integrated evaluative judgement of the degree to which empirical evidence and theoretical rationales support the adequacy and appropriateness of inferences and actions based on test scores or other modes of assessment (Messick, 1989: 13). Messick who writes the 'Validity' chapter in the 1989 edition of *Educational measurement* argues:

> ...because content- and criterion-related evidence contribute to score meaning, they have come to be recognized as aspects of construct validity.... This leaves only one category, namely, construct-related evidence. Yet in applied uses of tests, *general* evidence supportive of construct validity usually needs to be buttressed by *specific* evidence of the relevance of the test to the applied purpose and the utility of the test in the applied setting.... 'What is needed is a way of cutting and combining validity evidence that forestalls undue reliance on selected forms of evidence that highlights the important though subsidiary role of specific content- and criterion-related evidence in support of construct validity in testing operations...and that formally brings consideration of value implications and social consequences into the validity framework' (Messick, 1989: 20, emphasis in original).

Messick unequivocally defines validity in terms of score interpretation and use. He anchors the argument being developed in construct validity and formally calls attention to social considerations (*value interpretations* and *social consequences*).

Messick's writings have been described, elaborated and adapted in various manners, all in an attempt to unpack the meaning of the concepts presented. For example, the concepts articulated in the often cited and discussed progressive matrix, shown in Table 4, are loaded and require a great deal of clarification to guide a research programme. The cells of the matrix include concepts that do not present straightforward explanations and need to be deconstructed and elaborated. Messick emphasises, as argued in various bullet points above, an integrative notion of validity and in this regard every cell in the progressive matrix comprises construct validity, implicitly or explicitly. No single validity-related evidence offers adequate documentation of score interpretation and use. The matrix proposes two sources of justification for a testing system research

	Test Interpretation	**Test Use**
Evidential Basis	Construct Validity	Construct Validity + Relevance/Utility
Consequential Basis	Value Interpretations	Social Consequences

Table 4: Messick's progressive matrix (1989: 20)

programme: evidence and consequences. Both sources of justification are to be martialled to support the two functions of any given testing system, i.e., interpretation and use.

At a basic level, whereas evidence to support test interpretation attends to score meaning or interpretation, consequences document the quality of scores in terms of fairness issues, e.g., differential item/test functioning (DIF, DTF) analyses that pertain to the values attached to labelling (score designations), etc. Evidential support for test use supports the alignment between test purpose/setting and the obtained scores; criterion-related research is an example of research in this area. Consequences with regard to test use call for research into practices that document intended and unintended construct-related consequences of score uses, interventions/treatments provided, allocation of needed resources, societal impact, among others.

Messick's chapter generally reaffirms numerous points articulated by Cronbach who, as already described, endorses moving away from isolated, discrete validity studies and affirms a more integrated, coherent, systematic approach to validation research. For example, Messick:

- Rejects a trinitarian representation of validity as content, criterion and construct.
- Maintains that content- and criterion-related investigations provide necessary but not sufficient information about score meaning and as such are recognised as features of construct validity.
- Argues for a unitary concept of validity.
- Contends that all validity is construct validity.
- Endorses Cronbach's thinking that validity has to address the meaning as well as the use of test scores. 'Cronbach (1971) distinguishes between using a test to describe a person and using it to make decisions about the person' (Messick, 1989: 21). Messick writes that validity research has to provide information about how scores appropriately, adequately and meaningfully describe a person's ability. Validity also, he argues, has to attend to score use, i.e., the particular data/information assembled to support decision-making.
- Offers some limited support for the view that constructs can be seen as nomological networks that can be used to underpin validation. Messick (1989: 23) writes: 'nomological networks are viewed as an illuminating way of speaking systematically about

> the role of constructs in psychological theory and measurement, but not as the only way'.

Messick allows multiple avenues for developing theoretical structures of constructs or nomological networks. Messick considers epistemologies such as positivism, relativism, rationalism, realism and constructionism. He presents detailed analyses of the nature of knowledge, how it is gained, how specific propositions are generated and their limitations, and articulates the validity implications of various knowledge perspectives. His contributions in this area remain singular in the validity literature. In language testing, the work of Fulcher (2014, 2015) – elaborations of different philosophies that underpin various approaches to knowledge accumulation and theory development – is also a worthy contribution. These philosophies represent epistemological differences in terms of validity conceptualisation – e.g., a positivistic versus a post-positivistic orientation to validity (Moss et al., 2008). Epistemological orientations also denote differences in arguments sought and methodological approaches accepted.

Concerns with Messick's validity representation, which are well documented in the literature (see Kane, 2006), include lack of guidance with regard to how to structure the validity research, i.e., guide a research programme. Additionally, Messick's emphasis on the ongoing nature of validity offers no guidelines on when to terminate the process of gathering evidence. Notions such as 'appropriateness' and 'adequacy', included in a quote above, still offer no clear guidelines in operational terms. The language testing Listserv in the '90s witnessed many exchanges on this point. It is typically argued that the extent to which appropriate and sufficient validity documentation has been amassed is a judgement similar, at a simplistic level, to that needed by raters to evaluate open-ended test responses. The process is also described as being similar to how a case is presented/judged in a court of law. Another central criticism is Messick's lack of delineation with regard to who exactly should provide this judgement. Researchers increasingly ask: what individuals/group should provide judgement regarding the appropriateness and adequacy of evidence and rationale? Is this evidence and rational appropriate and adequate for any and all? Is it sufficient to have the psychometric or measurement professional decide? Recent research argues for the need to investigate how different stakeholder groups might react to and/or what they might value in a validity research programme (Chapelle, 2012; Berry, O'Sullivan & Rugea, 2012; Chalhoub-Deville, 2016; O'Sullivan, 2016).

	adequacy of…	appropriateness of…
inferences made from test scores	depends on multiple sources of empirical evidence	relates to impact considerations/consequences of tests
the design decisions derived from the interpretation of empirical evidence	is reflected in the usefulness/utility or (domain relevance of the test)	will enhance and anticipate the social justification and political defensibility of using the test

Table 5: Weideman's matrix (2012: 1)

Many professionals, especially in the language testing field, have heralded Messick's publications as a notable advance in the conceptualisation of validity. Messick's progressive matrix has offered an especially appealing organisational format for tackling and expanding Messick's concepts. We have selected two such representations to focus on here. One is by Weideman (2012) and the other by McNamara & Roever (2006). While these authors attempt to elaborate Messick's concepts, they also overlay their own commitments to a broader social perspective in terms of validity research.

Weideman's (2012) matrix (Table 5) offers a view on what Messick's cells mean within the scope of '*adequacy of*' and '*appropriateness of*' the evidence needed. The 'adequacy of' column calls attention to more traditional sources of validity evidence, e.g., the sources highlighted in the AERA et al. (1999, 2014) *Standards*. Whereas the notions in the 'adequacy of' column are widely supported in the measurement field, those in the 'appropriateness of' column are widely challenged. Many argue that research focusing on consequences does not fall under the purview of validity and/or is the responsibility of the test publisher. The *Standards* affirm that test publishers are responsible for consequences that pertain strictly to construct representation and relevance issues.

McNamara & Roever (2006) adapt Messick's matrix and give prominence to issues of consequences as they pertain to interpretations and uses of scores (Table 6). The first row of the matrix speaks to evidence sought to support score fairness claims in terms of interpretation as well as use. These two cells are generally accepted in the measurement literature as part of the test publishers' research documentation responsibility. The second row, on the other hand, is problematic for test publishers at large who, on the whole, shy away from embracing a social, value-grounded orientation and uphold a more technical, psychometric agenda when it

	What test scores are assumed to mean	When tests are actually used
Using evidence in support of claims: test fairness	What reasoning and empirical evidence support the claims we wish to make about candidates based on their test performance?	Are these interpretations meaningful, useful and fair in particular contexts?
The overt social context of testing	What social and cultural values and assumptions underlie test constructs and the sense we make of test scores?	What happens in our education systems and the larger social context when we use tests?

Table 6: McNamara & Roever's matrix (2006: 14)

comes to validity research. Though it has received widespread support on the conceptual level in the literature (Shepard, 1993; McNamara & Roever, 2006; Moss, 2016) Messick's inclusion of consequences within the scope of validity has been criticised for being too ambitious and unwieldy (see Cizek, 2011; Mehrens, 1997; Popham, 1997) and too vaguely defined to be adequately operationalised (O'Sullivan & Weir 2011).

The Weideman (2009) and McNamara & Roever (2006) matrices represent ambitious interpretations of Messick's thinking with regard to consequences. Their work is not strictly in line with Messick's (1989) orientation to issues of consequences. With regard to consequences, Messick zeroes in essentially on issues of the construct. He highlights two areas where social consequences can be said to *invalidate a test*: construct under-representation and construct-irrelevant variance. Messick writes:

> If the adverse social consequences are empirically traceable to sources of test invalidity, then the validity of the test use is jeopardized. If the social consequences cannot be so traced...then the validity of the test use is not overturned (Messick, 1989: 88).

Additionally, if it is found that issues of consequences pertain directly to a compromise in terms of construct relevance and representation, then measurement professionals are to be held responsible and they need to intervene. Other aspects of consequences, while critical, do not fall under the purview of test developers and measurement professionals. It is interesting to note that this circumscribed responsibility for consequences is endorsed in the consensus-seeking publication, the *Standards* of 1999 as well as the most recent 2014 edition.

The Standards of 1999 and 2014

Given the broad scope of input solicited and endorsement obtained, as typically described in the first few pages of every edition, the *Standards* represent a professional consensus perspective. Despite their expansive endorsements and enduring existence, however, the *Standards* remain primarily **suggestive** on what and how validity research, among other areas, can be pursued. The various editions of the *Standards* have never been employed to enforce professional compliance. The *Standards* also do not seem to have any preferential position in the US courts. Despite the lack of a regulatory function, the *Standards* have continued to play a central role in the profession, particularly in the US and countries/regions in which the US assessment philosophy has been influential (e.g., Japan, Korea, etc.).

Since the 1990s, the *Standards* have been published twice (AERA, APA & NCME, 1999, 2014). In these publications, the definitions of validity share features which have largely remained in line with Messick's thinking in terms of a focus on score interpretation and use. However, a comparative analysis shows that the 2014 *Standards* have subtly but significantly changed conceptualisation of validity arguments and research. To assist with the comparative analysis, we put side-by-side quotes from the two editions of the *Standards* in Table 7. Our comparison explores several areas: definition of validity, validity as a unitary concept, construct validity, validity research and ongoing validity research.

The 1999 AERA, APA & NCME *Standards*	**The 2014 AERA, APA & NCME *Standards***
'Validity refers to the degree to which evidence and theory support the interpretations of test scores entailed by the proposed uses of test' (p. 9).	'Validity refers to the degree to which evidence and theory support the interpretations of test scores for proposed uses of tests' (p. 11).
'It is the interpretations of test scores required by proposed uses that are evaluated, not the test itself' (p. 9).	'It is the interpretations of test scores for proposed uses that are evaluated, not the test itself. … It is incorrect to use the unqualified phrase "the validity of the test."' (p. 11).

Table 7: Definition of validity in the *Standards* (1999 and 2014)

For all intents and purposes, the 1999 and 2014 editions of the *Standards* offer the same definition of validity. The definition quotes are strongly reminiscent of Messick's thinking. The 'degree to which' phrase in the two quotes indicates that validity is not all or nothing but a matter of degree. Validity research involves both theoretical arguments and empirical evidence to support score interpretations as intended by given uses. The 2014 *Standards* are explicit in terms of pushing against the common practice of referencing 'the validity of the test'. The focus of validity is clearly on scores versus, for example, the content of the test/assessment/instrument. Content is relevant as part of the evidence/argument to support score interpretation and use.

The 2014 *Standards* reaffirm the need to coalesce validity evidence and reject a popular reference in professional circles to various types of validity. This orientation is characterised in the 1999 *Standards* as: 'validity is a unitary concept'. The 2014 *Standards* shy away from using the word 'unitary'; however, the lack of an explicit mention of a unitary concept does not mean a reversion to the category approach observed in earlier editions of the *Standards*. The 2014 *Standards* emphasise that validity encompasses different evidence types as opposed to different validities (note the first quote in the right-hand column of Table 8).

The 1999 AERA, APA & NCME *Standards*	**The 2014 AERA, APA & NCME *Standards***
'Validity is a unitary concept' (p. 9).	'Like the 1999 *Standards*, this edition refers to types of validity evidence, rather than distinct types of validity. To emphasize this distinction, the treatment that follows does not follow historical nomenclature (i.e., the use of the terms content validity or predictive validity)' (p. 14).
'Because a validity argument typically depends on more than one proposition, strong evidence in support of one in no way diminishes the need for evidence to support others' (p. 11).	'Because an interpretation for a given use typically depends on more than one proposition, strong evidence in support of one part of the interpretation in no way diminishes the need for evidence to support the other parts of the interpretation.... When propositions have been identified that would support the proposed interpretation of test scores, one can proceed with validation by obtaining empirical evidence, examining relevant literature, and/or conducting logical analyses to evaluate each of the propositions' (p. 13).

Table 8: Validity as a unitary concept in the *Standards* (1999 and 2014)

While bringing evidence together is important to help form an argument, the 2014 *Standards* have moved away from an inclusive validity documentation. The *Standards* contend:

> each type of evidence…is not required in all settings. Rather, support is needed for each proposition that underlies a proposed test interpretation for a specified use. A proposition that a test is predictive of a given criterion can be supported without evidence that the test samples a particular content domain (AERA, APA & NCME, 2014: 14).

It seems that while the term validity is reserved for an integrated collection of evidence to support intended score interpretation for a given use, test developers and researchers are to pursue the type of evidence they think is best needed to make the argument. This approach represents a departure from Messick's established thinking as well as arguments advanced by notable researchers in language testing such as Weir who writes:

> Validity is multifaceted and different types of evidence are needed to support any claims for the validity of scores on a test. These are not alternatives but complementary aspects of an evidential basis for test interpretation…. No single validity can be considered superior to another. Deficit in any one raises questions as to the well-foundedness of any interpretation of test scores (Weir, 2005: 13).

A strong emphasis on integrating the types of validity evidence and subsuming it under construct validity was a historic reaction to the more selection-from-a-menu approach observed in testing programmes. 'The very variety of methodological approaches in the validational armamentarium, in the absence of specific criteria for choosing among them, makes it possible to select evidence opportunistically and to ignore negative findings' (Messick, 1989: 33). A more selective approach gathering evidence to build a validity argument is arguably a response to the widely shared concerns about the feasibility and cost of an all-inclusive approach. Given the preeminence of the *Standards* as a source of professional guidance, we need to be watchful of how this shift in 2014 will impact validity research affiliated with testing systems. To what extent it will endanger the profession by adopting an opportunistic (e.g., convenient and favourable evidence) approach to building validity arguments to is worthy of attention.

The 1999 AERA, APA & NCME *Standards*	**The 2014 AERA, APA & NCME *Standards***
'**construct validity** A term used to indicate that the test scores are to be interpreted as indicating the test taker's standing on the psychological construct measured by the test. ... In the current standards, all test scores are viewed as measures of some construct, so the phrase is redundant with validity. The validity argument establishes the construct validity of a test' (p. 174).	Not mentioned (though the glossary includes several entries for content and criterion, e.g., content-related validity evidence and criterion-referenced score interpretation). In the chapter on Workplace Testing and Credentialing, the document references construct validity as a historical notion – '...evidence subsumed under "construct validity" in prior conceptualizations of the validation process...' (p. 173).

Table 9: Construct validity in the *Standards* (1999 and 2014)

Related to the issue of the *unitary concept* is the shift away from the concept of *construct validity* as the overall anchor to validity. This represents a radical change from the 1999 *Standards*, which anchor validity in construct validity. As Table 9 shows, the 1999 *Standards* state: 'all test scores are viewed as measures of some construct, so the phrase is redundant with validity' (p. 174). The 2014 *Standards* do not include construct validity in the glossary or in the validity chapter, as was the case with the 1999 edition. In the chapter on workplace testing and credentialing, the document references construct validity as a historical notion, now disregarded – '...evidence subsumed under "construct validity" in prior conceptualizations of the validation process' (2014: 173).

Readers will be hard pressed to find the term *construct validity* in the glossary, the index or the text itself of the 2014 *Standards*. The *Standards* (2014) do not offer justification for dropping *construct validity* and the powerful ideas it held as a subsuming concept. They simply replace the notion of a *unitary concept* with a strong emphasis on the coherence of an argument. They indicate under the heading of **Integrating the Validity Evidence**, 'A sound validity argument integrates various strands of evidence into a coherent account of the degree to which existing evidence and theory support the intended interpretation of test scores for specific uses' (AERA, APA & NCME, 2014: 21). (This coherence criterion is also observed in Kane's chapter entitled 'Validation', published in the influential *Educational measurement* of 2006.)

The change, it could be argued, is basically a response to criticisms levelled against Messick's more abstract construct validity conceptualisation. 'Validity theory...seems to have been more successful in developing general frameworks for analysis than in providing clear guidance on how to validate specific interpretations and uses of measurements' (Kane, 2006: 18). The latest edition of the *Standards*, probably as a response to this perspective, has reframed validity away from 'construct validity as the whole of validity theory' (Shepard, 1993: 405) and more in terms of testable propositions, which are definable, at least in principle, by test professionals/publishers and are investigated as part of validity research.

The question that arises here is how much practical improvement does the move to propositions and testable hypotheses offer? Shepard (1993) contends that what the *Standards* offer in this regard is not much better than what Messick has presented through his publications. Although her remarks are intended for an earlier edition of the *Standards*, they are relevant for the later editions as well. Shepard (1993: 429) writes:

> The complexity of Messick's model and chapter creates the same difficulty as nearly every other treatise on construct validity before his. Each emphasizes that construct validation is a never-ending process, because there are so many hypotheses to be tested across so many settings and populations and because the generalizability of findings decays over time. While the never-concluding nature of construct validation is a truism, the sense that the task is insurmountable allows practitioners to think that a little bit of evidence of whatever type will suffice. Current Standards do little to help prioritize validity questions. Validity Standards are not organized in a coherent conceptual framework. Therefore, they do not help answer the question 'How much evidence is enough?' nor do they clarify that the stringency of evidential demands should vary as a function of potential consequences.

The quote makes several important points. It affirms the complexity of a construct validity approach to document the quality of a testing programme with regard to its score interpretation for particular uses. But the problem is not restricted to a construct validity conceptualisation. The quote points out that the difficulty arises because 'there are so many hypotheses to be tested…' but the range of hypotheses depends on the stakes or the 'potential consequences' of a testing programme, among other things. The wide scope of hypotheses does not go away even if we abandon construct validity as a guiding concept. Anchoring the endeavour in construct validity serves as a strong reminder to pay attention to theoretical representation of entities targeted. This argument is fleshed out in Chalhoub-Deville (2009b), when responding to the call by Lissitz & Samuelsen (2007a, b) to abandon construct validity in favour of content validity conceptualisation and research. The quote also raises the important issue of the lack of guidance with regard to prioritising the evidence for different purposes/uses and the termination point of the research. These issues are taken up next.

Finally, whereas the 2014 *Standards* have abandoned the term construct validity, they continue to pay attention to constructs. The term *construct* appears in the *Standards* (1999: 173; 2014: 217). It refers to 'The concept or characteristic that a test is designed to measure'. Elsewhere in the 2014 *Standards*, we also note references to the role of constructs in a testing operation. They state:

> The proposed interpretation refers to the construct or concepts the test is intended to measure.... To support test development, the proposed interpretation is elaborated by describing its scope and extent and by delineating the aspects of the construct that are to be represented.... The detailed description provides a conceptual framework for the test, delineating the knowledge, skills, abilities, processes, or characteristics to be assessed (AERA, APA & NCME, 2014: 9).

The term construct, as represented in the above quotes, avoids discussion of nomological networks or nomothetic spans. In fact, the characterisation presented in the *Standards* is quite simple, and reminiscent of the *traditional* definition presented above. What is most pertinent here is that they kept the construct concept but abandoned the term construct validity.

The above set of quotes signals a different orientation to how validity research is to be conducted. Instead of an emphasis on a unitary concept, which has been described as vague and unwieldy, the 2014 *Standards* underscore the importance of laying out arguments that are then verified. 'Validation can be viewed as a process of constructing and evaluating arguments for and against the intended interpretation of test scores and their relevance to the proposed use' (AERA, APA & NCME, 2014: 11). The terms 'constructing' and 'evaluating' seem to suggest a two-step process, which is reminiscent of Kane's (2006) approach. This observation about a two-step approach is also evident in the quotes: '...propositions are articulated and evidence is gathered to evaluate their soundness' (AERA, APA & NCME, 2014: 12) and 'When propositions have been identified...one can proceed with validation...' (2014: 13).

The 2014 edition of the *Standards* articulates validity more explicitly as a process that comprises propositions, which need to be articulated and then examined as a coherent argument to support score interpretation(s) for particular use(s). The shift towards proposition and arguments is undoubtedly an endorsement of Kane's thinking as represented in the chapter entitled 'Validation' (2006). Kane contends that he seeks to unpack the unitary concept of validity and to offer a more practical approach to validity research. As explained in more detail in the next section, Kane suggests first laying out the claims that are said to support intended score interpretation and use, which he calls the interpretive argument (IA), and then pursuing investigations to support those claims. He calls this latter phase the validation argument.

The *Standards* (2014) offer no guidance on what constitutes coherent validity research, how to marshal evidence and arguments to make a case for a particular interpretation and/or use, and what research might look like for differing testing programmes with different stakes (high-low). The *Standards* do present, however, specific sources of evidence to guide validation practice. The sources of evidence basically define the scope of evidence that can/may be put together to articulate the validity argument. Both the 1999 and the 2014 *Standards* identify the following five sources of validity evidence: content, internal structure, external relationships, process and consequences. These delineations have generally been welcomed in the US in terms of practical guidance. Table 10 presents the sources of evidence along with examples of research that could be undertaken in each of the five areas.

More than any other source, 'consequences' as a source of validity evidence remains highly controversial and extensively delimited in terms of its scope of research in measurement circles and in the 2014 *Standards*. For example, it is interesting to observe how the headings for the other four sources of evidence follow the same pattern but that for consequences differs. The headings for the four other sources start with **Evidence Based on...** while the heading for consequences reads **Evidence for Validity and Consequences of Testing**. The 'and' could be interpreted as a signal that consequence is an add-on to validity rather than part of the concept. This represents the continued confusion about

Evidence Based on Test Content
- Alignment with learning and/or content and performance standards
- Evaluation of content fidelity and representation
- Mapping of items to intended content domain/domain of generalisation
- Accessibility of content to various groups in intended population

Evidence Based on Response Processes
- Think-aloud protocols to document construct representation and relevant processes
- Eye movement tracking
- Response time
- Drafts of work showing development of a response

Evidence Based on Internal Structure
- Psychometric properties of scores
- Dimensionality analyses, e.g., factor analysis
- Composite score weights
- Cross validation

Evidence Based on Relations to Other Variables
- Correlational and regression analyses
- Convergent and discriminant evidence
- Validity generalisation
- Benchmarking

Evidence for Validity and Consequences of Testing
- Documentation of intended benefits
- Cultural sensitivity reviews
- Access and opportunity to learn content/skills
- Fairness and differential item/test functioning to document fairness

Table 10: Sources of validity evidence with some examples (from the *Standards* of 1999 and 2014)

consequences, its role in validity research, the scope included in validation, who is held responsible for what part, among other issues.

The *Standards* seem to offer a more utilitarian approach to validity, which is guided by the five sources of evidence. Despite the more practical five-sources-of-evidence approach, the *Standards* fail to explicate what an argument that integrates these sources looks like, how an argument is put together, and how much evidence is necessary/adequate for any specific purpose. It also ignores a key element of any argument – the audience to whom that argument is presented.

Another prominent change in the conceptualisation of validity research is the established notion that validity research is ongoing. The 2014 edition of the *Standards* contests this formulation of ongoing validity research. The 2014 *Standards* are explicit and direct in their contention that validity research, at some point, comes to an end. They represent a significant departure from the 1999 edition on this point. To facilitate a comparative analysis of this issue, Table 11 offers text from the two editions of the *Standards*.

Under the heading of **Integrating the Validity Evidence**, the 1999 and 2014 editions of the *Standards* include two identical paragraphs that speak to the validity argument and technical quality of a testing programme. The discussion of when validation ends, as represented in the 2014 quote, is simply not included in the 1999 edition. The side-by-side comparison clearly shows that the latest edition of the *Standards* clearly opposes a popular notion (e.g., Messick, 1989; Chapelle, 1999) of ongoing research. It is disconcerting that the document actually refers to 'the validation study'. Unless the word 'study' here means programme, this language harkens back to the early days of validity research! The notion

The 1999 AERA, APA & NCME *Standards*	The 2014 AERA, APA & NCME *Standards*
Integrating the Validity Evidence No text is provided with regard to the end of a validation process.	**Integrating the Validity Evidence** 'It is commonly observed that the validation process never ends, as there is always additional information that can be gathered to more fully understand a test and the inferences that can be drawn from it.... However a test interpretation for a given use rests on evidence for a set of propositions making up the validity argument, and at some point, validation evidence allows for a summary judgement of the intended interpretation that is well supported and defensible. At some point, the effort to provide sufficient validity evidence to support a given test interpretation for a specific use *does end.* ... Legal requirement may necessitate that the *validation study* be updated...' (pp. 21–22, emphasis added).

Table 11: Formulation of validity research in the *Standards* of 1999 and 2014

of ongoing validity research was a powerful concept, strongly advocated by Messick (1989) to deter test publishers and other groups involved in the development/administration of assessments from taking on some research and claiming that validity has been attained. It is too early to tell how this change in guidance from the *Standards* is changing practices. Our guess, guided by history, is that it will change practices and not necessarily for the best. The 2014 *Standards* take a pragmatic approach that explicitly states that validation research does come to an end.

Suggestions (e.g., Moss, 2003) have been made to make use of case studies to provide examples on how to develop validity arguments for different types of testing programmes, score interpretations and score uses. We believe that test publishers could utilise information readily available to them, based on their research efforts, to contribute to the knowledge base in this area. An example of this is the work currently undertaken by the British Council in the UK. The British Council's Aptis testing service has connections in different arenas of testing around the world and the localisation core concept of the programme yields information and validation plans that can serve as benchmarks to fill the void observed in the field. (See the section on the British Council approach as reflected in the Aptis service below.) Another interesting example of the use of such a case study can be found in Read (2015), who describes the rationale behind the introduction of a post-entry English language test for students at the University of Auckland, New Zealand. His observations on the changing university population profile (from primarily users of English as an L1, to a mixed-language population), and on the need to comply with national legislation, demonstrate the critical importance of a clearly described context to validation arguments.

A more practical orientation to validity, as observed in the *Standards*, does invite a more serious engagement in consequences. The move away from constructs can be perhaps justified if a more meaningful and realist engagement in the world is a credible outcome. In today's world, particularly in places where we are increasingly engaged in accountability testing systems, scores are used in ways that impact students, teachers, schools and communities. Consequences need to be a central part of the scholarship of test development. Research with regard to consequences needs to document how testing programmes and related scores impact individuals, groups, and larger educational and societal structures (see Chalhoub-Deville, 2016). Validity research plans need to pay thoughtful attention to consequences. This issue is explored later in the monograph.

Kane's argument-based validity approach (ABV)

Since the early '90s, Kane (see 1992) has emphasised a conceptualisation of validity as an argument-based approach. Validity, according to Kane (2006, 2013), is not about construct validity or an inherent property of an assessment but the building of coherent arguments to support score interpretations and uses. Kane (2012a: 67) writes: 'I don't use construct language much, because I do not find it useful.' He explains that 'the uniform model based on construct validity is elegant and conceptually rich and suggestive, but it is not easy to implement effectively, because it does not provide a place to start, guidance on how to proceed, or criteria for gauging progress and deciding when to stop' (Kane, 2012b: 7–8). Kane pursues a validity line established by Cronbach where validation concerns itself with building arguments to support explicitly described intended score interpretations and uses. Cronbach (1971) expressed concern that the lack of strong construct theories to guide validity research renders construct validity research an unwieldy open-ended pursuit; 'a lengthy, even endless process' (Cronbach, 1989: 151). In his 2006 chapter, Kane states that validation involves delineating a network of inferences and then undertaking research to evaluate – support or refute – those inferences. The *Standards* adopt similar language in terms of 'constructing' and 'evaluating' propositions using various sources of evidence.

Kane (2006) advances an argument-based validity (ABV) approach that includes an interpretive argument (IA) and a validity argument (VA). His approach starts with delineating the IA, which specifies the network of inferences and assumptions or a chain of claims underlying intended score interpretation and use. The IA starts essentially with observed performances and progresses to decisions. The VA, simply put, is an evaluation of the proposed interpretive argument. The VA speaks to amassed evidence to support or refute the intended inferences embedded in score interpretations and planned uses.

> To claim that a proposed interpretation is valid is to assert that the interpretive argument is coherent, the inferences are reasonable, and the assumptions are plausible (Kane, 2006: 23).

This argument approach to validity specifies a starting point, how to proceed, and when to end. Researchers lay out the argument in terms of claims regarding scoring, generalisation, explanation, etc., i.e. the IA. Research is then undertaken focusing on the specified claims, i.e. the

VA. Judgement of the quality of the IA and VA references the coherence, completeness, clarity and plausibility of the IA and VA put together. An essential aspect in validation is that the types of evidence collected will depend on the purpose of the test interpretation. The goal is to gather relevant evidence to justify or refute intended interpretations and uses of test scores. Kane (2006, 2012b) points out that this process is less as a cookbook approach and more as structure to help organise the claims and systematise the research without engaging in validation research *forever*. With Kane's ABV approach, connection to formal theories is optional. The claims laid out in the IA become the *theory* of interest. This approach, as discussed Chapter 5 in this monograph, has been later characterised as a measurement argument (Bennett, Kane & Bridgeman, 2011; Sabatini, Bennett & Deane, 2011).

Kane (2006) presents a graphic, shown here as Figure 2, to explicate how the IA is laid out for trait-based interpretations. Kane's IA and VA focus on claims that pertain to the right side of the figure. An IA specifies the network of inferences and assumptions starting with the sample of observed performances and concluding with trait interpretation. These inferences have also been metaphorically referred to as bridges that need to be supported to allow the links sought. (It is important to note that the path does not have to end with interpretation but can be extended as appropriate for a given measurement or assessment system.) What follows is a description of the inferences as posited by Kane's (2006) IA:

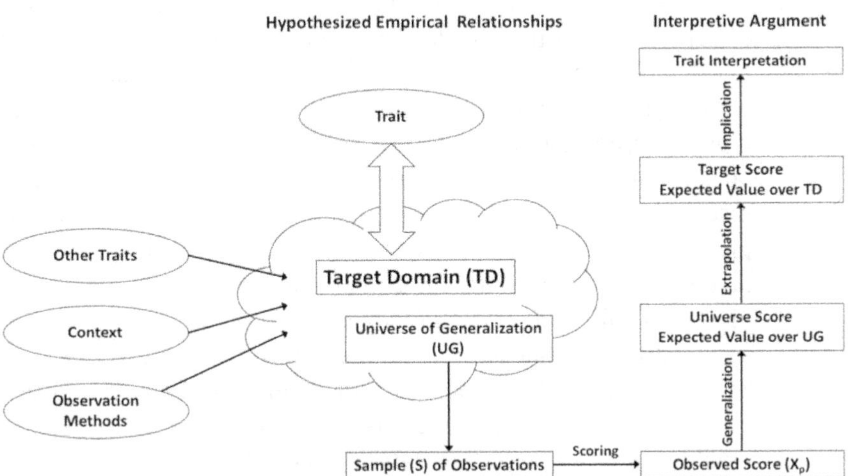

Figure 2: Kane's measurement procedure and interpretive argument for trait interpretations (2006: 33)

1. Scoring inference: The scoring of performances/observations inference refers to procedures such as standardisation of scoring operations, e.g., appropriate coding and/or use of rubrics, adequacy of scales, rater training, etc. that help yield an observed score (OS), which is in line with intended score interpretation. Claims, for example, about inappropriate scoring rubrics, inadequate rater training, or poor administration conditions compromise claims that scores are adequate and appropriate representation of performances and jeopardise later inferences along the path.
2. Generalisation inference: Generalisation enables converting an observed score (OS) to a universe score (US) based on claims of random samples of observations from the intended universe of generalisation. This inference would be addressed by classic psychometric research such as studies of the extent to which the OS is representative or generalisable to similar test tasks under similar conditions. These include generalisability analyses or reliability analyses to document standard error of measurement, and item response theory analyses to support claims about item and person reliability, i.e., the consistency and dependability of scores. Analyses also attend to claims about item and person separability. Claims are compromised and threaten the other links in the IA if, for example, *bad* variability is observed in scores that can be attributed to inadequate sampling of tasks, raters, etc.
3. Extrapolation inference: This inference depends on claims such as relevance and representation of the content, processes, tasks in the target domain that need to be scrutinised to justify transforming a US into a target score (TS). Fidelity studies that document the correspondence between test tasks and those in the target domain can support extrapolation inferences. Utility-based research, e.g., predictive studies, could be relevant depending on the purposes of the testing system. DIF results could be undertaken to show how different groups engage with the domain as identified. DIF can produce evidence as to whether the attributes assessed are similar across groups with regard to the intended target domain. Evidence that documents serious disparities between the universe of generalisation and a given target domain would compromise extrapolation from US to TS and imperil subsequent IA inferences.

4. Implication inference: Implication can be said to represent claims about particular interpretations given TS attributes. The intent at this juncture is to endow scores with meaning. Meaning claims pertain to verbal descriptions based on content standards and performance level descriptors/labels that explicate the meaning of a given performance. Theoretical arguments and evidence-based studies are warranted to support claims for intended interpretations of observed patterns or regularities in performances.
   Claims underlying the implication inference closely link test scores to potential intended and unintended consequences. Investigations of achievement of intended positive outcomes and attendance to unintended negative consequences, soundness of policy implementation and quality of learning opportunities are germane to the validation process.

Kane's attention to scores pertains to score meaning or semantic interpretation as well as score use or decisions. Although the graph does not portray a decision inference, his writing in the chapter does. 'For many test-based decisions, semantic interpretation and the decision are distinct and sequential' (Kane, 2006: 51). Kane calls for research to accommodate score use. In his latter publications (e.g., Kane, 2013), he reformulates the IA as Interpretive and Use Argument (IUA) to explicitly call attention to use. The following is a characterisation of a decision inference.

5. Decision inference: This inference encompasses claims that move beyond semantic interpretation of performance to focus on how scores are employed as grounds to make decisions or take action. Investigations of standard setting claims are typically dealt with at this juncture. Claims are posited regarding the credibility of the standard setting procedures employed, criteria adopted to set cut scores, as well as the inclusion of and representation of appropriate stakeholder groups on the standard setting panels, etc. Kane (2001: 85) states: 'Standard setting still can not be reduced to a problem of statistical estimation. Fundamentally, standard setting involves the development of a policy about what is to be required for each level of performance. This policy is stated in the performance *Standards* and implemented through the cut scores.'

Kane's inferences represent essentially a *measurement* network, which documents investigations to help support or show compromises in the path from observations of student performances to the interpretations and decisions envisioned. This IA portrayal of validity research is increasingly popular in the US and in other parts of the world. The following is an example that illustrates how Rasch analyses, which are prevalent in the language testing field, have been construed in terms of IA links or inferences. The example in Figure 3 by Aryadoust (2009, 2013) uses terminology commonly observed in Kane's IA writings, e.g., warrants and backing. Simply, warrants refer to the evidence or indices obtained at given inference points to support claims and allow the link or the bridge. Backing here refers to test theories, psychometric models, measurement studies that give rise to particular evidence(s)/to facilitate the warrants.

The IA laid out in Figure 3 showcases the scoring, generalisation, extrapolation and implication inferences. Once this chain of inferences is laid out, the VA stage or validation commences with empirical studies and theoretical explorations to provide backing for these inferences. This example clearly denotes an adaptation by Aryadoust (2009, 2013) of Kane's IA approach. However, it is not identical to the inferences laid out in the previous Kane (2006) figure. This is not a violation of Kane's formulation per se. Kane's inferences offer an example of a roadmap to be utilised as needed by a given testing programme. What Kane provides is a relatively flexible system that identifies key inferences following

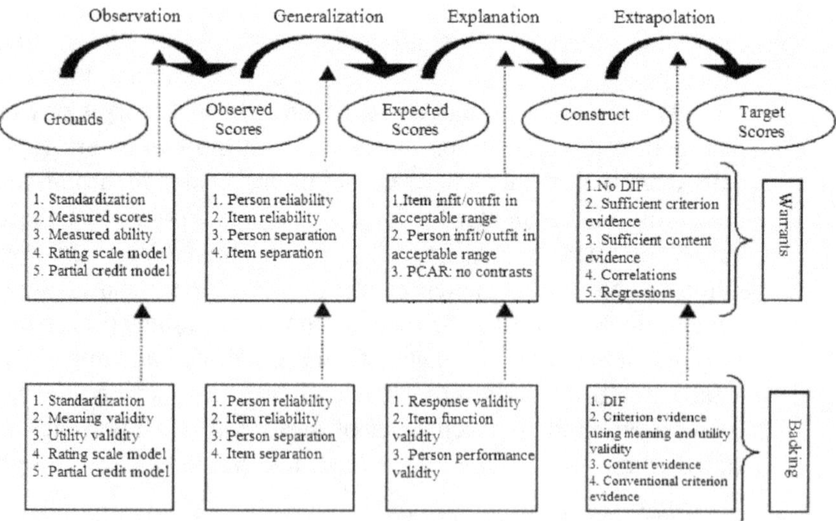

Figure 3: Kane's (2006) IA approach adapted by Aryadoust (2009: 1193; 2013): mapping Rasch-based measurement onto the argument-based validity framework

a sequence of measurement and psychometric operations in a testing programme.

Kane's ABV offers a more applied approach that systematises the formulation of the research into a plan, which comprises an IA and a VA (Kane, 2006, 2013; Kane, Crooks & Cohen, 2013). This is an improvement over the guidance offered by the *Standards*. As pointed out earlier, whereas the *Standards* (1999, 2014) present five sources of evidence and recommend that these be integrated into a coherent argument, they offer no guidance on how to do the sequencing of research, the stopping of the research or the integration of argument. The *Standards* state: 'A sound validity argument integrates various strands of evidence into a coherent account of the degree to which existing evidence and theory support the intended interpretation of test scores for specific uses. It encompasses evidence gathered from new studies and evidence available from earlier reported research' (AERA, APA & NCME, 1999: 17). The *Standards* add:

> Ultimately, the validity of an intended interpretation of test scores relies on all the available evidence relevant to the technical quality of a testing system. This includes evidence of careful test construction; adequate score reliability; appropriate test administration and scoring; accurate score scaling, equating, and standard setting; and careful attention to fairness for all examinees (1999: 17).

As they stand, the five sources of evidence or the research studies represent an assortment of evidence that needs an organisational system. Perhaps the role of a document like the *Standards* is to offer a *macro-level view* of how to approach validity research. The *Standards* provide the essential ingredients but remain removed from specific applications. They are engaged more with a big picture that remains relevant to different disciplines and applications. The extent to which such thinking is useful is up for debate.

The IA does not promote any given interpretation or score use but asserts the importance of laying out the inferences pertinent to the proposed interpretation and use. Kane asserts that more ambitious interpretations entail more inferences or claims to be laid out and demand more research backing and justification. While Kane's ABV does not demand conformity in terms of the inferences and hypotheses specified, he does hold firm on the need to maintain a two-step process, i.e., a unified argument-based approach – IA and VA. We state the IA and then proceed to evaluate it, i.e., the VA. Finally, and as explored next, Kane distinguishes between the design-development stage and the appraisal phase when the assessment programme is operational in terms of the nature of validation undertaken.

IA and VA at the development versus at the operational stage

Kane's ABV proposes different orientation to validity research at distinct stages of test development. Kane's (2006) two-step process is different in nature during the design and development phase versus when the system is up and running. Table 12 provides a summary of the stages and related IA and VA arguments. At the design and development stage, test developers are still in the process of operationalising the construct, delineating content domain, elaborating test specifications, creating items and tasks, setting administration conditions, establishing scoring codes, creating rating mechanisms, pilot and field testing, as well as working to establish related operations and support systems. At this design and development stage, research is undertaken to ascertain and refine all aspects of a testing programme. IA is constructed to specify the network of inferences and related claims inherent in the interpretation and use and research is undertaken to improve the quality of development. A VA at this stage seeks to *confirm* the quality of the testing programme before it goes live and becomes operational.

Validation research undertaken at the development stage is meant to pursue support for the inferences associated with test score interpretations given intended uses. Research at the development stage tends to produce rationales and evidence to support intended psychometric and measurement features. Kane labels this type of research as confirmationist in nature. Validation results are plugged into the refinement of assessment processes being developed to improve the quality of the assessment tools and services and render desirable score attributes. Publications by Chapelle, Enright & Jameison (2008, 2010) provide excellent examples of validation at the development stage. These publications provide extensive documentation of IA specifications and related VA research undertaken at the design and development of iBT TOEFL.

In summary, the intent at this design and development stage is to engage in constructive criticism that allows professionals to continue to refine the testing programme until desired measurement and operational properties are attained. Validation continues until test publishing professionals

Testing System Phases	Assessment Programme Under Development	Assessment Programme Developed
Nature of Engagement	Support	Appraisal
Interpretive Argument (IA)	Development of interpretation and use in terms of inferences and assumptions	IA treated as a proposal to be critically evaluated
Validation Argument (VA)	Evidence obtained tends to be confirmationist	Evidence obtained tends to be critical

Table 12: Nature of arguments (Kane, 2006)

make the decision that the argument to support the IA inferences meets their expectations and they are satisfied that they should proceed to test administration.

At the point at which the development of the testing programme has been completed to the degree that the test is live, the nature of the research pursued changes. At this operational phase, Kane (2006) characterises validity engagement as more critical. He argues that the IA and validation research at the appraisal stage need to be more challenging (devil's-advocate-like) with regard to ongoing operations. At this operational stage, research challenges, for example, the theories that underpin the testing programme, the scope of the target domain, the nature of predictions made, the practical aspects of the operation, the appropriateness of intended score interpretations, the impact of intended use, etc. Unintended and negative types of consequences observed are pursued as part of validation at this stage as well. Recently published research by Cheng & Sun (2015) illustrates an argument-based approach to validation at the appraisal stage. This validation research was conducted in the context of the Ontario Secondary School Literacy Test. The research undertaken posits the IA from the test developers' perspective who then carry out impact research that they utilise to critically engage in the inferences and claims articulated in the IA. Cheng & Sun's (2015) study zeroed in on issues of explanation and utilisation and underscored the empirical support for the extrapolation inference. This research offers guidance on how to design more critical types of appraisal validation.

Kane's differentiation of the development and appraisal phases of validation represents a significant contribution to the field. Such differentiation clarifies the role research serves at different stages of the life of a testing programme. The differentiated stages also articulate clearly that while a confirmatory approach to validation is necessary to enhance the quality of the assessment products, services, interpretations and outcomes, it is not sufficient. Critical engagement that challenges the various aspects of the operations is also needed. This line of thinking reflects rationales proposed by earlier researchers such as Cronbach (1988) and Shepard (1993). For example, Shepard (1993: 429) posits three questions to help organise validity research and argument:

1. 'What does the testing practice claim to do?'
2. 'What are the arguments for **and against** the intended aims of the test?'
3. 'What does the test do in the system **other than what it claims**, for good or bad?' (emphasis added).

The questions point to validation that clearly includes a confirmationist approach, *arguments for* and *intended claims*, as well as a critical approach, *arguments against* and *other unintended claims*, to be pursued when formulating a validity argument. The explicit attention to critical research at the appraisal stage represents an important contribution by Kane. Such research may generate meaningful and important evidence, and enhance testing practices and impact of score meaning and outcomes.

Argument quality criteria and pitfalls

The overarching criteria typically discussed in the literature with regard to Kane's approach focus on clarity, coherence and plausibility. The following description by Lane (2014: 128) characterises Kane's three suggested criteria as follows:

> Kane (2006) provided three criteria for the evaluation of IU arguments, including clarity, coherence, and plausibility. A clear IU [interpretative and use] argument is stated as a framework for validation in that 'the inferences to be used in getting from the observed performance to the proposed conclusions and decisions, as well as the warrants and backing supporting these inferences, should be specified in enough detail to make the rationale for the proposed claims apparent' (Kane, 2006: 29). A coherent argument logically links the network of inferences from performance to conclusions and decisions, including the actions resulting from the decisions. The plausibility of the argument emphasises that the assumptions underlying the assessment and score inferences

should be credible and judged in terms of supporting and conflicting evidence.

The clarity criterion basically looks at the scope and explicitness of the IU inferences and the research posited to support these inferences. The coherence criterion, perhaps similar to that in writing assessment, speaks to how logical the connections among the inferences are. Coherence targets the quality of the links, which bind the inferences together as they move from student performances to interpretations and decisions. The plausibility criterion denotes the extent to which the assumptions underlying an argument are credible or worthy of acceptance.

Kane (2006, 2013) also differentiates between criteria used to judge the quality of semantic and decision interpretations. Semantic or meaning-clarifying interpretations call for empirical backing, true versus untrue judgements, plausibility, coherence, logic and arguments, etc. types of meaning-driven corroboration. Decisions, on the other hand, call for value judgements of outcomes. Evidence of use may require utility research where outcomes and consequences are judged typically as effective versus ineffective.

Fundamental to this ongoing description of criteria is the notion of who is making the judgement with regard to the argument. The criteria in general specify principles, which are likely to be viewed differently by different stakeholder groups. One has to assume that the criteria are intended to target primarily test publishers and research professionals. Other stakeholder groups such as students, parents, teachers, principals, employers, etc., however, have to be considered. This is especially the case with testing systems observed in accountability testing (see Chalhoub-Deville, 2016). The type of judgement that Kane calls for is not likely to be uniformly rendered across different stakeholder groups.

Next, we address problems potentially associated with arguments, as discussed by Kane. 'The specification of the IUA clarifies what is being claimed and a carefully developed validity argument can provide a reasonable basis for accepting or rejecting these claims, but the process is not automatic...it requires judgement and it can go wrong' (Kane, 2013: 18). Kane warns against fallacies such as gilding the lily, begging the question, overgeneralisation or spurious material, reification and the straw-man. Here, we provide an explanation of some of these fallacies, which may not be readily comprehensible or are typically observed in practice.

The gilded lily fallacy occurs when the VA embeds support for inferences and interpretations which are readily perceived to be plausible. This fallacy references attempts to evoke more confidence by unnecessarily generating research to garner more support for an argument already perceived to be good.

Begging the question refers to arguments built on some questionable inferences. It can also denote basing the totality of the IA on some parts of that argument. Begging the question occurs 'when some critical inference or assumption in an argument is simply taken for granted, or "begged"' (Kane, 2013: 18). The fallacy refers to arguments where a conclusion is based on a premise that lacks support or the assumption is false or far-fetched. Begging the question is also related to circular logic/ arguments. Circular logic or arguments have been commonly observed, for example, with testing programmes developed to be closely related to some hierarchical descriptors – guidelines or frameworks. Evidence is sought to speak to how faithfully the test scores replicate the intended descriptors. Such a system of development and confirmation is closed to any external verification.

The straw-man fallacy denotes an argument that 'goes in the opposite direction and adopts an [IA/IUA] that is more ambitious than it needs to be, given the proposed interpretations and uses' (Kane, 2013: 18). A straw-man fallacy denotes an exaggerated or a misrepresented argument. The fallacy cautions against IAs which tend to stack the evidence beyond what is warranted by the claims, interpretations and uses. Having said that, Kane does emphasise that ambitious interpretations and uses require more augmented support. 'More-ambitious claims require more support than less-ambitious claims' (Kane, 2013: 3). Ambitious claims are typically observed with standardised admissions and accountability testing systems. We need to be careful to differentiate a true need to accumulate more evidence from a straw-man fallacy where the evidence accumulation is gratuitous and superfluous.

In their 2010 publication Bachman & Palmer present a validity model that reflects many of the tenets advanced by Kane (2006). They, however, contend that Kane's 'two arguments' approach, i.e., IA and VA, is confusing to assessment practitioners. Kane (2013) addressed this issue when responding to the same complaint presented by Sireci (2013) and Newton (2013). Kane asserted that the separation of the IA from the VA helps make clear what the argument and claims are and what the evidence to support each of these comprises. Those evaluating the argument can then point to weaknesses in the claims included, e.g., in terms of relevance, coverage and complexity, amount, etc. as laid out in the IA presented, or they may question the research undertaken to support those IA inferences.

Kane's central tenets, e.g., an argument-based approach to validity, an optional attention to constructs, a practical plan for laying out claims, have shaped validity in language testing in the US. The two-step ABV helps make the process of laying claims and pursuing inference support more transparent and amenable to evaluation. Kane's ideas have been positively received in language testing particularly in the US.

Revisiting construct validity

Messick basically positioned constructs as the fulcrum for all types of validity research. Kane has expressed concerns about the impracticality of a construct validity approach as advanced by Messick. He also expressed concerns about the state of constructs in the social sciences in general. This point has been made in language testing by researchers such as McNamara (2006) and Chapelle (2012) who point out the lack of strong theories or constructs in the field and characterise a second/foreign language (L2) ability as a weak construct. Bachman & Palmer (2010) move the field away from Messick's thinking, which has dominated the language testing field for decades. It is very telling, for example, that Bachman & Palmer do not even include the term *construct validity* in their index. This change is of great significance.

In his various publications (e.g., Bachman, 1990; Bachman & Palmer, 1996), Bachman has followed the tradition established in the widely-accepted measurement publications, pushing the field of language testing in the direction of construct validity research. While his earlier works promoted and elaborated on Messick's thinking and progressive matrix, this has changed in recent years. Bachman & Palmer in their 2010 book, even before the publication of the 2014 *Standards*, abandoned anchoring research in construct validity in favour of a pragmatic validation approach, very similar to what Kane suggests with his ABV. Bachman & Palmer do not offer any explicit rationale for this major change.

Interestingly enough, the *Standards* of 1999 include the term 'construct validity' in the glossary (the definition is presented in the definition table in the first part of this monograph and repeated here for readers' easier access), offering the following description:

> **construct validity** A term used to indicate that the test scores are to be interpreted as indicating the test taker's standing on the psychological construct measured by the test. A construct is a theoretical variable inferred from multiple types of evidence, which might include the interrelations of the test scores with other variables, internal test structure, observations of response processes, as well as the content of the test. In the current *Standards*, all test scores are viewed as measures of some construct, so the phrase is redundant with validity. The validity argument establishes the construct validity of a test (AERA, APA & NCME, 1999: 174, bold in original).

The quote highlights theoretical and psychological constructs, which are hypothesised from various sources of investigations. It also reaffirms that all scores are representations of some intended construct, which in turn anchors the validity argument. As confusing as anchoring validity in a concept which it also embodies may be, the *Standards* (1999), a decade after Messick's (1989) influential publication, enshrined validity arguments in construct validity. Anchoring all evidence in construct validity underscores the centrality of *construct* and the important but supporting role other types of evidence play in such research. While the 1999 *Standards* solidly anchor validity in *construct validity*, the most recent edition, i.e.., *Standards* (2014) decidedly move away from constructs and from according construct validity an overarching role. The 2014 *Standards* do not include the term construct validity in the glossary. As a matter of fact, the entire document includes only one mention of the term and it is there simply to say it existed in a former publication: '… lines of evidence subsumed under "construct validity" in prior conceptualizations of the validation process...' (AERA, APA & NCME, 2014: 173). Similar to Bachman & Palmer (2010), the 2014 *Standards* offer no explicit explanation for the demise of construct validity.

What is clear, presently, is that the measurement and language testing communities have both moved beyond construct validity. The push, at least in the US, is to embrace a more pragmatic conceptualisation of validity research. This new orientation, while it resolves some of the challenges commonly observed with construct validity, introduces new challenges and concerns. It requires more close attention to inferences such as consequences, which are deemed contentious.

CHAPTER 3

PRINCIPLED DESIGN, TEST DEVELOPMENT AND VALIDATION

Principled design and validation: Illustrative models

Weir's (2005), O'Sullivan & Weir's (2002, 2011) and O'Sullivan's (2011, 2016) *socio-cognitive model* in the UK, and Bachman & Palmer's (2010) *assessment use argument* (AUA) in the US, both suggest a pragmatic, practical approach to validity. Both camps seek to pay more attention to test development aspects. Gone is any language of anchoring validity in construct validity, as suggested by Messick's (1989) *construct validity progressive matrix*. Constructs are optional, as suggested by Kane (2006, 2013). The socio-cognitive model and AUA seek to expand evidence to more prominently represent aspects of content and consequences in quality documentation of a testing programme. We build on these two notions of content and consequences in what follows.

Given the orientation of this monograph to better connect validity research to testing operations, we delve in this chapter into concepts and models that have been advanced by educational measurement professionals to expand score-based validity documentation. Works by Bachman & Palmer, Lissitz & Samuelsen, Mislevy, Embretson, among others, have been concerned with issues of test development and the role of validity. We first focus on AUA as it most closely builds on Kane's ideas and offers a bridge to the validity systems that emphasise that validity is design – validity needs to accommodate test development. We explore contentions that validity references internal test development features, as presented by Lissitz & Samuelsen. Discussed in this section is Mislevy's *evidence centered design*, which emphasises the importance of validity at the design stage of a testing system. Embretson's model, *universal validity evidence*, also promotes consideration of design and development categories of evidence, in addition to psychometric documentation. These authors offer approaches which portray different functions for validity but all nonetheless pay attention to test development practices. Given, again, the primary interest in this monograph to better align validation and testing system operations, the works of these authors address directly issues of interest.

Finally, the chapter explores issues of validity and consequences in the context of educational reform and accountability testing, which is increasingly driving instructional practices. Reform-seeking policies in the US have allocated funding for and dictated aspects of design for accountability testing systems. These policies articulate overarching goals and specify test design features to achieve intended goals. Documentation within such systems also directs attention to validity not only at the individual test taker level, but at the aggregate, group level, as well as the larger socio-educational structure levels.

Bachman & Palmer's assessment use argument (AUA)

The AUA, similar to Kane's validation approach, represents a pragmatic process. Bachman & Palmer's AUA differs, however, from Kane's argument-based validity approach in two fundamental ways. Unlike Kane's IA, AUA clearly proclaims test design and development operations as critical components in validation. Bachman & Palmer (2010) underscore the importance of design and development as part of the validation process. Also, unlike Kane's sequencing of the IA, which begins with scores, Bachman & Palmer argue that validation commences at the design level and is anchored in intended/actual consequence(s). AUA links inferences from intended/actual consequences, intended/actual decisions, intended/actual interpretations of test taker's language ability, as well as assessment records/scores to assessment performance and the embedded assessment tasks.

As indicated by Figure 4, which shows inferential links from consequences to assessment performance, Bachman & Palmer (2010: 91) posit two arrows to call attention to aspects of assessment development as well as interpretation and use. One arrow, pointing down, indicates that validation starts with assessment development. It basically anchors assessment design in intended consequences, decisions and interpretations, and moves to scores and performance features. The other arrow, pointing upwards, directs attention to a sequence that starts with that test taker's performance, converted to some record – score or description. This arrow focuses efforts on justification for actual interpretation, use and consequences. Kane's IA/IUA resembles the interpretation and use arrow, pointing upward. This test development arrow suggests that development is decidedly integrated into validity documentation. Kane

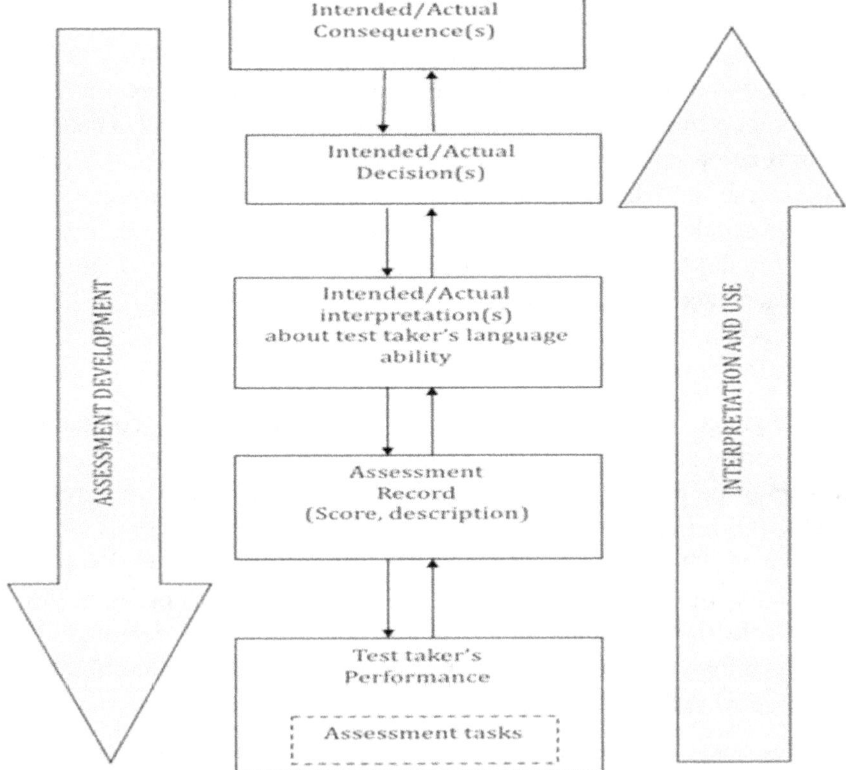

Figure 4: Inferential links from consequences to assessment performance (Bachman & Palmer, 2010: 91, Figure 5.1)

adopts more of what can be argued to be a measurement-psychometric stance where attention to research begins with converting performance to scores, and evidence is then related to or based on these scores. Additionally, and in comparison to Bachman & Palmer's strong affirmation of consequences as the cornerstone for the inferential links, Kane's commitment in this area is best characterised as work in progress.

At this point, we would like to explore three broad aspects of Bachman & Palmer's thinking and the AUA model: construct, consequences and justification. These issues are chosen because they represent clear points of departure for language testing from the prevailing measurement community. The first two notions also have been driving language testing publications and operations, especially in the US.

Constructs, tasks and validity

Given the long tradition in language testing to anchor validity in constructs, it is worth looking at how the language construct fares in AUA. Construct features could be said to be prominently represented in the AUA interpretation inference. This supposition is supported by AUA's inclusion of the term language ability in 'Intended/Actual interpretation(s) about test taker's language ability'. In addition, the Index includes an entry for abilities, which refers readers to look up construct. A language construct is viewed as 'a course syllabus, a needs analysis of TLU [target language use] tasks, a theory of language ability, or some combination of these' (Bachman & Palmer, 2010: 213).

The language construct in Bachman & Palmer's AUA is very comparable in its portrayal to what appears in earlier publications. While Bachman & Palmer do not refer to language ability as communicative language ability (CLA), as they had done in earlier publications (e.g., Bachman & Palmer, 1996), the language construct remains a representation of the interaction of language knowledge, topical knowledge, personal attributes, affective schemata and strategies along with task features. The authors offer no explanation for why they have abandoned the CLA term although what they present is essentially the same.

We do not see evidence, whether it is in terms of construct articulation or publications drawn upon, to denote much of a departure in thinking from CLA. To explain: in the Notes section at the end of the chapter, Bachman & Palmer also indicate that their construct representation builds on ideas and models advanced by authors such as Canale & Swain (1980), Hymes (1972), Savignon (1972, 1983) and Widdowson (1978, 1983). This body of literature is exactly what is referenced in Bachman (1990) as well as Bachman & Palmer (1996). An important question here is whether the abandonment of the label is of importance and merits the attention we give it in the present analysis. We contend that the change is emblematic of a significant shift in thinking, as discussed earlier, with regard to constructs and construct validity. Nevertheless, the absence of explicit terms and labels is not sufficient to conclude that Bachman & Palmer have actually altered their position with regard to constructs appreciably.

The above quote about the language construct presents a theory of language ability as one of the options that can be called upon to guide test development efforts and to anchor score interpretation. Abandoning the CLA label, we conjecture, is intended to demote constructs from the supreme status they have held for decades to a more 'it is an option' perspective. As an option, the theory of language ability, formerly called CLA, presented by Bachman & Palmer, provides support at a general level of the intended content, and the analysis of TLU helps articulate the specific construct and task attributes in the given domain of contexts of use, e.g., academic English language use in a university. It is interesting to note that this more flexible status of language ability theory brings the US and the UK perspectives closer. Where the US has traditionally pushed for the development of theoretical constructs, UK efforts, as described earlier, were more engaged in articulating syllabi and curricula to guide instruction and assessment. Now, the US and UK perspectives seem to be in broad agreement about the role of language theory to guide development and validation efforts – this is particularly the case in the socio-cognitive approach of Weir and O'Sullivan (see the following section), where language and social models are combined in reaching an understanding of the construct to be tested, and this feeds into all aspects of the development process, from task design, to assessment criteria, to interpretation of score meaning. Additionally, this shift in the status of constructs resembles the move away from Messick's construct validity to a more pragmatic approach as delineated in Kane's IA/IUA.

Bachman & Palmer (2010) assert that tasks are not to be conflated with constructs. They contend that scores on assessment tasks, even those that closely match intended TLU domain tasks, 'are of very limited use for making predictions. Scores from such assessment tasks cannot be interpreted as indicators of what test takers know and bring to their performance on the task' (2010: 220). Schwabe, von Davier & Chalhoub-Deville (2016: 307) elaborate in relation to this point:

> Anchoring scores in tasks affords us the expediency of inferences that seemingly connect assessments more readily to RL [real-life] situations. However, if not deliberately attended to at the design level, it is doubtful that such an approach will enable the extrapolation of L2 construct features – knowledge and processes – underlying performance, a critical consideration in the explication of scores (see research findings in Chalhoub-Deville, 2001). As the field moves forward, it is important to forge a more reasoned role for tasks in theoretical representations of the L2 construct.

We cannot assume that tasks readily afford transparency of underlying features and lend support to meaningful interpretation of scores. Salient task features need to be investigated and explicitly articulated in test specifications. The need to pay close attention to aspects of constructs and tasks and the nature of specifications is critical because they drive performance and scores/records obtained. Bachman & Palmer have customarily endorsed anchoring testing programmes in constructs, whether through CLA or more broadly defined in terms of a syllabus or some identified tasks. They continue with AUA this same practice. The authors emphasise the need to elaborate constructs in test development and in the justification research process.

Consequences and stakeholders

A significant feature that differentiates AUA from Kane's IA/IUA approach to validity is the call to attend to consequences and stakeholders throughout the process of validation. AUA is anchored in consequences. As part of the initial planning for a testing project, Bachman & Palmer prompt readers to consider 'Who are the intended test takers? How will they be affected? ... Who else will be affected? How will they be affected?' (2010: 450). Consequence claims generally speak to issues of beneficence. Bachman & Palmer adopt this notion from Kunnan (2000) who advances 'the principle of beneficence'. Bachman & Palmer (2010: 105) write: 'Following Kunnan, we define beneficence as the degree to which the consequences of *using* an assessment and of the *decisions* that are made promote *good* and are *not detrimental* to *stakeholders*' (emphasis added). Bachman & Palmer promote considerations of consequences of assessment use and decisions. They call on test developers (for example, see pages 105–110), to attend to consequences related to:

- individuals, e.g., experiences of test preparations, feedback received, equitability, etc.;
- teachers, e.g., washback and impact on instruction; and
- education systems and society, e.g., community values and legal requirements.

Bachman & Palmer encourage developers to attend to stakeholders to be affected by test use and decisions as well as those dictating use and making decisions. Research on engagement of stakeholder groups is still nascent, e.g., Chapelle (2012) and Berry, O'Sullivan & Rugea (2012). An agenda that outlines the investigations and documentation that ought to be pursued to systematise the lines of inquiry into validity/justification research and to integrate areas of communication, however, is still needed.

AUA's attention to aspects of consequences is pervasive. It includes statements that speak to how beneficial a testing system is to individuals, teachers/groups and societal/educational systems: reports (scores and decisions) are confidential; information is communicated appropriately and provided in a timely fashion; testing supports and promotes instruction and learning; values are considered and legal requirements are adhered to; decisions are technically sound, impartial and afford uniform decision processes; equitable treatment is promoted as well as various aspects of fairness and bias being considered. Given this encompassing attention to consequences and the call to engage stakeholders broadly, Bachman & Palmer (2010: 213) promote differentiated communication. They write that the construct 'should be stated in terms that the stakeholders reading the AUA can relate to and understand…', adding that 'the construct definition may be defined in technical terms for the test developers, as part of the Design Statement or Blueprint, while it will typically be stated in more general language for other stakeholder groups'. Table 13 includes quotes taken from Bachman & Palmer (2010: 158–160, *Table 8.1: Assessment Use Argument claims, warrants and rebuttal*). These quotes show that in various, principal areas of AUA, Bachman & Palmer have referenced the importance of attending to stakeholder groups. AUA is anchored in consequences and communication plays a critical role in turning technical documentation into information/actions that relevant stakeholders can utilise. Bachman & Palmer's attention to differentiated communication for stakeholder groups represents a meaningful and important advance in thinking in this area. The field and the public would benefit if our scholarship pays more attention to these matters.

Bachman & Palmer (2010: 110–111) are explicit in terms of the need to address not only intended but also unintended consequences – one can reason that they mean negative unintended consequences. On this point, they write:

> Given the almost infinite range of possible unintended consequences of using a particular assessment and of making a decision based on this, even the most conscientious and diligent test developer cannot possibly anticipate or guard against all the potential unintended consequences of using a particular assessment. Thus, the real issue here is that of determining which, out of all the possible unintended consequences, need to be anticipated.

The authors explicitly call attention to intended as well as unintended consequences, an approach that befits AUA's pragmatic orientation to validation. They do not, however, explain how risks can be identified

Claim 1: **CONSEQUENCES.** The consequences of using an assessment and of the decisions that are made are **beneficial** to stakeholders

A. Warrants about the **beneficence** of the consequences of *using the assessment*:

1. The consequences of using the assessment that are *specific to each stakeholder group* will be beneficial. …
3. Assessment reports are presented in ways that are clear and understandable to all stakeholder groups. …

B. Warrant and rebuttal about the **beneficence** of the consequences of the *decisions that are made*:

2. Warrant: The consequences of the decisions will be beneficial for *each group* of stakeholders. …

Claim 2: **DECISIONS.** …

B. Warrants about the **equitability** of the decisions that are made: …

2. Test takers and other affected stakeholders are fully informed about how the decision will be made and whether decisions are actually made in the way described to them. …

Claim 3: **INTERPRETATIONS.** …

A. Warrants about the **meaningfulness** of the interpretations:

7. The test developer communicates the definition of the construct to be assessed in terms that are clearly understandable to all stakeholders. …

Claim 4: **ASSESSMENT RECORDS.** ….

NB: The output part of this claim is an 'assessment record', which is reported to the relevant stakeholders, along with the interpretation from Claim 3 above. …

(Bachman & Palmer, 2014, presentation at the British Council, London)

Table 13: Attending to stakeholder groups in Bachman & Palmer's AUA (2010: 158–160, emphasis added)

and engaged in to remedy potential negative impact. More guidance is needed with regard to practical matters such as:

- the nature of adequate and appropriate documentation of actual consequences;
- the process/framework to identify and isolate any factors that may influence the desired outcomes;

- the causal links or relationships between the testing activities and the desired outcomes;
- the allocation of responsibility for the various aspects of consequence-related research within a testing organisation/programme and outside in relevant policy, societal, etc. circles;
- the need to identify potential unintended consequences;
- the stakeholder group to be held responsible for a given intended/ unintended consequence-related matter; and
- the financial resources required.

In summary, Bachman & Palmer's unequivocal anchoring of the AUA conceptual framework of validity in issues of consequences is notable. Consequences are the first issue to be dealt with during assessment development and the last issue to be accommodated when attending to interpretation and use. This commitment to consequences is not widely embraced in the measurement community. More on consequences in the measurement literature later.

Justification versus validation

Another notable difference between Bachman & Palmer's AUA and Kane's IA is the nomenclature they adopt for their frameworks. Bachman & Palmer reject the term validation in favour of justification. They also emphasise their preference for the term justification versus argument. One could remark that this difference is not substantive. After all, AUA's concepts of claims, warrants, backing and rebuttals are reminiscent of Kane's (2006) presentation of these concepts. However, the term justification begins to move the concept of validity beyond the technical scope of psychometric analyses of scores and performance-related data. The term justification encompasses operations that attend to test design and development. As Bachman & Palmer (2010: 95) write, a process of justification 'guides the development and use of a given language assessment and provides the basis for quality control throughout the entire process of assessment development'. Unlike Kane's IA/IUA approach, AUA's justification refers to quality control, which is not restricted to psychometric, score-oriented analyses. AUA's justification emphasises quality documentation of testing operations throughout design and development.

This attention to documentation of quality at the development level is likely to be embraced more by language testing professionals, as compared to Kane's audience, which tends to be more measurement and psychometric professionals. This is because we would normally expect language testing professionals who have a background in areas such as language teaching, linguistics and acquisition to be more inclined to attend to test design and development operations. Measurement professionals, especially psychometricians, given their training, are more preoccupied with score and data analysis. Consequently, the type of documentation that each group attends to shifts to accommodate their professional backgrounds and training.

The other point that could be said to support the term justification is the distinct and compelling representation of consequences in AUA. Consequences in Kane's IUA is one of the eventual links in an argument. The inference related to consequences appears after scoring, generalisation, extrapolation and implication inferences have been attended to. 'Consequences' in AUA, on the other hand, serve as the foundation for test design and development. AUA anchors all inferences in aspects of consequences. Intended consequences, to be fleshed out at the design level, are said to anchor planned decision(s), interpretation(s), scores and descriptive statements, and task features. Once the test is operational, investigations of consequences resembles IA's progression of performance quality documentation. However, because AUA posits a statement of consequences at the design level, eventual investigations of consequences are more focused and targeted. Investigations of actual consequences are confirmatory in nature. Said differently, the articulation of intended consequences enables purposeful research of actual uses, outcomes and practices.

It is interesting that Embretson (2007, 2008) also opts to use a different label to denote research that attends to quality beyond interpretation, but more on Embretson later. For now it is most relevant to point out that, in her *universal validity model*, Embretson uses the term *significance* to refer to categories that support test score utility, impact, etc. Again, if quality control pertains to all operations in a testing system, then maybe we do need a different label to denote the research that attends to aspects of consequences. Validity could be the label to use for research to support score interpretation, and justification or significance to support intended and actual uses, decisions and consequences. As we contemplate the merits of adopting different labels, we need to consider whether differential labelling really matters and in what ways. Would, for example, the adoption of different terms be used to denote more transparent activities to be undertaken? Bachman & Palmer (2010: 95) do not articulate differentiated roles for test developers and user groups with regard to these activities. They, for example, note when arguing in favour of adopting the term justification in assessment:

> It [justification] provides the basis for test developers and decision makers to be held accountable to those who will be affected by the use of the assessment and the decisions that are made.

adding that:

> It is important for test developers and test users, or decision makers, to realize that they may be held accountable by any stakeholder group at any time for the uses of an assessment they have developed and used.

These quotes offer blanket statements of comprehensive responsibilities. Who is responsible for what research to support different aspects of an assessment, related scores and ensuing consequences, however, is a point of huge contention (see Chalhoub-Deville 2009a, 2016 for a discussion of this point).

Bachman & Palmer's justification presents a very distinctive approach to documenting quality assurance in a testing programme. The AUA approach raises critical questions with regard to the scope of quality documentation. For example:

- Where does quality assurance begin and what does it include?
- Do we need different terms for the same set of evidence when addressing different stakeholder groups?
- How practical is it to have determined roles and differentiated responsibilities for varied documentation of consequences?
- Do language testing and measurement professionals have the expertise and discipline training needed to engage with issues of consequences?
- What structures can help us delineate the embedding of consequences into various aspects of our testing operations?
- To what extent can reform-oriented testing achieve the ambitious consequences intended by accountability-based policies?

These questions deserve attention as the field deliberates the inclusion of consequences in test in all stages of test development, including test design and score use.

Lissitz & Samuelsen: Validity with internal features

In the lead article of a special issue of *Educational Researcher*, Lissitz & Samuelsen (2007a, b) present a model that anchors validity in content matters and does away with construct validity. In their model, shown in Figure 5, the authors differentiate between internal features, which include latent processes, content and reliability, and external components that comprise network (nomological networks), utility (concurrent and predictive) and impact. They view internal features as part of validity and thus test developers' responsibility. External areas represent research outside the purview of validity and the responsibility of test developers. External components' research is to be undertaken by test users and related stakeholders.

The internal components refer to aspects that connect most closely with test design and development, i.e., the 'process of the creation of instruments that measure something of interest' (Lissitz & Samuelsen, 2007b: 442). In this regard, validity is considered a property of the test in terms of its representativeness of content specific to some domain and its documentation of reliability. Such representation brings back old notions

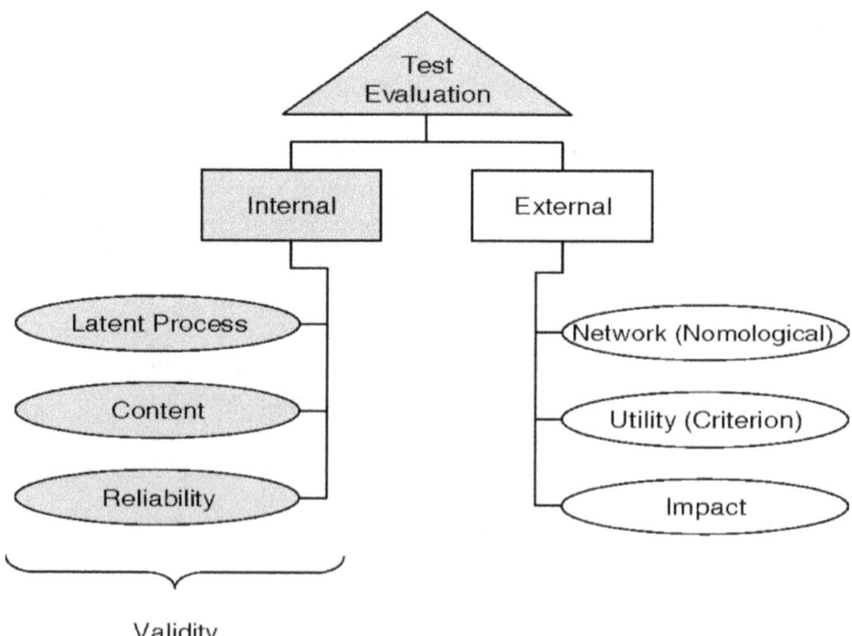

Figure 5: The structure of the technical evaluation of educational testing (Lissitz & Samuelsen, 2007a: 438)

of validity and reliability. However, it is the inclusion of cognitive processes that renders this model different from those in the past. 'This focus on person response processes, rather than simply on test items, set the conception of content validity apart from others and provided a basis for considering tests of differential item function and factor analyses (as examples) under the umbrella of content validity.' In essence, and in line with the *Standards* (1999, 2014), which consider response processes to be one of the five sources of evidence, Lissitz & Samuelsen (2007a) move away from only sampling the domain of interest (curriculum, *Standards*, tasks related to a job, etc.) and target latent processes, which detail the type of engagement test takers have with the content sampled.

Lissitz & Samuelsen (2007a, b) flesh out their conception of the investigations to be undertaken to support internal test development operations. In Table 14, which we have reproduced from their article, the authors outline questions and related sources of evidence pertinent to each of the three categories: content, reliability and latent processes. While the questions raised and the evidence suggested are not novel, they do provide practical guidance on some core investigations to be undertaken to support test development practices. As we can see from what is omitted from the table, Lissitz & Samuelsen classify the nomological network associated with theoretical development or construct as external to test development operations and not a validity consideration. Criterion utility and impact are also excluded from validity. Relating the test to, or differentiating it from, other measures or exploring its effect is worth pursuing by *someone* but is certainly not a test development concern, Lissitz & Samuelsen assert. The authors write, for example, with regard to consequences:

> We think the impact of a test is sometimes an important consideration and sometimes worth studying, but if a test is later shown to have some impact that is unintended or unwanted, that observation should not be considered relevant to the question of whether the test is valid. …consequential validity suggests that there is a belief that if a test leads to unacceptable or unwanted ends, the test…was not acceptable or valid. The argument can also go in the other direction, where positive consequences can be seen as justifying the use of a particular assessment device. We reject that argument (Lissitz & Samuelsen, 2007b: 445).

Lissitz & Samuelsen essentially contend that a nomological network, criterion utility and impact are less under the control of test developers

Perspective	Sample of questions asked	Potential sources of evidence
Practical		
Content	Does the assessment encompass the full range of the content *Standards*? Does the assessment properly reflect the cognitive complexity of those *Standards*? Is the same emphasis reflected in the assessment as in the *Standards* and in the classroom? Are the items appropriate for the purpose of the assessment? Are the items properly constructed? Are there criteria and mechanisms in place for scoring the items?	Analysis of the curriculum Creation of a table of specifications or test blueprint Documentation of match between items and blueprint Documentation that students have the opportunity to learn Documentation of the qualifications of the item writers and raters (including their training) Review of items and scoring rubrics for quality Examination of item characteristics (difficulty, discrimination, option selection) from pre-test, pilot or field test
Reliability	When matched on ability, do students from different racial groups perform similarly? Genders? Are the test items appropriate for students with limited English proficiency? Students with disabilities? Do the different test forms provide the same information? Does the test provide the same information on different occasions? How accurate are the test scores?	Bias and sensitivity review DIF analysis Review of the accommodations offered Analysis of the scores of accommodated students Test-retest reliability Parallel-forms reliability Internal consistency reliability Examination of the standard error of estimate for total score and subtest scores Rater consistency

Theoretical		
Latent process	Are the tasks eliciting the expected knowledge, skills, and abilities from the students? Do tasks that are supposed to work together do so? Do tasks that are supposed to provide unique information do so? Are the item difficulties at the expected levels, and are the distracters functioning as expected?	Review of the item performance data Examination of pattern of intercorrelation of items Examination of item, testlet, and total test score relationships Convergent/divergent evidence from correlations Factor analysis Results of verbal reports or think-alouds Cognitive analysis of student responses

Note: DIF = differential item functioning.

Table 14: Internal factors that should be considered for the systematic evaluation of content validity (Lissitz & Samuelsen 2007a: 6)

and more the purview of researchers and user groups. Therefore, they argue that research into these external areas should realistically be the responsibility of researchers in the field at large and test use stakeholders. Additionally, while these components are important for test evaluation, they fall outside the purview of validity research, and their documentation has no bearing on *test validity*.

Basically, researchers who were invited to contribute to the special issue of *Educational Researcher*, edited by Lissitz & Samuelsen (2007a, b), tended to concur that more attention to aspects of test development is well warranted. These researchers endorse the need for more explicit guidance and articulation with regard to test development. This is a point that Chapelle (2012) also made when discussing Kane's IA. The network of inferences that Kane lays out focuses on the set of assumptions at key points in the measurement process, as opposed to the test development part of assessment. The UK position in the past was very much aligned with Lissitz & Samuelsen's (2007a, b) core argument. The more practical approach to quality documentation, generally prevalent in the UK before the development of the socio-cognitive approach, endorses validity as an articulation of test development practices. The socio-cognitive approach broke with UK tradition. It recognises the importance of clearly defining the construct, as well as clearly articulating the links between the operationalisation of the construct in the form of a test task or item, the scoring system used to assess performance, and the relative value of the ultimate decision. As we will see in the next chapter of the book, this approach demands that language tests be built on a language-in-use model and a measurement model.

While contributors to the 2007 special issue of *Educational Measurement: Issues and Practice*, referred to above generally agreed that the field needs to pay more attention to test development operations, they expressed serious reservations about Lissitz & Samuelsen's *test validity* proposal. Comments by respondents, e.g., Sireci, Embretson, Mislevy and Moss included arguments such as:

- Test developers need to attend to external variables because these too invariably offer important insights about internal aspects of test development.
- Test development is an articulation of construct representation and therefore construct-related research should be part of validity.
- Validity has been richly enhanced by considerations based not only on content but also on test score investigations.

Sireci (2007) contends that the *Standards*' call to integrate an argument based on the five sources of evidence (content, internal structure, external relationships, process and consequences) offers a more constructive approach. Sireci (2007: 479) writes: 'Although the guidance provided in the Standards is not perfect, I believe that this integrated characterisation is more beneficial to those who seek to evaluate tests than is the framework being proposed by Lissitz and Samuelsen.'

Lissitz & Samuelsen (2007a: 440–441) suggest that constructs be replaced by standards and tasks. 'Test standards, in typical large-scale educational testing, have been written to try to specify the domain in question. A test then can be defined to measure that particular content defined by the standards....' They add (2007a: 441): '...the test is a combination of tasks and these tasks are the operational definition that is captured (or is supposed to be) by the name and description of the domain to be measured by the test'. Lissitz & Samuelsen (2007a), however, do not consider any of the concerns that arise when using standards and related tasks (such as in language testing, the ACTFL Guidelines, the CEFR, and the Common Core State Standards) as target content domains from which to sample for test development.

Chalhoub-Deville, as part of an invited paper at the October 2008 University of Maryland Ninth Annual Maryland Assessment Conference, organised by Lissitz, which later appeared as a chapter in an edited book (Lissitz, 2009), undertakes an exploration of validity research in terms of standards- and task-based assessments in language testing. Her investigation makes clear how complex and questionable such an approach can be. Chalhoub-Deville (2009b: 251) writes:

> Content frameworks, as operationalized by the ACTFL Guidelines and the CEFR, have benefited the practice of foreign language learning and testing. These frameworks have contributed significantly to advancing curriculum, instruction, textbook content, and assessments…. These frameworks, nevertheless, lack a credible body of professional evidence to support their current formulations. …they lack what most researchers and developers consider to be a content domain based on accumulated theoretical knowledge and grounded research.

Standards/frameworks/guidelines tend to represent more popular and experiential depictions of ability at different proficiency levels. These structures have been promoted by policy and related powerful endorsements more than by credible theoretical arguments and scientific evidence. In defence of the CEFR, the development process involved gathering and scaling a series of language descriptors based on evidence from a large population of experienced language teachers across Europe. The CEFR, however, is being pushed/adopted in areas outside Europe. This spread to other areas is questionable given its European-based research foundations.

Basically, there are no easy answers to defining the content-construct domain, which is what Lissitz & Samuelsen were trying to do by redirecting attention to content. One can argue that a weak theory still posits testable hypotheses that are more in line with scientific thinking than these hierarchical assertions. On the other hand, there are many who would very much disagree with this assertion, arguing that any test built on a weak theory can only offer a representation of the underlying construct by chance.

Another consideration with regard to Lissitz & Samuelsen's (2007a, b) contention is the practical reality of who is to be held responsible for the ousted external components. What difference does it make, if what Lissitz & Samuelsen call external features fall within or outside validity?

One reason relegating these components to an area outside validity is critical because it impacts whether such research is actually undertaken and by whom. As important as Lissitz & Samuelsen say research into the external components is, once test developers relegate that research to test users – who are not likely to have the training to undertake needed research, relevant documentation is ignored or discounted because it lacks rigour. Alternatively, other scholars may take on research of external components. Again however, once 'outside' validity documentation becomes optional, research undertaken by scholars in other fields becomes easier for psychometricians or measurement professionals to ignore or to lose touch with.

Chalhoub-Deville (2009b) reaffirms that content-related validity is critical for the documentation of test quality. She argues, however, that this is necessary but not sufficient evidence. Considerations of theory remain relevant to support score interpretation and use (see also Chalhoub-Deville, 1997).

> I wholeheartedly support the need to focus attention on developing arguments and procedures closely associated with content validity. I contend, however, that an exclusive focus on content offers a fragmented and an incomplete perspective with respect to the theoretical rationale and empirical evidence needed to appropriately examine the qualities of test content, and the interpretation and uses of test scores, the consequences of proposed score interpretation and use, and theory refinement. I understand that these issues are a tall order for psychometricians and researchers to undertake, but as argued by many, the higher the stakes associated with a given testing program, the more extensive the documentation [needed] (Chalhoub-Deville, 2009b: 242).

This position, again, is in line with prevalent thinking in the language testing literature, at least in the US. Chalhoub-Deville (2009b) endorses the more encompassing representations of validity. Her position is more in line with argument-based models (e.g., IA and AUA), which envision a broader scope to validity research – whether it is called validation or justification. Next we discuss the works of Mislevy and his colleagues. Mislevy endorses the importance of paying attention to design and development as critical, maintaining that such research represents important documentation towards establishing the validity of the test scores.

Mislevy's validity by design

What differentiates Mislevy's work from most measurement models is its concerted attention to the design aspects of testing systems. Mislevy laments the use of measurement models (e.g., Rasch) that do not make explicit the features and processes engaged in a test task and thus offer little information of the abilities or knowledge and skills underlying performance and captured in a score. Such psychometric approaches, he contends, weaken validity arguments. Mislevy (2007) calls for practices that help render *validity a matter of design versus aspiration*.

Similar to Lissitz & Samuelsen (2007a, b), Mislevy takes issues of design and content development to be of great importance to validity formulation. However, he rejects Lissitz & Samuelsen's focus on content and the exclusion of construct validity. In his article 'Validity by design', Mislevy critiques Lissitz & Samuelsen's approach and advances:

> work that makes more explicit the underlying principles of assessment design, thereby providing conceptual foundations for familiar practices and supporting the development of new ones. By structuring design activities around assessment arguments, the test developer accrues evidence in passing for what Embretson (1983) calls 'construct representation' argumentation for validity (Mislevy, 2007: 463).

Mislevy endorses a validity conceptualisation, which includes construct considerations. He is interested in an argument that starts to accumulate technical evidence at the design level to support the ensuing scores. In comparison to the model advanced by Kane, who directs attention to validation analyses at the performance level, Mislevy directs attention to validity evidence at earlier stages of research and development. His publications (e.g., Mislevy, 2018) continue to refine a systematic and detailed approach of documentation, commonly referred to as *evidence centered design* (ECD). Mislevy's validity is an argument with an all-inclusive evidence system that comprises test design, development and administration operations.

ECD promotes the construction of 'educational assessments in terms of evidentiary arguments' (Mislevy, Almond & Lukas, 2003: i) and this thinking has influenced major testing efforts in the US. For example, ECD concepts anchor research and development efforts of the two major educational achievement testing consortia associated with the accountability system of the *Race to the Top* policy programme. In 2010, the

US Secretary of Education awarded grants to the Partnership for the Assessment of Readiness for College and Careers (PARCC) and the SMARTER Balanced Assessment Consortium (SBAC) to develop assessment systems that are largely aligned with the national Common Core State *Standards* (CCSS). These consortia have embraced ECD tenets.

> Both consortia, SBAC and PARCC, have adopted the evidence-centered design (ECD) to develop and validate their summative assessments of CCSS curricular. The ECD has frequently been used for the development of large-scale assessments and focuses on accountability. It is based on the view that an assessment is an argument derived from imperfect evidence of performance/learning, which is then framed as an operational process (Mislevy, Steinberg & Almond, 2003; Mislevy & Haertel, 2006). The ECD, drawing inspiration from complex systems analysis in architecture and software engineering, identifies five interacting layers: Domain Analysis, Domain Modeling, Conceptual Assessment Framework, Assessment Implementation, and Assessment Delivery. Interaction and refinement is encouraged within and across layers (Caccamise, Friend, Littrel-Baez & Kintsch, 2015: 94–95).

Figure 6, reproduced from Mislevy, Steinberg & Almond (2003: 6), presents a schematic representation of Mislevy's ECD. ECD is an evidentiary structure that targets the sequence of operations from design, to observation, on to inference. The main interacting models and processes target the test design, development and administration stages. Research undertaken considers construct and/or traits, and what Bachman & Palmer (2010) call the TLU domain connections. ECD is interested in the creation of systems that connect student and task variables, the development of task/item banks and scoring systems, item calibration and the conditions for the administration of the testing system. The major areas highlighted in the ECD approach are described next.

Domain analysis involves research of construct/domain of interest given test purpose. At this point, research is concerned with identifying pertinent ability attributes by investigating the published literature, instructional materials, relevant content and performance *Standards*, job domains, etc. Mislevy et al. write that this first stage of domain analysis marshals information from a variety of substantive sources and proceeds to organise accumulated theories, research, experiences, subject-matter expert

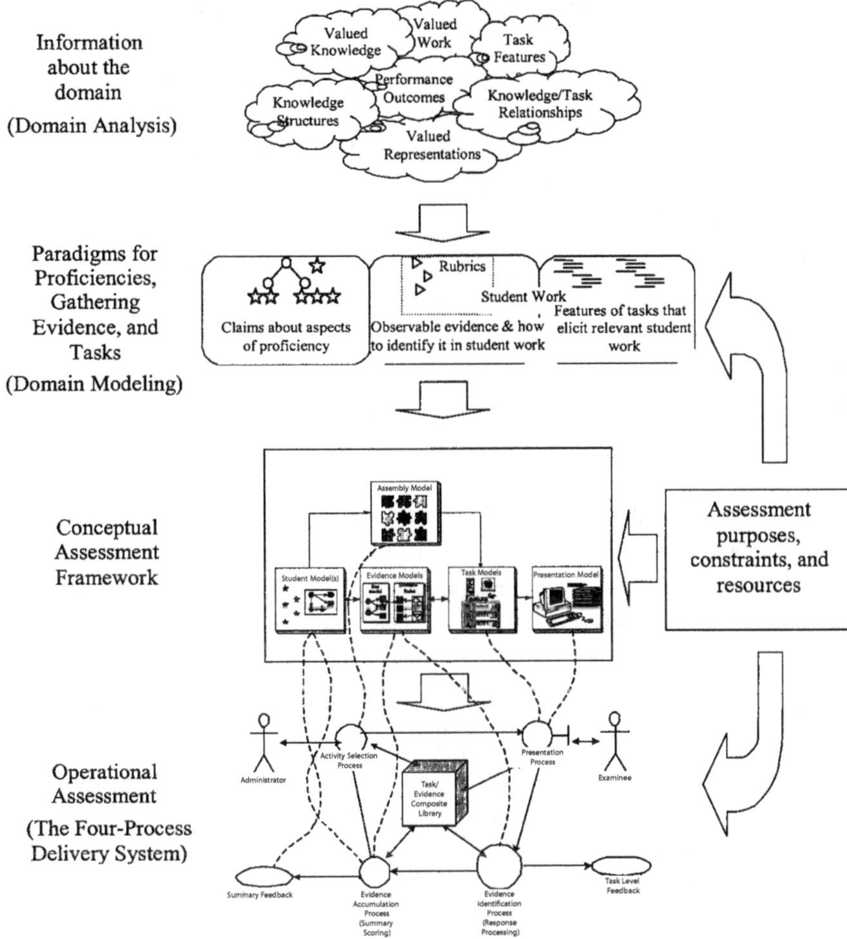

Figure 6: Schematic representation of test design evidentiary structure (Mislevy, Steinberg & Almond, 2003: 6)

beliefs, curricula and related teaching materials, exemplars from related assessments, among others. At this stage, test developers basically seek a broad spectrum of information, which comes from theoretical as well as practice sources to start to shape a more targeted assessment domain.

Domain modelling articulates findings from the research stage to the structures or *paradigms* of a testing system. These paradigms represent a formal framework intended to support development and score inferences. Mislevy, Almond & Lukas (2003: 6) believe that

> this information is organized in terms of design objects called paradigms: Structures that organize potential claims about students and aspects of proficiency they reflect (proficiency paradigms); the kinds of things students might say or do that would constitute evidence about these proficiencies (evidence paradigms); and the kinds of situations that might make it possible to obtain this evidence (task paradigms).

In the domain modelling stage we seek to systematically connect the intended ability/proficiency features to salient student characteristics and relevant task variables. To use ECD terms, test developers focus on the connections between the student model or *proficiency paradigm* and the *task paradigm* using the *evidence paradigm*. These stages represent a rough draft of the features of a given testing system. Mislevy et al. describe how at this design stage research seeks to identify the evidentiary interrelationships that connect student/test taker characteristics with task attributes as these interactions are likely to occur in real-world situations. This documentation resembles the connections to intended TLU domains, that Bachman (1990) and Bachman & Palmer (1996, 2010) have long called for.

Basically, *domain analysis* and *domain modelling* involve not only measurement professionals and psychometricians but also language testing and other subject matter experts. ECD makes room for a team with broad set of skills to collaborate to ensure a coherent and systematic approach to the development of an assessment framework. This was observed, for example, in the development of the TOEFL 2000 project, which became TOEFLiBT.

A *conceptual assessment framework* (CAF) moves work into the specifics of the testing operation at hand and the particular structures of the assessment programme. A CAF considers design and development, given the assessment's intended purposes, available resources and recognised constraints, as the specifications and operations are being developed. CAF transforms information gleaned in the various proficiency models, the domain modelling stage, into development and implementation specifications. Specifications detail how to utilise salient task features to target and externalise test takers' intended ability attributes. This also entails administration, rating/scoring, psychometric and other implementation specifications.

> The CAF models provide the technical detail required for implementation: specifications, operational requirements, statistical models, details of rubrics, and so on. In brief, the student model specifies the variables in terms of which we wish to characterize students. Task models are schemas for ways to get data that provide evidence about them. Evidence models contain two components, which are links in the chain of reasoning from students' work to their knowledge and skill: The evaluation component of the evidence model contains procedures for extracting the salient features of student's performances in task situations – i.e., observable variables – and the measurement component contains machinery for updating beliefs about student-model variables in light of this information. These components correspond roughly to task scoring and test scoring. The assembly model describes the criteria by which multiple tasks are selected for gathering evidence from students, as an assessment. Finally, the presentation model gives specifications for presenting tasks, managing interactions with students, and capturing their work (Mislevy, Almond & Lukas, 2003: 6–7).

A CAF addresses elements that includes specifications for operational assessment delivery, including test *assembly, presentation models and other administration features*.

The four-process delivery system represents the administration and delivery aspects of an assessment. It also pertains to and accommodates a variety of test delivery platforms. As Figure 6 shows, this delivery system includes the following processes: item/task selection, presentation features, response algorithms and performance summary or scores. The selection process identifies a task/item according to pre-specified criteria, which the presentation system then displays. Upon task completion, response algorithms/rating mechanisms parse out/evaluate response features and summarise the information as a score record. Mislevy, Almond & Lukas (2003: 13) suggest that:

> The Four-process Delivery Architecture…[is] essential to making the observations and drawing the inferences that comprise an assessment argument. This is true whether some of the processes…are collapsed or…in a given system, and regardless of whether they are carried out by humans, computers, or human-computer interactions.

These processes are the basis for the evidentiary links that connect observations with the inferences of score meaning and are the building blocks that support the assessment argument.

ECD posits a validity-through-design approach where claims about obtained scores are made explicit at the design stage. Through the various operations, from domain analysis, to domain modelling, to the actual construction of and delivery of the specifics of a testing programme, an evidentiary structure is accumulated. Accumulated evidence helps formulate an argument to provide support for score inferences. In terms of the scholarship of validity, Mislevy, similar to Kane, views validity as the construction of arguments and utilises Toulmin's structure to build the argument. However, unlike Kane who seems to focus the argument on the analysis of observations, Mislevy expends a great deal of effort to articulate systematic connections among frameworks and processes at the design and development stages. In Mislevy's ECD, task features that can be employed to elicit these intended performances are targeted in task selection and/or construction and the various assessment framework models and processes are created to enable linking claims to observations. An evidentiary argument with warrants, backing and rebuttals is accumulated to formulate the argument.

Mislevy's call for attention to the initial stages of development is mirrored in Bachman & Palmer's (2010) justification scheme. Mislevy as well as Bachman & Palmer promote a principled design approach that emphasises documentation of an alignment of construct or some domain representation, assessment approaches, psychometric models and intended inferences. Actually, the field of language testing is quite rich in terms of publications that have advocated the development of systems to articulate a more methodical approach to test design and development, e.g., the Cambridge University Press Applied Linguistics series edited by J. Charles Alderson & Lyle F. Bachman (e.g., Alderson, 2000b; Douglas, 2000; Read, 2000; Buck, 2001; Luoma, 2004).

Mislevy's front-end approach to validation is in line with what Lissitz & Samuelsen (2007a) call for in terms of attention to test content and development. However, ECD provides a far more elaborate and systematic articulation of processes of test development. Additionally, ECD does not stop at the development stage but proceeds to accrue evidence to support inferences based on performances and score interpretation as per intended uses. In this regard, ECD resembles Bachman & Palmer's approach to validity. AUA asserts the importance of evidence in terms of assessment development and test takers' performance, i.e., the left and right sides of Figure 6. The ECD and AUA approaches, however, differ in significant ways. Whereas Mislevy's ECD anchors development in construct and task features and is concerned with scientific – probabilistic – measurement operations, Bachman & Palmer's AUA anchors the various stages of development in intended consequences and the concept of beneficence. 'Consequences' is the starting and ending point in AUA and the justification argument constructed. Consequences tend to play a secondary role in ECD and their scope tends to be more psychometric, e.g., traditional fairness and bias issues.

The Embretson (2007, 2008) *universal validity system* (UVS) presents a structure that could be said to coalesce the ideas promoted in Lissitz & Samuelsen's internal validity, Mislevy's ECD and Bachman & Palmer's AUA approaches to validity. The model is explored in the next section.

Embretson's universal validity system

Embretson (2007, 2008) offers a seemingly all-encompassing approach to validity entitled the *universal validity system* (UVS). The model is *universal,* she explains, because it is said to be appropriate for educational and psychological testing systems. It could be said then that the model is also broadly relevant to language testing systems. The UVS model includes a wide range of evidence categories. The model targets constructs and latent processes, accommodates operational conditions, includes item and test development, connects scoring and psychometric models, considers other measures and utility, as well as integrates impact research. The wide-ranging categories of the model can be viewed in terms of test design, development, administration and operational research programme segments. Just like Bachman & Palmer (2010) argue with regard to AUA, the relevance of Embretson's various categories and their particulars differ in terms of how pertinent they are for testing systems with varying stakes or considerations for score meaning and intended use inferences.

Figure 7 and the associated tables (Tables 15–17) explicate Embretson's (2008) thinking. In this system of validity, Embretson puts categories into different segments in terms of the roles they play in moving test development along and the type of evidence they provide. UVS comprises three interrelated segments. The central segment is the core of a test development operation. It includes test specifications along with scoring and psychometric models. Test specifications are directly supported by a domain structure and item design principles. Test development operations are informed by a theory, latent processes and the testing context. These categories: relevant theories, latent process studies and test administration conditions could be said to represent the second segment. The third segment addresses scoring. Scoring models dictate relevant psychometric systems given entailed assumptions about the dimensionality of the construct/content represented in the scores, selection algorithms and

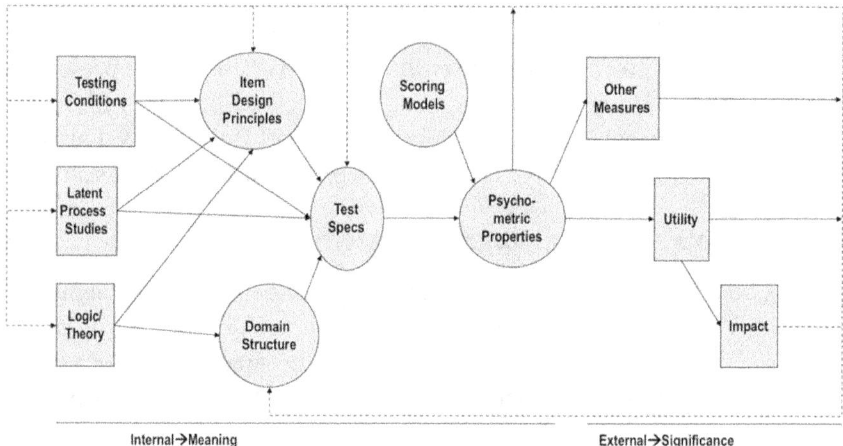

Figure 7: A universal validity system (Embretson, 2008)

Internal categories of evidence	Core parts of test design and development operation
Test specifications	Blueprints specifying domain structure representation, constraints on item features, specification of testing conditions
Psychometric properties	Item intra relationships, DIF, reliability, relationship item psychometric properties to content and stimulus features, reliability
Scoring models	Psychometric models and procedures to combine responses within and between items, weighting of items, item selection *Standards*, relationship of scores to proficiency categories, etc. Decisions about dimensionality, guessing, elimination of poorly fitting items, etc. impacts scores and their relationships

Table 15: The UVS test development and operational segment

issues of exposure, scoring of complex performance and independence assumptions, dependability of test items, etc. Given the role of these segments, and as Figure 7 shows, they are identified as internally- and meaning-focused. These internal-meaning segments and related feeder categories help shape and directly impact test specification.

Here is how we understand the input categories to work, given the graphic in Figure 7 and related descriptions in Tables 15 and 16: basically, the input categories connect theories, analyses of intended domain, scientific knowledge, available resources and testing requirements with item and test design. Prevailing theoretical arguments in a given subject area, e.g., language use constructs and/or some content standards/frameworks/guidelines, contribute to a target domain structure delineation and to item functions. A domain structure specification then informs test specifications. Testing conditions, e.g., test centre specifications, delivery platforms, and time allocation, also help define test specifications. Latent processes also contribute to item design and specifications by identifying cognitive, affective and strategic processes that show appropriate engagement in item/task performance. Item design principles, which also shape test specifications, are themselves constrained by intended theories/logic, latent process studies and testing conditions.

Internal categories of evidence	Theoretical rationale, empirical studies, knowledge and experience, and resources available
Logic/Theoretical analysis	Theory of the subject matter content, specification of areas and their interrelationships
Latent process studies	Studies on content interrelationships, prerequisite skills, impact of task features and testing conditions on responses, etc.
Testing conditions	Available test administration methods, scoring mechanisms (raters, machine scoring, computer algorithms), testing time, locations, etc.
Item design principles	Scientific evidence and knowledge about how features of items impact the KSAs applied by examinees – formats, item context, complexity and specific content
Domain structure	Specification of content areas and levels, as well as relative importance and interrelationships

Table 16: The UVS meaning-oriented segment

External Categories of Evidence	
Utility	Relationship of scores to external variables, criteria & categories
Other Measures	Relationship of scores to other tests of knowledge, skills and abilities
Impact	Consequences of test use, adverse impact, proficiency levels, etc.

Table 17: The UVS significance-directed segment

The input and test development segments in UVS include eight categories and pertain to a large portion of test design and development work. In essence, these two segments contribute arguments and evidence to support intended inferences regarding score meaning. They comprise the research and design undertaken to substantiate the claims we make about students' knowledge, skills and ability, given test purpose. These two segments can be said to resemble most closely Mislevy's ECD models and processes. We contend that Mislevy's work presents richer information about the nature of the work and how to systematise it for operational test design, development and documentation. This is the case, most probably because Mislevy's thinking has been operationalised, elaborated and tested in a variety of projects, including TOEFL 2000 and the Race to the Top educational testing consortia. ECD and UVS are, nonetheless, in alignment with regard to making explicit the important role these components play in the accumulation of validity evidence to support score meaning.

Whereas the interpretation of test score/performance meaning is shaped largely by the input and test development segments (what Embretson labels as internal categories of evidence), test significance is largely dependent on evidence from external sources of information. The external categories, described in Table 17, focus on evidence that connects the scores to other measures and documents their utility and impact. External categories of evidence include utility or the familiar criterion research (concurrent and predictive) where test scores are examined in terms of their relationship to other intended test scores. External evidence also examines patterns of relationships between test scores and knowledge, skills and abilities of interest. The external category of evidence also speaks to issues of impact, which includes adverse consequences. External evidence can provide information about the adequacy of evidence garnered from internal sources in terms of use and decisions made. Concerns are likely to arise when certain expectations are not met or hypotheses not confirmed, or if adverse impact or unintended consequences are documented in terms of test score use(s).

It is noteworthy that the whole system of categories is interactive. Test specifications and the psychometric properties of the test, for example, influence the types of relevant investigations to be carried out with regard to external relationships of test scores with other variables and/or tests. Also, when scores are analysed in terms of relationship with external variables and/or test scores of interest, and impact, evidence is available to feed back to the system at various point of test development, e.g., to revise domain structure or item design.

Embretson's system characterises validity as the accumulation of evidence in terms of test development progression. Representation of validity evidence is more closely tied to actual test operations. UVS articulates a role for theoretical constructs to inform domain structures and item design, which in turn contribute to test specifications and development. With such a characterisation, UVS has roots in Messick's thinking, but unlike Messick, it articulates a more transparent flow of validity evidence in terms of test operations. Another distinctive feature of UVS is its broad definition of validity. It includes evidence that contributes to both score interpretation and use. Interestingly, Embretson thinks it important to award the differentiated sources of validity evidence different labels, internal → meaning and external → significance.

This differentiated labelling brings up Bachman & Palmer's replacement of *validity* with *justification*, to emphasise a more expanded scope of evidence to support score meaning and use. AUA's *justification* and UVS's *significance* point to issues of impact and consequences as integral to quality assurance in a testing operation. Their commitment to consequences as part of technical documentation is remarkable, given the contentious views with regard to consequences. What is not clear with UVS, however, is who is supposed to undertake research on consequences. Whereas Bachman & Palmer indicate that impact and consequence-related research is to be undertaken by test developers, Embretson does not provide a clear position.

A comparison of validity to support test development

The models highlighted in this chapter have all addressed matters of importance to the ongoing discussion of validity in terms of test development. At this point we would like to provide a comparison of how the models explored issues such as the presentation of inferences in various test development phases, attention to constructs, importance of consequences or impact, and the labels employed to define different operations.

Compiling evidence across phases and categories of test design and development

Bachman & Palmer (2010), Lissitz & Samuelsen (2007a, b), Mislevy, Almond & Lukas (2003) and Embretson (2007, 2008) are interested in laying out a system of validity evidence to support inferences, which pertain to test development. Embretson's UVS resembles Mislevy's ECD and Bachman & Palmer's AUA whereby all three systems attempt to conceptualise validity, more or less, in terms of actual test development operations. Their explicit attention to sequencing evidence to support scores is in contrast to the more or less loose category approach depicted in the *Standards* (e.g., 1999, 2014) and by Lissitz & Samuelsen. UVS, ECD and AUA specify the distinct categories of the models, delineate the sequence of evidence, and show how the categories/inferences relate to one another. UVS, ECD and AUA are more transparent in their modelling of how evidence at various phases of test development compiles to support score meaning and use. Another important characteristic of these three systems is their interactiveness. As their graphics show, evidence in any one category seems to shape directly or implicitly the other categories. The adequacy of the evidence compiled is cumulative; based on the interrelatedness of features and documentation across the categories. Of all the models explored, Mislevy's ECD provides the richest articulation of structures (or models as he calls them) involved in test design and development.

Attention to constructs

UVS, ECD and AUA systems make room for a construct articulation to inform test specifications and test development. This is in contrast to Lissitz & Samuelsen's push to drop that pesky term *construct* and to Kane's objections to its use in validity research – though for a different reason: he is primarily concerned with the use of a term which has had many different, often contradictory understandings. Both Mislevy and Embretson have strong interests in constructs in various psychology and educational testing areas. Through their various publications over the years, Bachman & Palmer have also worked with language test constructs. Given their historic elaboration of the L2 construct, i.e., CLA, the downplaying of CLA in terms of validity characterisation in the 2010 publication is conspicuous and puzzling. Embretson's UVS and Mislevy's ECD articulate approaches that shadow test development operations and research and articulate a prominent role for constructs. Mislevy and Embretson's models, it could be argued, continue to reflect Messick's commitment to constructs as anchor for testing operations and validation. AUA, on the other hand, represents a clear departure from that line of thinking and is more akin to Kane's IA approach. 'Our conceptualisation of an Assessment Use Argument builds on the work of Michael Kane on validity and validation (Kane 2002, 2006; Kane, Crooks, and Cohen 1999)' (Bachman & Palmer, 2010: 135). The presence of traits and constructs in IA and AUA is optional and depends on the test developers' and users' interests.

Consequences/impact and validity

Mislevy's ECD does not speak to issues of impact or consequences beyond the more psychometric aspects of fairness and bias (e.g., DIF). AUA and UVS, on the other hand, do. While ECD tends to focus more strongly on aspects of score interpretation as a foundation for validity, UVS features score interpretation, use and impact in validity. UVS attends to internal and external categories of evidence, which is reminiscent of Lissitz & Samuelsen's conceptualisation. Embretson differentiates between the internally-focused evidence that supports score interpretation and the externally-focused categories, labelled *significance,* which provide evidence related to score use and impact. Unlike Lissitz & Samuelsen, Embretson makes the case that not only the internal but also external categories of evidence support validity claims. She states that meaning is supported by internal sources of information and the importance or impact of testing relies on external sources, all of which are germane to validity documentation. AUA is even more resolute about the focal role of score use and consequences in the entire operation of development and documentation of quality.

Impact, in Embretson's UVS, is the last category represented and is said to be informed by investigations of how the scores relate to external measures and variables. Impact seems to be most closely connected to the utility category (see the hard line that travels from *utility* to *impact*). This graphic connection and the language presented in Table 17 may suggest that UVS's impact, similar to ECD, pertains to issues of fairness and bias. Impact in UVS seems to be the only category represented with a dashed versus a hard line in terms of how it feeds into the loop that links back to the input and test development segments. This representation is in sharp contrast with the AUA proposal where consequences anchor the entire justification process. Consequences in AUA are the starting point and are meant to guide the testing process from conception to eventual use and decision-making. Also investigations carried out to feed into an AUA justification ultimately focus on how those intended consequences are realised, i.e., actual consequences, once a testing system is operational.

Labels: Validity, justification and significance

UVS and AUA include a sequence of evidence to support score interpretation and use. UVS offers different labels, however, to differentiate between the internal and external validity evidence and the roles they play to support scores. Embretson puts forward internal evidence to support score meaning and external evidence to denote the *significance* of their impact. Bachman & Palmer do not even utilise the term validity, opting instead for the term *justification*. The rationale for this decision is that the core of the AUA approach involves identifying how use and consequences both drive the entire design and development operation and anchor quality documentation.

What is not clear with AUA is whether *justification* can be said to coexist with validity. Bachman & Palmer see validation in the language testing literature as a term which relates to the collection of evidence to 'support the link between the assessment and the interpretation' (2010: 135). They seek to expand and reframe validity. *Justification* is said to capture 'the notion that what we investigate in this process is not simply the assessment-based interpretation, but the extent to which the intended uses of the assessment are justified' (2010: 135). AUA's *justification* pertains to aspects of intended score meaning and uses. This notion of meaning and use as integral to quality of a testing programme is similar to validity in UVS, where Embretson integrates evidence that pertains to score meaning as well as significance. The point here is not to argue that AUA and UVS are the same in terms of attention to the type of evidence. As repeatedly stated, AUA is driven by aspects of consequences and the need to attend to stakeholder groups. This is not the case with UVS, which offers a more traditional representation of consequences. What is key to AUA and UVS is that both models:

- include consequences as part of test development – directly or indirectly;
- reason that a different label is needed to call attention to the different role that consequences play in terms of evidence collected;

- indicate that consequences/impact should be a source of information for test development and improvement; and
- demand that evidence with regard to impact and consequences be part of the technical documentation of a testing programme, i.e., what traditionally has been termed validity.

In conclusion, given that consequences could be included in validity, the need to adopt a different label, *justification*, is not warranted. Anchoring documentation of validity in a more expansive scope of consequences may be more of a compelling argument for adopting a different term. Publications such as those by McNamara & Roever (2006) and Chalhoub-Deville (2016) that explicate validity in terms of more ambitious consequences, however, cast doubt on the need to abandon validity terminology. Differentiated labels such as *justification* and/or *significance* may be useful to distinguish research pertaining to score use(s) if such research becomes the responsibility of separate groups of scholars with different skill sets or if it affords better communication with intended individuals and groups. But these differentiated labels are still subsumed under validity.

A US-UK Comparative Outlook

The UK and the US have operated with different perspectives with regard to the role validity should play in testing programmes. Differing cultural assumptions and operational practices have guided divergent approaches with regard to the nature of the validity evidence needed, the role it should play in teaching and learning, professional publications held as guiding sources, etc. Table 18 provides a quick comparative overview of some issues as they exist in the UK and US.

Table 18 shows that there has been a systematic difference in approaches to validity thinking on the opposite sides of the Atlantic, what O'Sullivan (2006) described as the 'Atlantic Divide'. This difference can be traced to the emergence of the standardisation movement in the US, which spread from Columbia University in New York in the first decade of the 20th century and quickly saw educational testing emerge as a major industry within little more than a decade (see Johanningmeier & Richardson, 2008). The standardisation movement was facilitated by the introduction of the multiple-choice item type by Kelly (1916). These conditions set the scene for the parallel emergence of theoretical support for the approach taken in these tests that had as its basis the psychometric-structuralist approaches already extensively used in psychological testing,

UK	US
Validity-related work is less visible in publications in the 20th century, only really emerging in the first decade of the 21st century with the work of O'Sullivan & Weir (2002) and Weir (2005).	Validity-related publications accelerated in the 20th century, e.g., *Educational measurement* and the *Standards*.
No agreed-upon central publication offers guidance for practice.	The various editions of the AERA, APA & NCME *Standards* (e.g., AERA, APA & NCME, 1999, 2014) offer broad professional guidance.
Language testing operations incorporate educational and psychological measurement practices but are not driven by them – instead they focus on learning and the curriculum.	Language testing operations tend to be guided by educational and psychological measurement practices.
Validity innovations pay attention to developments in US publications but are driven primarily by curriculum/ syllabus development and learning.	Validity innovations are guided by developments in educational and psychological measurement.
Validity is intertwined with test design/ development best practices in both assessment and instruction.	Validity emphasises a more psychometric paradigm.
Validity concerns both the test itself and the inferences drawn from scores.	Validity in recent history focuses on inferences from scores.
Consequences are critical to validity thinking.	Consequences represent a contentious topic.
Attention to alignment between instruction and formative assessment.	Attention to alignment between instruction and benchmark assessment.
The construct in language testing practices has been historically more strongly anchored in instructionally-relevant materials, e.g., syllabi/certificates. Increasingly we observe a push for *standards*-based testing.	The language testing construct has traditionally distanced itself from any specific instructional programme/materials. This has changed. Increasingly we observe a push for standards-based testing.
Evidence is shaped to attend particularly to test development and instructional practices.	Evidence is geared to address the professional measurement and language testing community.
Validity operations are more socially-grounded; attention to more cognitive-psychometric features have emerged in recent times.	Given its historical roots, validity systems have tended to be anchored in a cognitive-psychometric paradigm; social aspects remain exploratory.

Table 18: Comparison of some validity issues in the UK and the US

which had also sprung from the work of people such as James McKeen Cattell and Edward Bradford Titchener at Columbia University. The type of evidence that was accepted as demonstrating the validity of a test increasingly turned to statistical evidence of similarities in structure between hypothesised traits and the data that emerged from test administration. This has remained the mainstay of educational measurement in the US and a number of other countries influenced by the US approach (e.g., Holland, Japan, etc.). In recent years, however, there has been a growing awareness that there are significant issues with the approach that markedly limit its value when assessing language (or in fact any skill or ability that is demonstrated through usage, e.g., driving a car, playing tennis, building a piece of furniture or playing football). This is due to the complexity of language use; since it is at the same time both a cognitive and a social activity – an interaction of both.

Thinking in the UK around validity tended to take a very different approach to that prevalent in the US. As we will see in the Commentary section at the end of this chapter, the focus in the UK has always been on the relationship between learning and testing. Unlike the situation in the US, where the two were deliberately separated, in the UK, they were deliberately connected. In fact, test validity came to be associated with establishing a meaningful connection between the content and approach taken in the test and the classroom. Developers in the UK came to rely to a more and more significant degree on what became known as content validity. While organisations such as Cambridge were claiming what they described as a VRIP (validity, reliability, impact and practicality) approach to test development, they did not offer an operationally appropriate definition of validity within this approach. The earliest inkling of an emerging UK testing philosophy driven approach to validity came in the early work of Weir (1988, 1993) where he began to develop his ideas that were later to come together as a series of frameworks (one for each skill) that formed the basis for his seminal book (Weir, 2005).

In applying these frameworks across a range of development and validation projects, O'Sullivan demonstrated the undoubted strengths in Weir's frameworks, while at the same time recognising that there were a number of limitations on their applicability. By stripping the frameworks back to their basic underlying concepts, O'Sullivan, first with Weir (O'Sullivan & Weir, 2011) and then alone (O'Sullivan, 2011, 2014, 2016) argued for the recognition that they were supported by an underlying model which was on one level simpler that the original frameworks, but on another level quite a lot more complex. The simplicity is apparent in the reduction of the number of elements from Weir's original six (candidate, cognitive, test, scoring, criterion and consequential) to three (candidate model, test model and scoring model). The complexity lies in the recognition that consequence cannot be seen as an afterthought to development, but is integral to the entire development process (much in agreement with Bachman & Palmer, 2010). It is also apparent in the recognition that the context of test development and use (as defined by the stakeholders who comprise that context) will also contribute to the way in which the underlying construct is defined, and (again, in agreement with Bachman & Palmer, 2010) in the implication that the needs of these stakeholders should be addressed in any validation arguments.

It is to this more recent socio-cognitive model that we now turn. The next section provides an example of how an L2 testing system is developed with validity evidence integral to test development activities. This example showcases the UK prevailing tradition that validation is development. Also, the example highlights connections to US validity, mainly to Messick's writing.

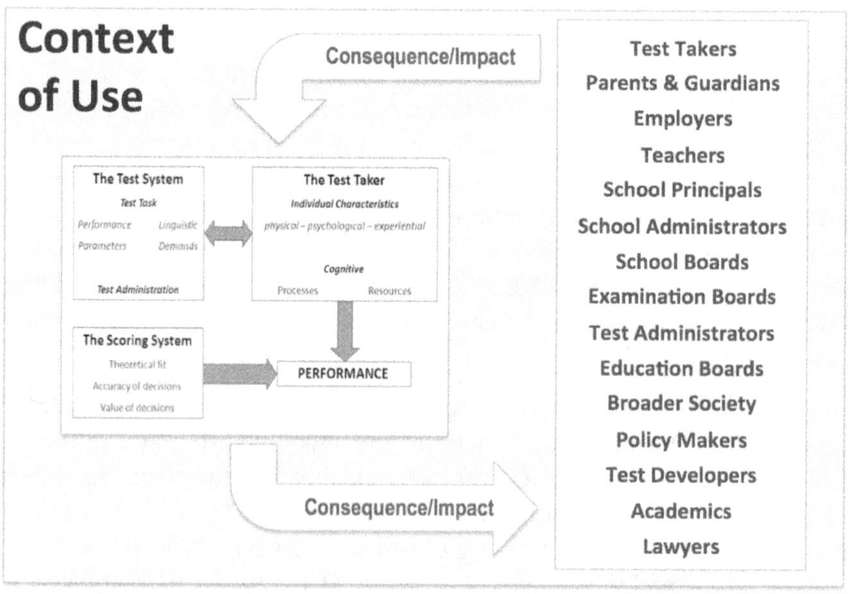

Figure 8: Revised test validation model (O'Sullivan, 2014)

An updated socio-cognitive model

The application of the socio-cognitive model to the development of Aptis marks the first time the model was used as the basis of a commercial test development project *ab-initio*. The development team made the decision to apply O'Sullivan's interpretation of the model well before the development project started and it was then used to inform all development decisions from the consideration of test takers to the preparation of the specifications. It also formed the basis of the research and dissemination agenda designed to add technical and theoretical support for the test.

The updated model, shown here as Figure 8, will be presented and discussed in detail below.

The core elements

The core elements of the model remain the same as the earlier model presented by O'Sullivan (2011) and include three central elements: the test taker, the test system and the scoring system.

The Test Taker

We consider the test taker from two perspectives; their individual characteristics and the cognitive model of the trait or ability being tested.

Individual characteristics were first defined by O'Sullivan (2000a) as relating to three areas. These are presented and briefly discussed below.

Physical	This includes variables such as age and gender as well as variables that can relate to either short-term ailments (e.g., flu, migraine, etc.) or long-term or permanent disabilities (e.g., dyslexia, limitations to hearing or sight, etc.). Decisions related to these variables can include:	
	Age	The age of the test population should always be taken into consideration when making decisions around test design, timing, topics, cognitive complexity of input and expected complexity of output.

One example of how a test should take the age of test takers into account comes from the development of Aptis for Teens. This test is a variant of Aptis General and was designed to meet the needs of a younger population than the original test; 13 to 16 year olds as opposed to 15 plus. When younger learners were asked to take the original test, it was noted that quite a few had some difficulties with some of the higher-level tasks; with the speaking paper, for example, the abstract nature of the final (B2) task and the cognitive complexity entailed when responding to three different aspects of a task. As part of the development project, a new B2 task was developed with significant support from experts in assessing young learners. This was trialled extensively before inclusion in the operational test.

Gender

There is little evidence of any significant differences related to tests of speaking or writing – though Lumley & O'Sullivan (2002) suggest that task topic with strong male or female bias might well impact on test performance. For this reason, it is essential to ensure that the test specifications make it clear to item writers and quality assurance experts that test topics are reviewed for likely gender bias.

	In addition, it is likely that any bias would be exacerbated when dealing with a younger population. This emphasises the need to consider test taker individual characteristics not just individually but also as part of a more complex multifaceted matrix.
State of health [short term]	Short-term ailments such as flu can negatively impact on test taker performance to a significant degree. For the developer, this means a decision on whether to allow ill test takers to re-sit the paper at another time is required. If the decision is to allow re-sits, then the developer will be required to prepare multiple parallel test versions for each administration, more than would be the case where no re-sits are allowed. While this may not have a direct negative impact on test takers (unless there are problems with the equivalence of the multiple versions), it will add significantly to the resources required of the developer and may add to the cost of the test – thus impacting indirectly on test takers!
State of health [long term]	Any long-term or permanent disabilities must, by law in most countries, be addressed by the developer. Typically, additional time is allowed for test takers identified as dyslexic, for example, while other measures require different accommodations such as an amanuensis for a blind or physically challenged test taker.

- ***Psychological*** This can include a wide range of variables such as memory, personality, cognitive development, affective schemata, concentration, motivation and emotional state. Consideration of these variables may entail:
  - *Memory* Ensuring that test tasks do not entail the storing of information in short-term memory. Such a task might mean reading a paragraph of 75 words and then not allowing test takers access to the paragraph when asked to respond to an item. Other memory-heavy tasks include story retelling (written or spoken) or listening items presented after the input. The impact of memory demands are likely to be felt most significantly on younger (Hasselgreen & Caudwell, 2016) or lower-level candidates (Prat, 2011).
  - *Personality* Reflecting on research by O'Sullivan (2000a, 2008) and Berry (2007) who demonstrated that test taker personality can have a significant impact on their performance, particularly in tests of speaking. Berry demonstrated that introverts tend to perform less well when partnered with more extroverted test takers in group tasks, while performing well on one-to-one or monologue tasks. O'Sullivan looked at the perception of test takers of their partners in paired tests (relative degree of extroversion and relative language level). He found that the variable interacted in complex and difficult to predict ways. This suggests that we should try to ensure that test takers are exposed to a number of

	different task formats (e.g., paired, group, solo) and that we should, where feasible (e.g., in classroom assessment) ensure that test takers are paired with appropriate partners.
Cognitive development	This affects the way individuals think, perceive and remember information, or their preferred approach to using such information to solve problems. We therefore need to consider the potential impact on test takers of requiring them to respond to tasks that are set at too high a level of cognitive challenge. This variable is clearly linked to others such as age and disability.
Affective schemata	This refers to how a candidate reacts to a task. We must understand that there are likely to be occasions when test takers react negatively to aspects of the task – we know for example that learners from some cultures may perform well in speaking tests when partnered with a friend, while the opposite can be true of other cultures. Test takers can also react negatively to the content of test input. For that reason, most test developers maintain a list of 'taboo' topics (such as death or disease).
Concentration	Realising that overly long tests can result in some learners, particularly younger or cognitively challenged, losing concentration and failing to perform at their best. One option is to create tests that deliberately change focus after a set time. In Aptis, this is achieved by creating tasks with different response formats and different input. The 'down

		time' between tasks allows the test taker to switch off momentarily and prepare mentally for the next part of the test.
	Motivation	Building motivation into the test by ensuring that the topics, tasks and responses are both stimulating and offer enough variation to keep test takers motivated. It also helps to balance the test, with relatively easy items/tasks coming early on and more difficult and challenging items/tasks coming later.
	Emotional state	Taking into consideration the fact that a test taker's emotional state can change relatively quickly. This is clearly linked to a whole series of other variables; it may be a long-term condition or it may be caused by test anxiety (pre-test) due to previous failures or bad experiences with tests or negative feedback from parents or teachers. Test developers can work to ensure that the test taker experience when sitting the test is as positive as possible, with clear instructions and demonstrations of what is expected of them in the test. Examples of this in Aptis include test-taker-friendly instructions (pre-trialled with test takers), demonstration tests available online, sample tests and immediate pre-test practice demos.
Experiential	This will include variables such as education (formal and informal); experience of examinations in general; experience of this particular examination; factors such as exposure to the target language through movies, games, target language, country of residence, etc.	

Education	When developing a test for use within a specific education system, it is important to link the test (in terms of content, format, approach and underlying philosophy) to that system. Tests for learners that straddle a number of education systems are somewhat more challenging, as it is quite difficult to make assumptions about the test taking population regarding education – it may well be that test topics and tasks are simply beyond the experience of learners who then fail to demonstrate the best of their ability.
Examination experience	It is clear that experience taking examinations prepares test takers for the challenges involved; it helps them devise a personal examination schema. In large-scale international examinations such as Aptis we cannot always be certain that test takers will have developed this schema, or if they have that it will be of use to them. An example of this is the over-reliance, in many countries, on tests of language knowledge (i.e., grammar and vocabulary) which are delivered using multiple-choice questions. Test takers who only experience this type of educational test will find the European practice of including a broad range of test tasks and formats which assess their ability to use the language immensely challenging. Openly available practice opportunities help alleviate this issue.

	Experience of this examination	Developing a comprehensive understanding of how a particular test is constructed, a similarly comprehensive understanding of what type of responses are expected and a how these responses will be scored are all critical skills to learn when engaging in test preparation programmes. With Aptis, the candidate guide offers a comprehensive overview of the test that is designed to allow individual test takers the opportunity to develop these skills.
	Target language exposure	While the test developer cannot control for this set of variables, they are likely to have an impact on language performance through their influence on a range of the psychological variables presented above. The Aptis candidate guide recommends a whole range of learner orientated materials, including language and test preparation apps and study resources, often based on real-world language use situations.
Cognitive	The socio-cognitive approach calls for a clearly described model of the underlying trait or ability being tested. This has been operationalised in a number of ways: the Art Competency model that supported the Portuguese Ministry of Educations National Art Curriculum (Torres Pereira de Eça, 2005); the updated Bloom's Taxonomy for the International Council of Ophthalmology Fellowship Examinations (Taylor, O'Sullivan & Quilter, 2009) and for the testing of science in Sri Lanka (Selvaruby, 2006; Selvaruby, O'Sullivan & Watts, 2008). Other, more explicitly cognitive construct models have been proposed: for example, the British Council's Aptis test has looked to the model of reading progression proposed by Khalifa	

& Weir (2009) and that for listening progression proposed by Field (2014, 2019). An example of how the Khalifa & Weir model was adapted and operationalised in the Aptis reading paper can be seen in Table 19.

Reading *Shaded cells indicate the targeted processes for Aptis Task 4 (aimed at an upper intermediate reader – CEFR B2 level)*	Cognitive processing Goal setting	Expeditious reading: local (scan/search for specifics)	Careful reading: local (understanding sentence)
		Expeditious reading: global (skim for gist/ search for key ideas/detail)	Careful reading: global (comprehend main idea(s)/overall text(s))
	Cognitive processing Levels of reading	Word recognition	
		Lexical access	
		Syntactic parsing	
		Establishing propositional meaning (cl./sent. level)	
		Inferencing building a mental model	
		Creating a text-level representation (disc. structure)	
		Creating an inter-textual representation (multi-text)	
		Features of the input text	

Table 19: Cognitive dimension of Aptis Reading Task 4 (O'Sullivan & Dunlea, 2015: 47)

As we can see from the above overview, the receptive skills have been interpreted in a primarily cognitive way in the Aptis development project. In fact, where the socio-cognitive model has been operationalised the interpretation has tended to be primarily cognitive, see for example Shaw & Weir (2007), Khalifa & Weir (2009), Taylor (2011), Geranpayeh & Taylor (2013). The issue of ensuring that reading tests (for example) have an appropriate social component is most likely to be associated with text content (appropriateness to population and purpose: e.g. topic, genre) and as such is more likely to be associated with the *test system* though the link across to the *test taker* and the underlying construct model should be clear to the reader.

The Test System

Performance parameters These are parameters such as timing, preparation, score weighting, knowledge of how performance will be scored, etc.

Purpose This refers to the requirements of the task. A clearly defined and conceptualised purpose allows candidates to choose the most appropriate strategies and determine what information they are to target in responding to a task. It can facilitate both ***goal setting*** and ***monitoring*** activities – critical to successful task completion.

Response format How candidates are expected to respond to the task (e.g., short answers or essay). Different formats can impact on performance; see for example Lissitz, Hou & Cadman Slater (2014).

Known criteria Knowing how a test performance will be scored is highly likely to impact the performance. Letting candidates know how their performance will be assessed is therefore critical to allow for equitable test delivery. It is possible that where some test takers have experience or knowledge of the scoring system they will be significantly advantaged. One way of achieving this is to make rating criteria for speaking and writing freely available beforehand (e.g., rating scale available on the test's web page).

Weighting Similarly to known criteria, knowledge of any test item or task weighting can have a significant impact on performance as item or task ***goal setting*** can be affected if candidates are informed of differential weighting before test performance begins.

Order of items Tests are often designed to reflect a continuum of expected difficulty, with easier items or tasks appearing early in the event. This is to allow the test taker to grow into the test and is expected to facilitate the concept of testing for best. Due to the nature of test design and delivery it is usual to find that in speaking and listening tests the order of presentation is set. Though this may not always be the case in a reading or writing test, in computer-delivered tests the order tends to be set.

Time constraints This can relate either to pre-performance (e.g., planning time), or during performance (e.g., response time). Much literature has been devoted to the impact on task difficulty of manipulating the time constraints; see Skehan (1996, 1998), Skehan & Foster (1997), Foster & Skehan (1996, 1999), Wigglesworth (1997) and Ortega (1999). The findings of these various studies have demonstrated that the provision of appropriate planning time in particular is critical to task performance.

Linguistic demands This refers to the language or other stimulus of the input and the expected language of the output.

Channel In terms of input this can be written, visual (photographs, artwork, etc.), graphical (charts, tables, etc.) or aural (input from examiner, recorded medium, etc.). The input can include more than one of the above.

Output demands will depend on the ability or skill being tested. It is usual that the demands will increase as the level of language being tested increases – so the output for a task aimed at a low-level test taker will be considerably shorter than would be the case where the task is aimed at a high-level test taker.

Discourse mode	Includes the categories of genre, rhetorical task and patterns of exposition. The suggestion here is that discourse mode can impact on later performance in a number of ways: • It is probable that descriptive as opposed to argumentative input will be easier to comprehend for most learners, thus impacting on responses (e.g., Elder, Iwashita & McNamara, 2002). • There is evidence that the age of the test taker will confound the effect of discourse mode (see McCann, 1989).
Text length	It is important to control for the amount of input/output to tasks as this may have a significant impact on performance – e.g., affecting working memory and negatively affecting the performance of younger or lower-level test takers in particular.
Nature of information	The degree of abstractness of the task input has been demonstrated to affect test taker performance (e.g., Skehan & Shum, 2014). Since more concrete topics/inputs are less difficult to respond to than more abstract ones, the test developer should take into consideration this variable when designing tasks (see Robinson, 2011).
Topic familiarity	Greater topic familiarity tends to result in superior performance (Bui, 2014). This is an issue in the testing of all sub-skills and is typically addressed in one of two ways: • Ensure that the topics included in the test are familiar to all test takers. An example of this is basing national examinations on the topics included in the major textbooks only.

		• Select topics that are very unlikely to be familiar to any test takers.
Social Demands	We first refer to the interlocutor or audience in a productive skills test (writing or speaking). Typical variables might include:	
Writing	*Writer/ reader relationship*	Setting up different relationships can impact on performance, e.g., responding to a known reader of a specified age relative to the writer will result in significantly different written responses depending on the age of the intended reader (see Porter & O'Sullivan, 1999). In the Aptis writing paper, this relationship is clearly described in the higher-level tasks, and implied in the others.
Speaking	*Speech rate*	Output was once expected to reflect that of an L1 speaker (e.g. Council of Europe, 2001) though it has now moved towards a high-performing L2 speaker norm. Input may be adjusted depending on level of candidature. However, there is a danger of distorting the natural rhythm of the language, and thus introducing a significant source of construct-irrelevant variance. It is also likely that the speech rate of the input will impact on later performance (see Haake et al., 2014). According to the British Council's Learn English website, the fluency and coherence criterion on the IELTS rating scale refers to 'how good the candidate is at keeping talking at the right speed', suggesting that the speech rate of test task output is likely to impact on test score or grade.

Variety of accent	This can be dictated by the construct definition (e.g., where a range of accent types is described) and/or by the context (e.g., where a particular variety is dominant in a teaching situation). In many international tests (e.g., Aptis or TOEFL) it is common to hear a variety of accents, though the issue of accent and comprehensibility is critical (Xu, 2011; Harding, 2011).
Acquaintanceship	There is evidence (e.g., O'Sullivan 2000a, 2002) that performance improves when candidates interact with a friend (though this may be culturally based). In most international tests in which a paired or group task is included, test takers are randomly assigned in an attempt to control for this variable.
Number	This variable is likely to be related to candidate characteristics, particularly personality type. These is some evidence that candidates with different personality profiles perform differently when interacting with different numbers of people (Berry, 2007).
Gender	There is some mixed evidence that candidates tend to perform better when interviewed by a woman (again, this can be culturally based), and that the gender of one's interlocutor in general can impact on performance (O'Sullivan, 2000b; O'Loughlin, 2002). It is important when developing a test to keep this in mind, particularly where the test is developed for use in a specific local context where knowledge of the test taking population is likely to be far higher than would be the situation with an international test.

	Topic	While topic will interact with many of the variables referred to above (e.g., for writing see Lumley & O'Sullivan, 2002; Hidi & McLaren, 1991), it is quite likely that the topic of the task input (and expected output) will have an impact on test taker performance (see Brantmeier, 2003; Hidi, 2001). Note that topic may also have some significant impact on performance on reading and listening tasks.
Receptive skills	We should not dismiss the potential impact of social demands in the receptive skills – though clearly these are likely to be weaker than with the productive skills. Typically, social impact will relate to the themes and topics included in the test paper, but will also include reference to images and general presentation of the paper.	
Integrated tasks	*Writer/ reader and speaker/ listener relationship*	As with the productive skills, integrated tasks will involve an act of communication. We would expect that the audience for this communication is clearly described in the task instructions. In the first test to include such integrated tasks in an English for Academic Purposes setting, the Test of English for Academic Purposes (Weir, 1983), the audience for the productive element was clearly identified for the candidate.
Administrative demands	This refers to the language of the input and the expected language of the output and can also include reference to the audience or interlocutor where appropriate.	

	Security	This refers to systems that are put in place to ensure the security of the entire administrative process. The demonstrable security of a test is vital to any validation argument, as without strictly controlled and monitored criteria and regulations, the essential validity of any test-based decisions cannot be guaranteed. In traditional test settings, test developers ensure that highly detailed test delivery handbooks are strictly adhered to. This situation is changing in some ways as online proctoring becomes a reality – though regulations around the proctoring are as strictly enforced as with more traditional systems. These systems will include:	
		Pre-test	Training and monitoring of staff in areas such as: • Registration identity checks • Test paper handling and storage
		In-test	Rigorous training and monitoring of all staff to include: • Candidate identity checks (e.g., in high-stakes tests such as IELTS this will include fingerprint analysis and/or facial feature recognition) • Invigilation of the event, including pre-defined responses to candidate requests (e.g., to leave room, paper-related questions, etc.)

		• Monitoring of test venue (e.g., not allowing invigilators to remain seated during the event, etc.) • Ensuring that regulations regarding the opening and later collection of test papers and notes are followed. Where tests are computer-based, this might involve checking of computers and candidate seating areas.
	Post-test	Training and monitoring of staff to include: • Paper collection, storage and delivery to developer for scoring • Maintenance of regulations around divulgence of test content
Physical organisation	This refers to a range of activities, including: • Informing candidates of test plans pre-test (times, location, requirements – pen, pencil, laptop, etc.) • Room set-up – e.g., set-up for face-to-face interview should reflect the pre-determined standards • Signage outside and inside the event	
Uniformity	All of the above systems are set in place in order to ensure that administrations of the test are replicated as exactly as possible for all candidates, regardless of location or time. Additional initiatives include the use of a strict invigilator or examiner script to ensure that all spoken interactions related to the test event are controlled for.	

The Scoring System

Theoretical fit	The way in which test performance is assessed must fit with the conceptualisation of the ability being tested. This goes beyond a key or rating scale to inform the philosophical underpinning of rater and examiner selection, training and monitoring.	
	Linking to the test taker	Since the socio-cognitive model recognises that the ability or trait we are testing, i.e. the construct, is a characteristic of the test taker, it is critical that the scoring system has as its basis a direct and evidenced link. While this link is more readily demonstrated in an objectively scored test of listening or reading, it is nonetheless important that the test developer demonstrates in the validation argument, that the answer key reflects the underlying construct. In tests of the productive skills, the situation is probably more critical. Here, the rating criteria (or rubric) must be shown to be based on the theory of language progression outlined in the Test Taker section above. They should also reflect 'actual' language production for the task or tasks included in the examination.
	Linking to the test system	As with the link to the test taker, it is equally critical that the criteria used to evaluate test or task performance are directly linked to the various elements of the test system. This link between the three central elements of the test is critical to the validity of the test and any disconnect will fatally impact on the validity of any decisions that will be based on the test performance.

Accuracy of decisions	Encapsulates the old idea of reliability, though broadening this to include all aspects of the scoring functions related to a test.	
	Rater training	There is evidence that training improves consistency and ability to stay on standard (see Rethinasamy, 2006). Training has traditionally been undertaken in live sessions, though there is an increasing trend towards online training systems; see Knoch, Fairbairn & Huisman (2015) for an examination of the system developed for Aptis.
	Standardisation	As part of any training regime, raters must internalise the criterion level (e.g., pass/fail boundary) and this should be checked using a standardisation procedure. As with rater training, this is now increasingly undertaken as an online activity. Standardisation is particularly important when ensuring that raters are familiarised with new test tasks or new task versions. The Aptis testing service uses a *control item* (CI) system to build standardisation into the system. This is where raters must first successfully rate a pre-rated sample before gaining access to the rating portal proper. In addition, they are exposed to a number of additional CIs at random as they proceed through each rating event.
	Rating conditions	Attempts should be made to ensure that all rating/examining takes place under optimal conditions. Where possible, these conditions should be set, so that all examiners have an equal opportunity to perform at their best. This is particularly important with high-stakes tests.

Moderation This involves monitoring the performance of raters to ensure that they stay on level. As indicated above, in the Aptis system this is achieved through the CI system, while in other tests scores are routinely checked to ensure that they are within pre-set bounds. Most high-stakes tests include real-time monitoring of rater performance and build in systems for re-rating where a rater drifts.

Analysis Statistical analysis of all rater performances will ensure that individual candidates will not lose out in situations where examiners are either too harsh/lenient or are not behaving in a consistent manner. Analysis can be seen as forming part of the monitoring system or as a post-hoc review of rater performance. It can combine these two, of course.

This is the part of scoring validity that is traditionally seen as reliability (i.e., the reliability of the scoring, or rating, system).

Raters When we discuss the candidates (in terms of physical, psychological and experiential characteristics) we should also consider what we know of the examiners in terms of these same characteristics. Little research has been undertaken in which these have been systematically explored from the perspective of the rater, though Zhang & Elder (2011) suggest that there is no systematic difference between native and non-native speaker raters in their study.

	Grading and awarding	The systems that describe how the final grades are estimated and reported should be made as explicit as possible to ensure fairness. These systems usually combine statistical analysis of results (including bias or DIF analysis) and qualitative analysis of the test itself. In some tests, the profile across the four skills achieved by the student is also taken into account.
Value of decisions	This relates to things like criterion-related evidence such as comparison with measures such as teacher estimates, other test scores, performance standards such as the CEFR.	
	Criterion evidence	This refers to the tradition perspective on criterion-related evidence and will include comparisons with: • Other forms of the same test • Other tests which focus on the same trait (the expectation is for a high level of similarity) or tests which focus on very different constructs (where the expectation is for a low level of similarity) • Other non-test related measures of the same construct such as teacher, peer or self estimates of ability. While O'Sullivan & Weir (2011: 24) suggest that this type of evidence might be considered as part of the scoring system, it is very important to note that it must be seen as a broader concept, to include a link not only to the scoring system but also to the underlying construct. Without this link any claim will be meaningless.

Standard setting	This refers to the linking of reported test performance (i.e., a score or grade) to an independent standard or framework. The act of standard setting is designed to add meaning to the test score by allowing it to be more broadly interpreted: see Dunlea (2016) for an excellent overview of the area. There have been a number of studies which have attempted to establish a link between a particular test and the CEFR. The main purpose of these studies appears to have been to establish evidence of the value and potential use of the test score or grade beyond the system devised by the developer. If I can establish that a grade 6.5 on my test can be equated to a CEFR level B2, then it is likely that test score users who are not necessarily familiar with my test will grant formal recognition as they are familiar with the CEFR levels. See Martyniuk's (2011) collection of related studies.

One aspect of the socio-cognitive approach which should be stressed is the expectation that a test should be based on a clearly defined model of language progression while at the same time it is supported with a clear measurement model. In the Aptis testing service, the British Council has looked to a number of sources to identify appropriate language models for the different papers. These were:

- Reading – Khalifa & Weir (2009)
- Listening – Field (2014, 2019)
- Speaking – Levelt (1989)
- Writing – Palmquist (1994–2012)

We will briefly focus on the way in which the first of these informed the Aptis approach to the testing of reading.

The Khalifa & Weir model (represented here as Figure 9) has been particularly influential in reading test development over the past decade. The model, itself updated from an earlier version by Urquhart & Weir

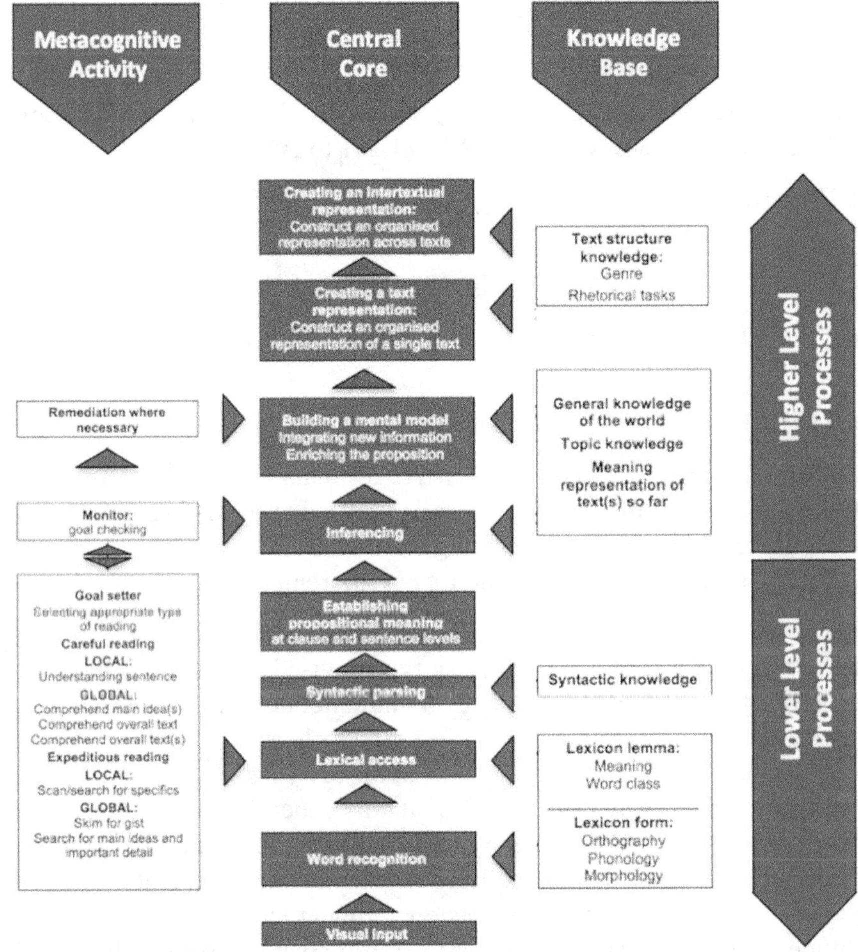

Figure 9: Khalifa & Weir's model of reading progression (2009: 49)

(1998), has informed the work of Cambridge Assessment English, the British Council and numerous tests by other exam boards around the world (e.g., CET in China, GEPT in Taiwan).

The British Council operationalised the model as follows:

CEFR C	Multiple Texts – Intertextual Comprehension
CEFR B2	Significant Single Text Comprehension (e.g., 750 words)
CEFR B1	Medium Single Text Comprehension (e.g., 250 words)

CEFR A2 Short Single Text Comprehension (e.g., 100 words)

CEFR A1 Sentence Level Comprehension Only

The test that emerged from this operationalisation of the model comprised four tasks, accessing CEFR levels A1 to B2.

CEFR B2 Matching headings to paragraphs (7 headings and 750-word text)

CEFR B1 Cloze (7 items from a 250-word text)

CEFR A2 Paragraph reorganising (6 items with a maximum 75-word text)

CEFR A1 Sentence comprehension (5 sentences)

Statistical analysis of trial and later live test data indicated that the four tasks were performing as planned and appeared to be distinguishing different levels of ability, thus meeting the expectation that the test should satisfy both language and measurement requirements.

However, concern was raised within the British Council's Assessment Research Group (ARG) that the task type devised to measure a test taker's ability read at the paragraph level might not be working as expected. The task type (a cloze task where test takers chose words from a selection greater than the number of blanks in the text) has long been criticised (see for example Alderson, 1979) as it was generally believed that test takers responded to the blanks by focusing only on local information on either side of a particular blank. Even though the measurement model for the test suggested that the task was operating at the appropriate level of difficulty, an eye-tracking study was commissioned to explore the actual behaviour of test takers. The study by Brunfaut & McCray (2015) clearly demonstrated that the concerns of Alderson (and others) were indeed supported as test takers systematically failed to read the entire test, and as such were unlikely to be able to demonstrate that they had comprehended it. As a result of the study, a new task type was devised, where it was hypothesised that test takers would be forced to read the entire text in order to respond appropriately to the items associated with it. This was duly trialled and found to work well in terms of measurement qualities, but in order to ensure that it met the expectations of the language model, a second eye-tracking study was commissioned from the Lancaster team (Brunfaut, 2016). The findings of this study supported the expectations of the ARG team, thus ensuring the integrity of the Aptis reading paper.

Considering consequence

With regard to the concept of test consequence, there are a number of points that should be taken into consideration:

- Consequence has never been clearly defined within validation models and has never been adequately operationalised in validation studies (see Kane, 2013).
- The link between stakeholders and consequence has not been described and as a result has not been adequately explored. One exception to this has been Chalhoub-Deville's (2016) identification of policy-makers as a specific audience for a validation argument.
- For some time now there has been some significant criticism of the failure of test developers to satisfactorily deal with the social and educational consequences of the tests they are responsible for (McNamara, 2008; McNamara & Roever, 2006; Shohamy, 2001, 2007). However, to date no practical solutions have emerged from this criticism, either from critics or test developers.
- The emphasis in early research on affective factors in language testing, which highlighted the impact on test performance of personal characteristics in the context of test-related social interactions, may have contributed to the limiting of our conceptualisation of the 'socio' aspect of the model by limiting it to the test itself, rather than recognising that it might also refer to the test within its social context (Berry, 2007; O'Loughlin, 2002; O'Sullivan, 2000a, 2000b, 2002; Porter & O'Sullivan, 1999; Porter, 1991a, b).
- Within the socio-cognitive approach, it can be argued that the social aspect has, in essence, lost out to the cognitive aspect, particularly with regard to the receptive skills. The conceptualisation of the socio-cognitive model suggested here attempts to deal with this situation by recognising that the social element is more likely to come to the fore in tests of language production and should be explicitly identified within the *test system* design. It can be argued that there is a social aspect to the receptive skills that is not always recognised. This is typically manifested by identifying the writer-reader or speaker-listener relationship but can also be highlighted by explicitly identifying elements of the input text (written or spoken) that require understanding of aspects such as pragmatic or cultural features of language use.

No test exists in a vacuum. Neither are any tests likely to emerge that have not been influenced by a number of factors. These might include political, social, commercial or theoretical pressures that can have a significant impact on the format, delivery and use of a test. It is therefore critical that we consider the contexts of development and use when considering how consequence should be operationalised in any validation model.

Contexts of development and use

The context in which a test is developed can influence key decisions around the construct definition and test approach and content. An example of this is the way in which the English Language Testing Service (ELTS) test was developed. Weir & O'Sullivan's (2017) account of the process, referred to above, shows how the conflicting approaches of the British Council's Test Development Research Unit (TDRU) and Cambridge saw the project conceived by the TDRU team led by Brendan Carroll and passed on to Cambridge for development, only for their proposed test to be rejected by the TDRU. To quote Alan Davies:

> Munby and Brendan [Carroll], fairly soon they decided that Cambridge and the other people, the other usual suspects on the committee, including me, were as it were too dyed in the wool in the past and they wanted something very different, and so the Council took it over completely
>
> (from Weir & O'Sullivan, 2017: 145)

While the TDRU team were keen on delivering an altogether new type of test, the Cambridge team clearly took a very different approach. Roger Hawkey (a TDRU member at the time) felt that

> They [Cambridge] would automatically start from their existing set of tests, so they would think, well, is this FCE or is it CPE, as a starter, rather than is this ESP or EAP or a Munby model?
>
> (from Weir & O'Sullivan, 2017: 145)

Test developers, therefore, should be seen as acting within a particular paradigm from which it can be extremely difficult to shift. This paradigm will have different elements, from the theoretical (as we saw in the above example, the two approaches to construct definition were radically different), to the practical (again with the given example, Cambridge felt they knew what would work, while the British Council's English Language Services Department felt they wanted to push boundaries), to the commercial (the Cambridge approach would likely have offered a less expensive service). It is not difficult to imagine how these different stresses would have a direct impact on test and scoring system related decisions that are needed during the development process. The historical overview of the way in which the European and US testing worlds developed in very different ways is another example of the relevance of the development context in the whole process.

Another issue that can impact on decisions made during the development process is the nature of the test, which can be seen as falling into three categories:

Commercial These are developed by companies that are keen to exploit an existing or potential market and fully commercially focused. The resultant tests are less likely to be supported by a costly long-term validation agenda than either of the other two categories, as commercial companies rarely if ever see the commercial need for this. This is particularly true of small-scale tests where developers simply do not have the resources to undertake even basic research. The probability is that a purely commercial test will have been developed with profitability to the fore in all decision-making. This can have a negative impact on the test itself.

Educational Developed by or for government departments to respond to the perceived educational needs of a country, and non-commercial in that it is free to the test taker. In situations such as the UK, the government outsources major examination development at some considerable cost. Interestingly, government-developed tests suffer from similar issues to the commercial tests in that compliance with existing regulations can significantly impact on test development – for example, considerations of local administration, often by untrained or inexperienced staff, must be taken into account. As we have seen in the discussion around test security, above, this can have a serious impact on validity, though efforts to limit this impact can mean a simplification and therefore under-representation of the construct. Much of the research into this type of test is undertaken by independent researchers. However, the breadth of work undertaken by Cambridge Assessment in validating their schools-focused tests is impressive (see http://www.cambridgeassessment.org.uk/our-research/).

Hybrid These are tests that are developed to meet the educational or social needs of a country, but which grow to have a significant commercial focus. The most prominent examples of this classification include IELTS and TOEFL. The organisations that are responsible for these two tests in particular have a long history of supporting validation research. A recent estimate for IELTS suggests that since 1989 there are more than 400 research studies which focus on the test (Cyril Weir, personal communication, April 2017), while TOEFL have regularly published official research reports since John Clark's study of native speaker performance on the test in 1977. Unfortunately, the same cannot be said of all tests in this category: witness the paucity of research work undertaken on the TOEIC test since its development in 1979.

These categories are necessarily broad and not all tests will fit easily into a category. We should also take into account the fact that the pressure on test developers to defend their tests through well-constructed research validation arguments or agenda will depend on the attitude of policy-makers. This is particularly evident in the different stances taken in the US, where there are quite well defined standards that must be adhered to, and the UK, where a visit to the Office of Qualifications and Examinations Regulation (Ofqual, 2017) website offers no indication of their position on validity or validation. Perhaps it is not surprising to see that neither of Britain's two major developers of examinations for the school system (AQA and Edexcel) include a link on their websites for research and validation, though the former supports the Centre for Education Research and Practice which undertakes and commissions validation projects.

It is clear that stakeholder values will play a significant role in the test development process. While we typically see key stakeholders as the people with the power to influence test development and use practice, it is important to recognise that the context of use in which a test resides is comprised of a number of stakeholders and stakeholder groups, all of whom will have some, however minor, influence. This influence ranges from the initial design to the reporting of test taker performance to the dissemination of information about the test. The different groups will have somewhat different perspectives, concerns and values and these will contribute in a number of different ways to the way in which a test is perceived. It is important also to recognise the fact that even well-placed policy-makers cannot act unilaterally Since they are subject to political, professional and personal pressures from other stakeholder groups it is critical for them that they make the most appropriate decisions in light of these pressures.

The appropriate consideration of stakeholder groups has been at the heart of the British Council's whole research and validation approach since they launched the test in 2012. Their Language Assessment Literacy Project, which has been in place since 2013, is seen as a vital element of the validation agenda, in which key internal (e.g., exams delivery, sales and marketing staff) and external (e.g., ministries and institutions that buy and use the test) stakeholders are helped to develop appropriate levels of competence in test theory and practice to inform their decisions. Stakeholder interests also drive the British Council's test localisation agenda, in which attention is paid to the context of use of the test by ensuring that the test is seen by these groups as being socially, educationally and culturally appropriate. There is also evidence that the necessary awareness among test developers of the needs of stakeholders is already beginning to happen in the US.

Baumann et al. (2017) describe how they ensured buy-in from key stakeholders by engaging with them throughout the process of change in assessment approach at the University of Chicago. Their stakeholders had to be convinced, using arguments and evidence that were meaningful to them, of the greater benefits of the new approach (a move from translation- to comprehension-based testing). Baumann et al. correctly identified this as a key assessment literacy issue, with critical implications for validation, recognising the importance of helping stakeholders to interpret test score meaning through assessment literacy training and through ensuring that all communication and literature around the test (reports, etc.) is accessible to them – in other words, it is written specifically for this audience using language and delivery formats that they are most comfortable with.

Constructing validation

Dunlea (2016: 53) argues that 'the socio-cognitive model is best placed to be the standard bearer of the key concepts promoted by Messick's unified model of validity, particularly in relation to language testing'. Table

20 outlines what Dunlea sees as 'the clear relationship that can be drawn between the components of the socio-cognitive model and Messick's six aspects of validity', highlighting the clarity of the relationship between the two approaches. Unlike other approaches to validation, e.g. Mislevy, Almond & Lukas (2003) or Chapelle, Enright & Jamieson (2008), the socio-cognitive approach is intentionally specific to language testing. It includes within the frameworks derived from the model sufficient detail to guide the user through the development process and make explicit the link between development and validation, Weir & O'Sullivan's

Messick	Socio-cognitive model
Content	Relates to test task and to the relationship between the test task and the test taker in context, where relevance and representativeness are seen as being locally appropriate
Substantive	Relates to the test taker, specifically to the definition of the ability being tested in the specific context
Structural	Relates to the relationship between the test taker, the test task and the scoring system – e.g., demonstrating the link between a rating scale/rubric, the task and the underlying trait or ability, and providing evidence that it is working as planned
Generalisability	Relates to the relationship between the test taker, the test task and the scoring system – e.g., demonstrating the appropriateness of test cut-scores in relation to a locally meaningful standard or Indicating how well the test will work when taken by different (though appropriate) populations or sub-populations or Indicating how well a test taker's reported score or grade predicts performance within the target domain
External	Relates to the scoring system and the context of use – e.g., demonstrating a link to a locally appropriate criterion
Consequential	Relates to the consequence/impact of using the test in a specific context for a specific purpose

Table 20: Linking Messick's six validation criteria to the socio-cognitive model

concept of validation=development. The overview of the socio-cognitive approach presented is not meant to be definitive, and includes examples of parameters from different skills frameworks rather than detailed frameworks for each skill.

As with the position taken by Messick, the socio-cognitive approach expects that the test developer will refer to all of the detailed parameters described in the frameworks derived from the model when constructing a validation argument. Again similar to Messick, the primary focus of a validation argument will be to clarify how all of these different pieces of evidence combine to offer a clear evidential link between the three aspects of the model (test taker, test task and scoring system). The socio-cognitive model contributes to Messick by indicating that this should be done within the context of test use, by attending to the needs, expectations and knowledge of the key stakeholders.

Commentary

We have observed in this overview of validity as seen from a UK/European perspective, that there is a fundamental difference in philosophical approach to the area of assessment and validation when compared to that of the US. This difference has been in existence since the dawn of modern language testing in the early years of the 20th century and was clearly recognised by UK-based scholars such as Roach, Wiseman and Thyne in the 1940s, 1960s and 1970s respectively. While Roach was primarily concerned with the practical impact of standardisation and measurement on the tests he worked on at Cambridge (1945), both Wiseman and Thyne recognised the limitations of the then current US-influenced approaches from a conceptual (as well as practical) perspective. Wiseman's (1961) concept of *efficiency* is of particular interest given the later recognition by US scholars (particularly Messick) of the need to look beyond the technical psychometrics of a test to consider its purpose, use and impact. He also uses the term *backwash*, a decade before Hughes' re-casting of the concept as *washback*, to describe the positive and negative impact of examinations on the classroom. Thyne recognised the need to gather a range of evidence to support any validity claim, arguing that we should not ask 'Is it valid?' but 'How valid is it?' (1974: 5). This question clearly implies the need for an evidence-based approach to validation that is not solely statistically derived.

While the primary concern amongst the scholars cited above was on the practical improvement of examinations, Weir, initially with the support of his colleagues in the Reading Group, was to take a more theoretical and at the same time practical approach to the area of test development and validation. Despite criticism from the US of his insistence on a *real-world approach* to both construct definition and test development, and later criticism in the UK of his decision to include explicitly defined cognitive models of language development in his socio-cognitive frameworks of the early years of the 21st century, Weir was to become the dominating influence on UK language testing.

The socio-cognitive model of test development and validation, as it is described here and employed by the British Council, not only demands that test developers take into consideration specific aspects of language, cognition and use but also understands that these are taking place in a social context of test development and use. This context is defined by its stakeholder groups and impacts on construct definition and validation reporting. It demands of test developers that they actively engage with stakeholders to help them more fully understand the nature of tests and the interpretation of the results reported on test performance. This is not a new position to take. In fact, it is clearly stated in the *Standards* (AERA, APA & NCME, 2014: 119) that:

> When test score information is released, those responsible for testing programmes should provide interpretations appropriate to the audience. The interpretations should describe in simple language what the test covers, what scores represent, and how scores are intended to be used.

In addition, and perhaps most critically, by placing the test taker at the centre of the whole approach to development and validation, the socio-cognitive model demands that tests are appropriate to this critical stakeholder group. In order to ensure that this is the case, it is therefore critical to involve these groups when attempting to develop an understanding of how the construct is to be defined and understood within this context. This will require some considerable knowledge of the culture and language-learning opportunities within formal and informal education of the test taker. It will also require knowledge of the social context within which the test will be used, so as to allow for some meaningful awareness of the consequences of using the test in this context. Localisation, the term by which this process is known, suggests that an understanding of a test's purpose-in-context, is the key validation factor. The concept of the international general proficiency test, with no defined test-taker population or context of use, is therefore called into question.

The term *Teaching of English for No Obvious Reason* (TENOR), coined by Abbott & Wingard (1981), can be adapted here as referring not to teaching but to testing. This is explicated in the context of seeing children being prepared for one such international test by studying words related to Christmas (Santa, reindeer, snow, etc.) in a school in a Mumbai slum. In that testing context, there was a lack of any awareness on the side of the teachers (an assessment literacy issue) or the organisation selling the test to this school (an ethical issue) of the real needs of these children. Projects in which the British Council's Aptis test service has been altered to ensure that it is appropriate for use in places such as India, the Kingdom of Saudi Arabia and Malaysia demonstrate that localisation can work when undertaken with partners who are expert in the local context.

The gradual movement away from large-scale, curriculum- and learner-free tests towards more localised and ultimately personalised examinations will mean that new conceptualisations of what validity means and how it can be established are needed. This will be most obviously seen in the way in which the target construct is defined, since the indirect, hypothesised approaches have failed to result in truly *efficient* tests (in Wiseman's terms). Vernon's suggestion that '[T]he psychologist might ponder on such facts that, although group tests of intelligence are more reliable than individual tests…yet the latter seem often to give I.Q.s much truer to real life' (1958: 2, referred to by Wiseman, 1961: 162) clearly has some resonance for modern-day language testing. The spread of technology-delivered tests has thus far often resulted in a retreat to the somewhat primitive forms of assessment castigated by Wiseman (1961) and Hoffman (1962). However, considered application of more *real-world* models of modern language use in test instruments offer a meaningful way forward towards the ultimate goal – a fully personalised assessment. Localisation is a goal worth our scholarly engagement despite current obstacles, e.g., requirements of standardisation in areas such as licensure and certification as well as educational reform-driven accountability assessment.

CHAPTER 4

VALIDITY AND CONSEQUENCES

Definition

Consequences have, more than any other evidence type, continued to be a contentious issue in terms of their status in a validity conceptualisation: 'Perhaps the most contentious topic in validity' according to Brennan (2006: 8). Many (e.g., Popham, Mehrens, Ebel and, most recently, Lissitz & Samuelson) have argued that consequences should not be considered part of validity, while others (e.g., Lane, Linn, Moss, Shepard, Brennan and Kane) have argued the opposite. The debate needs to be considered with an eye towards disputes such as the nature of issues that consequences comprise. Before we turn our attention to this debate, we explore the definition of the term consequences.

A few terms seem to coexist in the published literature that relate to consequences (see Cheng, 2008). Chalhoub-Deville (2009a, b, c, 2016) writes that *consequences, impact, washback and backwash* are labels that can be used interchangeably. Variations observed among these terms are predominantly attributable to disciplinary traditions or geographic preferences. However, in the area of language teaching and learning, *impact* is typically used in relation to society in general, while *washback/backwash* refers to the influence of tests on language learning. The term *washback/backwash* was addressed in the first chapter, 'Teaching and Testing', of Hughes' 1989 book.

While *impact* was generally used in Bachman (1990) and Bachman & Palmer (1996), it is the term *consequences* that Bachman & Palmer utilise in their 2010 publication. The word 'impact' does not appear in the index of their book. Fundamentally, these labels refer to various intended and/or unintended, negative and/or positive outcomes related to testing systems. In an article that addresses educational and social reform impact, Chalhoub-Deville (2009a, c) maintains that the term refers to the influence that a testing system and related practices have on individuals, groups and society. 'Impact could be examined at the micro or macro level. Investigations could be set up to study direct or indirect influences on test takers, the educational community or society at large' (Chalhoub-Deville, 2009a: 119). It is not our intention here to advocate for any one label. We simply would like to show that they share meaning and connote similar issues.

Deliberations of consequences address highly contentious issues. A central consideration is the nature of consequences that people agree or disagree to include in validity. Closely related to this point is what aspects of consequences are to be investigated and who is responsible for undertaking that investigation. Typically, a narrow view of consequences in validity is tolerated, i.e., consequences directly attributable to the way in which the construct is measured. This position is upheld by most professionals and is essentially what Messick advocated. 'It is not that adverse social consequences of test use render the use invalid but, rather, that adverse social consequences should be attributable to any source of test invalidity, such as construct underrepresentation or construct-irrelevant variance' (Messick, 1995: 748). Construct underrepresentation occurs when assessments do not cover all important aspects of the construct or a testing system misses features relevant to what should be assessed. Construct-irrelevance occurs when a testing system assesses features which are not part of the intended construct.

In this ongoing deliberation of the nature of consequences, it is interesting to compare Messick's view with that of Cronbach's. Messick (1989: 88) argued that:

> If the adverse social consequences are empirically traceable to sources of test invalidity, then the validity of the test use is jeopardized. If the social consequences cannot be so traced...then the validity of the test use is not overturned.

Cronbach (1988: 6) on the other hand, felt that negative consequences 'could invalidate test use even if the consequences could not be traced to any flaw in the test', because 'tests that impinge on the rights and life chances of individuals are inherently disputable'. By emphasising that any aspect that impacts on individuals negatively is worthy of investigation, even if it does not pertain to a construct flaw, Cronbach clearly goes beyond the characterisation offered by Messick. The two positions represent two ends of a continuum in terms of their engagement with consequences.

Representation of consequences in the *Standards*

The *Standards* (1999, 2014: 21) side with Messick when they indicate that '[E]vidence about consequences is relevant to the validity when it can be traced to a source of invalidity such as construct under-representation or construct-irrelevant components.' The 2014 *Standards* largely address issues of construct relevance and representation in a chapter entitled 'Fairness in Testing'. This chapter is part of the section called 'Foundations', which includes validity, reliability and fairness. The *Standards* address issues of fairness with regard to test development and administration to enhance valid score interpretations for intended test takers and relevant subgroups. They also discuss the use of accommodations to remove barriers to the assessment of the construct of interest and to support valid score interpretation for intended uses.

> Professionals may be justified in deviating from standardized procedures to gain a more accurate measurement of the intended construct and to provide more appropriate individual decisions. However, for other contexts and uses, deviations from standardized procedures may be inappropriate because they change the construct being measured, compromise the comparability of scores or use of norms, and/or unfairly advantage some individuals (AERA, APA & NCME, 2014: 53–54).

The *Standards* discuss differential item/test functioning (DIF and DTF) detection of potential bias towards or against different groups and the need to carry out investigations to better understand the reasons for the lack of consistent construct representation across groups.

Lissitz & Samuelsen who present a highly restricted notion of validity, as discussed in the previous chapter, endorse features the *Standards* discuss as part of fairness. Lissitz & Samuelsen (2007a: 441) specify the following as sources of evidence to document validity:

- analyses such as bias and sensitivity review,
- DIF analysis,
- review of the accommodations offered,
- analysis of the scores of accommodated students.

Fairness is argued to be ultimately about the validity of test score interpretations for intended uses for individuals and groups. The *Standards* exclude consequences that pertain to what McNamara & Roever (2006: 14) call the 'overt social context of testing' such as social equity or policy-related accountability that document the impact of testing practices on individuals, educational communities and/or societal structures. The upshot here is this: what the *Standards* advocate in terms of technical aspects of consequences or fairness represents a limited interpretation of consequences and while this position might be characterised as prudent, it might also be reasoned as taking the easy option. In offering a narrow definition of consequences and recognising evidence garnered primarily (if not only) from the psychometric qualities of the data generated in a test administration, the *Standards* do a disservice to test stakeholders by ignoring what McNamara & Roever have identified as complex and often non-quantifiable consequences.

Another clue that lends support to our evaluation of the 2014 *Standards*' position is the language adopted when labelling the five sources of validity evidence. While there are certain section headings – pp. 14–16 – that specify 'Evidence Based on Each of Test Content, Response Processes, Internal Structure', and 'Relations to Other Variables', the heading for consequences is markedly different. It states: 'Evidence for Validity and Consequences of Testing' (p. 19). The *Standards* include construct-related consequences as part of validity while excluding consequences that extend beyond intended score interpretation and use evidence, i.e., those that pertain to unintended consequences, or relate to policy evaluation. Throughout this chapter and, for example, in Chapter 13 of the *Standards* (2014: 20), 'Uses of Tests for Program Evaluation, Policy Studies, and Accountability', it is asserted that 'it is important to distinguish between evidence that is directly relevant to validity and evidence that may inform decisions about social policy but fall outside the realm of validity'. The point about this demarcation of validity scope is to delimit or absolve the test developer/publisher from being held responsible to engage in research and provide documentation to support the interpretation and use of test results in educational and social contexts. The *Standards* do not require test users to take responsibility for such research. Standard 13.8 states:

> Those who mandate the use of tests in policy, evaluation and accountability contexts and those who use tests in such contexts should monitor the impact and should identify and minimize the negative consequences (AERA, APA & NCME, 2014: 212).

So, policy-makers and test users, but not test developers are to be held responsible since they are better situated to address consequences that pertain to their own actions. However, a test developer is implicated in this process. As Kane (2013: 62) puts it: '...but a test developer who provides a test to the user shares this responsibility. In particular, test developers who suggest that a test can be used in a particular way have an obligation to support the claims that they make.' Basically, by responding to a call from an agency to develop a test, developers share in the responsibility for the consequences of intended uses, whether explicitly or implicitly stated.

We argue that a narrow view of consequences is offered in the *Standards* (2014). The *Standards* indicate that validity pertains to the degree to which intended benefits are realised, and comprises consequences which are directly due to the way in which the construct is measured. The *Standards* exclude arguments/evidence that pertain to other sources, e.g., policy from validity considerations. Next, we turn to examine the extent to which the models we have focused upon in the monograph embrace the viewpoint advocated in the *Standards*.

Representation of consequences in validity systems

The models presented by Mislevy and Embretson discuss validity as it shadows test design, development and use operations. Both ECD and UVS also offer a psychometrically- and cognitively-driven evidentiary documentation of validity. Validity within ECD is characterised thus:

> All must work in concert to create an assessment that is at once coherent and practicable. Toward this end, it will be of significant benefit to have a shared framework for talking about the roles that each facet of the design elements and delivery processes play in the support of a coherent assessment argument. Evidence-centered design provides such a framework, and can thus prove useful for understanding how innovations such as cognitive modeling, new measurement models, automated scoring, and technology-based tasks fit into assessment systems (Mislevy, Almond & Lukas, 2003: 17).

The quote underscores validity as an accompaniment to test development practices. We contend, given the notion of development=validation, that this is a strong feature of these models. Overall, however, the premise of validity (and consequences) is predominantly cognitive and psychometric in its orientation (McNamara & Roever, 2006). McNamara & Roever (2006: 9) write that validity has tended to be 'heavily marked by its origins in the individualist and cognitively oriented field of psychology'. Impact in ECD focuses on aspects of use as it primarily connects test performance – content and processes – to real-world environments. ECD is creating systems to advance 'a sound basis for organising observations and guiding actions in the situations for which it is intended' (Mislevy, 2007: 83). With this perspective, the apparent goal is to enhance prediction outcomes. This reaffirms more of a cognitive, and psychometric, orientation to validity.

In Embretson's model (2008), the impact category follows utility. A solid-lined arrow flows directly from utility to impact (see Figure 7 in the previous chapter). Impact is connected only indirectly, represented with dashed-lines, to the loop that provides interrelations among the categories. Her conception of impact could essentially be interpreted to address the effectiveness of score predictions and to comprise claims/questions such as the following:

- To what extent do test practices and related scores realise intended consequences, and primarily make accurate characterisations of individual constructs and outcomes?
- To what extent do relationships with other measures and variables contribute to adverse construct measurement?
- To what extent can unintended consequences of score use be traced to conceptualisations in the design and/or input categories?

Nowhere does UVS, or ECD for that matter, consider social structures along the lines envisioned by Chalhoub-Deville (2009a, b, c, 2016), McNamara & Roever (2006), Bachman & Palmer (2010), Moss (2016) or Kunnan (2018).

As described earlier, Bachman & Palmer's AUA model affords consequences a prominent role, thus is markedly different from ECD and UVS. AUA anchors its argument in beneficence and does not shy away from encouraging test developers to consider claims that speak to consequences at the individual, group and larger societal level, depending on the specifics of their testing programme. AUA calls attention to the need to tailor justification arguments to reach beyond test developers and researchers. Bachman & Palmer promote investigations of both intended and unintended consequences and argue that communication with different stakeholder groups is key to render technical information actionable.

The anchoring of AUA in consequences represents a significant shift in Bachman's (2005) own thinking. 'While researchers like Shohamy (2001) and Lynch (2001) argue for a critical examination of test functions and consequences as part of validation, Bachman (2005) deems such endeavors as impractical in validity research' (Chalhoub-Deville,

2016: 459). One can only surmise that the publication of Kane's (2006) chapter on 'Validation' in the influential *Educational measurement* contributed to the change observed from the 2005 Bachman publication to the Bachman & Palmer (2010) book. Overall, AUA clearly represents a meaningful contribution to the field and a step forward in terms of deliberations on consequences. With AUA, research on consequences is integral to validity/justification and is not an add-on.

When compared to codes of ethics or practice available in the field, AUA could also be said to provide the field with a stronger push to consider consequences. Davies (2008) entrusts codes of ethics and of practice with social and political accountability, an approach viewed with scepticism by McNamara & Roever, who write: 'we are uncertain whether the codification of ethical principle will have any measurable impact on the field' (2006: 253). AUA moves the field away from an appeal to consider codes, i.e., unenforceable documents, to a more systematic plan of researchable claims that need to be addressed by test developers as part of their technical documentation. It remains to be seen the extent to which language testing professionals will agree that the guidance AUA offers is appropriate.

The jury is still out on whether AUA presents more than a cognitive, individualist (as opposed to aggregate and system level) consideration of consequences. In addition, we need to consider whether information that AUA and related materials provide can help us construct research agendas that focus on various aspects of consequences. Here we are reminded of Shepard's (1993: 428) point:

> In my view, validity investigations cannot resolve questions that are purely value choices (e.g., should all high school students be given an academic curriculum versus being tracked into vocational and college preparation programs?). However, to the extent that contending constituencies make competing claims about what a test measures, about the nature of its relations to subsequent performance in school or on the job, or about the effects of testing, these value-laden questions are integral to a validity evaluation. For example, the question as to whether students are helped or hurt as a result of a test-based remedial placement is amenable to scientific investigation.

Related to this quote is the very complicated matter of engaging with complex social issues that our testing operations are at the heart of increasingly. In our accountability tests, for example, we need our scholarship to provide operational models of how to participate in social engineering types of test-centred policies. Also complicated is the idea of engaging relevant stakeholders, ferreting out responsibility for different aspects of consequences, and bringing together the multiplicity of views into an integrated argument. On the whole, AUA's engagement with consequences, while in need of more thought and development, is significant.

Compared to his 2006 publication, Kane (2013) increasingly speaks out about the importance of documenting use and paying attention to consequences. His evolving conception of the role consequences play in validation now views 'adverse impact and unintended systemic effects...as serious issues that need to be addressed in evaluating high-stakes testing programs' (Kane, 2013: 59). In a 2010 presentation, Kane questioned a definition of validity that engages with consequences only when they are related to the constructs measured. He commented:

> This formulation bothered me, because it seemed to say that consequences can invalidate an interpretation/use of test scores, but only if they were already invalid. The rationale for this formulation makes sense, because a test should not be faulted for exhibiting real group differences in performance, but it bothered me. It seemed that social consequences could only act as a reminder to check on validity, or to check more carefully. This is not a bad thing in itself, but does it have teeth?

Kane (2006: 54) asserts, following Cronbach's lead, that 'Consequences have always been a part of our conception of validity.... Traditional definitions of validity in terms of how well a testing program achieves its goals...necessarily raise questions about consequences, positive and negative.' A similar view has been endorsed by the US government's NCLB Peer Review Guidance on Consequences: 'In validating an assessment, the State must also consider the consequences of its interpretation and use. ... States must attend not only to the intended outcomes, but also to unintended effects' (U.S. Department of Education, 2004: 33). In his presentation, Kane (2010) concludes:

> As I see it, the real questions about social consequences are three:
>
> - What kinds of consequences should we focus on?
> - How should we evaluate consequences?
> - Who should be responsible for evaluating consequences?

We concur with this representation of the primary issues to address with regard to consequences. Testing professionals should be involved in discussions of consequences that address:

- the nature of consequences that need to be investigated;
- the types of evidence that should be pursued at different stages: as part of the test development process, test administration and the ongoing test use;
- the allocation of responsibility to different stakeholders with regard to pertinent research;
- criteria that speak to quality of evidence collected; and
- guidance in terms of how to incorporate consequence evidence and rationales from different test user groups into quality assurance and validity.

This conversation needs to involve relevant policy-makers, test providers and researchers, relevant professional groups (e.g., educators when the testing system pertains to school achievement or physicians when the testing systems pertains to medical license, etc.) and other groups and organisations. After all, '...perceptions about the seriousness of various kinds of consequences may be highly variable across stakeholders and across groups of stakeholders' (Kane, 2013: 48).

Moving forward: Investigations with regard to consequences

As scholars in the field, especially in language testing, continue to consider the undertaking of consequences in testing operations, they need to tackle several issues highlighted or alluded to in the published literature. We posit these issues below in the form of questions. To better guide thinking in this area, we present questions in five different areas of primary concern: nature of consequences, elaboration of claims, stakeholders' responsibilities, stakeholders' communication and unintended consequences. Neither the areas nor the questions are to be considered exhaustive. The point is to highlight how much work is needed and to encourage more focused scholarly activities with regard to consequences in test development and validity research.

Nature of consequences

- What is the nature of the consequences we should consider?
- Are there consequences common across different test purposes/uses?

- What aspects of consequences are salient for different test purposes/uses?
- To what extent should we move beyond the technical aspects of consequences, e.g., fairness as documented in the *Standards*, and deal with issues of consequences that traditionally have been relegated outside the realms of validity and thus more the responsibility of test user groups?
- To what disciplines, and additional areas, do we need to expand our scholarship to better attend to consequences at various individual, aggregate/group and system levels?
- Where should we place consequences in terms of a validity system – at the design level as suggested by Bachman & Palmer (2010) or at the tail-end of our test operations, as depicted by Embretson (2007, 2008)?
- What are the budgetary and resource implications of attending to this expanded notion of consequences?
- How are different types of consequences perceived by varied stakeholder groups?

Elaboration of claims

- What do consequences actually entail in terms of claims?
- What are the claims of consequences that are salient at different segments of a test development operation?
- What does a sequence of claims look like for different purposes/uses?
- Are all claims to be of equal significance?
- Which claims might need to be accorded more/less weight given test purpose/use?
- To what extent might the same set of claims be accorded different importance by different stakeholders?
- To what extent will claims related to different stakeholder groups differ?
- What procedures, rules and indices should we adopt to evaluate different claims?

Stakeholders' responsibilities

- Who are the stakeholders for a given testing programme?
- What frameworks or principles can help us identify relevant stakeholders, e.g., item writers, policy-makers, educators, the media, test takers, etc.?

- For which aspects of consequences are test developers and other relevant stakeholders to be routinely held responsible?
- What frameworks or principles can help guide the negotiation/allocation of responsibility for different consequences?
- How can resources be shared to undertake necessary research allocated for different stakeholder groups?
- What mechanisms are available/should be created to hold stakeholder groups responsible? The *Standards* and various language testing codes have no enforcement power.
- How do we bring the evidence accumulated by measurement professionals and other stakeholder groups together to create a coherent argument related to consequences?
- Do we need to change the way we educate measurement and language testing professionals to better prepare them for the changes we are espousing?
- How do we engage with colleagues from different disciplines or parts of a testing organisation to carry out needed work?

Stakeholders' communication

- Why is communication with stakeholders not considered an area of scholarship in the measurement and language testing fields?
- What do differentiated communication plans look like?
- What formats and platforms are user-friendly for different stakeholders?
- What specific pieces of information are relevant to different stakeholders?
- Who is responsible for developing the communication plans for specified stakeholders?
- Are test development specialists equipped to deliver a meaningful communication plan across a broad group of stakeholders using a variety of communication channels?
- How do we communicate evidence and related information within a testing organisation – to various item developers, test administrators, sales and marketing professionals, business managers, etc. – to improve test programme operations?
- How do we render performance data usable to stakeholder groups such as teachers to enhance the usefulness of testing for learning/teaching purposes?

Unintended consequences

- How do we make the case to relevant stakeholders for the need to marshal resources to attend to *negative* unintended consequences – are they unintended after all?
- What examples of *negative* unintended outcomes and/or consequences can be accumulated from various testing operations to create scholarly activities in this area?
- Should we not also engage in documenting *positive* unintended consequences?
- How to ferret out the scope of areas to investigate with regard to unintended consequences, e.g., classroom/instructional impact versus real-estate value?
- What is a meaningful time frame within which we pursue documentation of unintended consequences?
- How do different stakeholder groups perceive various aspects of *negative* unintended consequences?
- Who should be involved in documenting *negative* unintended consequences?
- Should we prioritise particular stakeholder groups (e.g., test takers) when considering unintended consequences?
- To what extent might any stakeholder prioritisation be related to an interaction between context of test use and test decisions or claims?
- When should we investigate *negative* unintended consequences – at the development stage or after the testing programme is operational?
- Should *negative* unintended consequences be attended to at every stage of development along with intended consequences?
- What frameworks can help design mitigation plans to anticipate and remedy potential unintended negative consequences?

Accountability testing, consequences and validity

Shohamy (2007) has been forceful in her arguments that tests are often used as a policy tool. Within that context, Chalhoub-Deville (2016) takes on the issue of consequences within an educational reform agenda that utilises testing as a principal component. Testing is increasingly being employed to drive accountability systems. The *Standards* (2014: 215) define accountability as 'a system that imposes student performance-based rewards or sanctions on institutions such as school systems or on individuals such as teachers or mental health care providers'.

Such ambitious reform-driven testing systems require radical changes in conceptualisations of validity. In such systems, it would be outlandish not to attend to issues of consequences. Reform-based testing initiatives involve score interpretation and use at the individual or group level as well as at the system level (e.g., educational, economic and social).

Testing programmes affiliated with educational reform initiatives move beyond traditional test purposes, individual level measurement and circumscribed technical documentation. Reform-based testing compels explicit interconnections among policy stipulations, complex testing systems and expanded stakeholder groups and structures. Within the context of validity for educational reform testing, arguments need to be fleshed out at different levels: individual test takers, teacher/provider groups and larger systems targeted – educational/societal. These activities will necessitate some considerable reflection on how the communication with and among these and other key stakeholder groups is planned, operationalised and managed. Also needed are scholarly engagements that acknowledge the social dimension to validity. What is proposed is understandably quite ambitious and the necessary technical documentation is complex. However, the complexity of the quality assurance should be/is congruent with the encompassing ambitions and claims of these reform efforts.

Validity argument localised

Chalhoub-Deville proposes a broad validity agenda that embraces Kane's IUA but is *localised* to attend to issues raised in a reform-style of assessment. Chalhoub-Deville (2016: 13) calls for engagement in research to 'articulate consequential research programmes and related analytic tools that address policy-driven accountability assessments'. A schematic representation of this agenda is presented in Table 21 and is intended to articulate a need to consider validity at the policy level, at the design level and various development stages, and subsequently when the testing system is operational. This approach integrates consequences as part of technical documentation undertaken by test developers. The approach to the evidence collected moves from being primarily confirmationist in nature, as typically observed with research when a testing programme is under development, to being critical when the programme is up and running. When engaged in a confirmationist mode of validation, results are employed to improve and strengthen the effectiveness of the policy or testing features under development. The critical stage affords validation to continue to be mindful not only of intended but also of unintended

CONSEQUENCES IN VALIDITY: REFORM-DRIVEN ASSESSMENTS	Score Interpretations & Uses at the individual level	Score Interpretations & Uses at the aggregate level	Reform: The Educational-Social Contexts of testing
Policy & Arguments Under Development	Social Impact Analysis: Measurement Argument	Social Impact Analysis: Measurement Argument	Social Impact Analysis: Theory of Action Argument
Specification of Claims – intended & potentially unintended	Interpretation & Use Inferences	Interpretation & Use Inferences	System Level Inferences
Validation Evidence	Confirmationist	Confirmationist	Confirmationist
Assessment Programme & Arguments Under Development	Measurement Argument	Measurement Argument	Theory of Action Argument
Specification of Claims	Interpretation & Use Inferences	Interpretation & Use Inferences	System Level Inferences
Validation Evidence	Confirmationist	Confirmationist	Confirmationist
Assessment Programme & Arguments Developed	Measurement Argument	Measurement Argument	Theory of Action Argument
Appraisal of Claims	Interpretation & Use Inferences	Interpretation & Use Inferences	System Level Inferences
Validation Evidence	Critical	Critical	Critical

Policy: Validation Evidence is Critical

Table 21: Conceptualising consequences within validity in reform-driven testing

consequences. O'Sullivan (2016) makes a similar suggestion, but in his case localisation is extended to the broad range of stakeholders who make up the context of test development and use (see his chapter 5).

The nature of the validity claims moves beyond the more traditional focus on individual test-taker performance. Claims are differentiated depending on the argument level: individual, aggregate/group or larger structures. The measurement profession has been adept at addressing technical issues such as (a) scoring, (b) generalisation, (c) extrapolation and (d) utilisation at the individual level. Increasingly professionals are also engaged in the development of claims and tools to address aggregate level arguments, e.g., hierarchical linear modelling, value added modelling, among others. See chapter 13 in the *Standards* (AERA, APA & NCME, 2014) for more information on the topic. Research remains scant when it comes to consequences and arguments at system levels, i.e., the educational-social contexts of testing.

Theory of action, social impact analysis, logic models and other evaluation-based approaches have been suggested to guide the development of claims and pursue investigations of meaningful policy outcomes. Measurement professionals, including language testers, are not typically familiar with such approaches. Nevertheless, it is such approaches that are needed to flesh out claims and pursue research at the larger educational/community/societal scale and we need to either retool, change how we prepare our future professionals, or formulate teams across disciplines to properly engage in needed research. In conclusion, reform-based testing offers an example of how the scope and particulars of validity and consequences, while still anchored in prominent thought in the field, need to be adapted in order to accommodate the particulars of a context of a testing programme.

Testing, especially with reform-driven systems, is policy-driven and is intended to effect fundamental and encompassing changes at the individual, group and societal levels. The more practical approach to validity espoused in more recent validity publications such as the argument-based models, e.g., ABV and AUA, have to be modified to flesh out claims entailed not only at the test design but at the policy design stage as well. The implementation of policy dictates in terms of test specifications, development and operation should then constitute an opportunity to further reflect on the policy, provide a critical appraisal of its particulars and inform better policy development. This is not delusional thinking. A responsible scholarship demands that we evaluate the real-world consequences of our testing programmes.

Roles and responsibilities negotiated

Taking on validity documentation of consequences-related validation necessitates close involvement of test developer and user groups, which is not typically done with validity research. It also necessitates moving beyond traditional *a priori*, fixed allocation of roles and involvement. The literature offers little guidance on how collaborations can be structured in more fluid test development and documentation circumstances. Traditionally test developers claim responsibility for research that directly relates to issues of the construct and practically everything else is deemed to be the responsibility of the users (AERA, APA & NCME, 1999, 2014). Increasingly researchers such as Kane (2013: 58) argue that 'test users generally are in the best position to identify unintended consequences, but test publishers also have the responsibility for the consequences of uses they explicitly or implicitly advocate'. While this push to rethink the circumscribed, fixed role of test developers is positive, it does not provide guidance on how to move along this path and accommodate the reality of testing, including educational reform testing.

Chalhoub-Deville (2016: 14– 15) states:

> This fixed, a priori allocation of roles for consequential research is not tenable with GERM [global educational reform movement] testing (Chalhoub-Deville, 2009a, 2009b; Nichols & Williams, 2009). For example and as already described with RTTT, the federal government and various state agencies, typically viewed as users, increasingly direct the development, interpretation and use of accountability assessment systems. Reform testing blurs the lines between test-taker and test-user groups. Issues such as role conflation necessitate a more flexible approach to the allocation of responsibilities for consequential research.

Chalhoub-Deville (2016) makes a case to move thinking beyond static role allocations that do not accommodate the reality of accountability testing programmes. She presents Figure 10 that stipulates key factors to consider at a broad level to assist with negotiated responsibilities in terms of consequences-related research. Key aspects of the figure include:

- Breadth of construct/domain;
- Intended score interpretation and use;
- The amount of time a testing programme has been operational;
- A flexible zone of negotiate responsibility (ZNR); and
- Two primary stakeholder groups – test developers and test users.

Test developers, as Figure 10 depicts, are said to play a larger role with consequences' research where the construct/domain is broad in scope and score interpretations and uses are in line with intended inferences. Test users play the larger role of undertaking such research when the

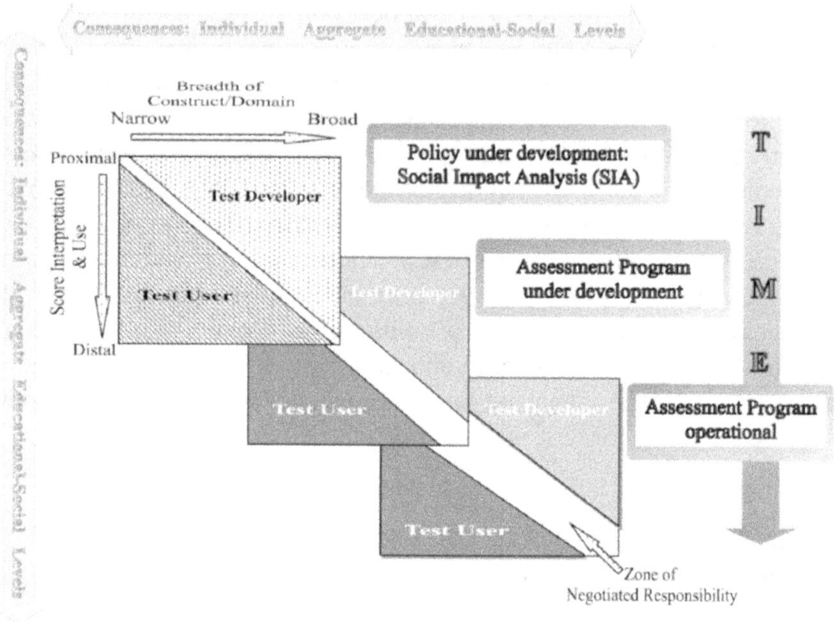

Figure 10: Role and responsibility allocation for consequences in validity (Chalhoub-Deville, 2016: 467)

scope of the construct is narrow but score interpretations and uses drift beyond intended inferences. Beyond these demarcated roles, developers and users have to negotiate the undertaking of research regarding consequences. Figure 10 features a ZNR to indicate a need to negotiate responsibilities for consequential research when roles move beyond those traditionally delineated.

Passage of time and related stages of testing operations are additional factors to consider when allocating responsibility. Chalhoub-Deville (2016: 16) writes:

> over time and with a successful operational testing program, users tend to devise new – typically towards the distal end of the continuum – interpretations of/uses for results. Test developers cannot hold on to the stance that such interpretations/uses are not originally intended. What might once have been characterized as distal has become common practice, which needs to be accommodated in the research agenda. Developers are likely to accrue financial benefits from these new interpretations/uses, because they tend to

> involve an increase in test administrations. Unless developers seek to stop unauthorized practices, then an argument could be made that developers 'implicitly advocate' (Kane, 2013, p. 58) these practices. Test developers have to assume research responsibility for this expanded interpretation/use of results and/or enter into negotiations to undertake necessary research.

In other words, holding to design statements about the purpose/intended inferences of a testing system is not tenable when a testing programme has been operational for a long while, its test taker numbers have increased substantially, and its uses have become fairly diverse. With expansions in volume and/or purposes as well as market share, responsibility is beyond what was originally envisioned. The figure shows that as a testing programme grows and evolves, the ZNR is enlarged, which indicates a greater demand to negotiate responsibilities for consequential research. Test developers cannot eschew their responsibility and a share of the research that needs to be undertaken. For more on the topic of accountability testing, validity and consequences, see Chalhoub-Deville (2016).

Again, the goal with the figure and related description is to encourage the field to undertake systematic thinking with regard to research related to consequences and to flesh out more realistic allocations of roles and responsibilities. Figure 10 presents initial thinking in this area. We foresee the model to be adapted in various ways to accommodate localised testing efforts. For example, in the case of accountability testing, we expect to differentiate among test user groups such as teachers and related educators versus professionals who are affiliated with departments of education/public instruction. These groups have different capabilities/resources and interests, which help dictate roles they can play and responsibilities they can undertake.

CHAPTER 5

AN INTEGRATED ARGUMENT-BASED APPROACH TO VALIDATION

Validation is an encompassing and complex endeavour that targets quality evidence. In essence, validation speaks to formal efforts put in place to accumulate evidence to uphold inferences and actions. Evidence is gathered to support the quality of the test development process, the test product, intended interpretation of scores, actions undertaken as well as the realisation of integral outcomes, e.g., as observed with policy-driven accountability testing. The validity literature can be said to offer rich conceptualisations of what quality represents. The present monograph has highlighted a variety of approaches to test development and validation in the US and the UK, in particular.

One approach, as presented in the various editions of the *Standards* (e.g., AERA, APA & NCME, 1999, 2014), attends to validity conceptualisation as a list of factors or sources. This approach does not explicate how these factors interact or combine in order to produce a coherent argument or make the case for the quality of a given testing system. The *Standards* offer guidance *from a distance* arguably to accommodate the variety of applications in different educational, psychological and employment settings, among others.

Messick (1989) offers construct validity as the concept that brings the various sources or types of quality evidence together. Validity is a unitary concept that speaks to issues of construct – score interpretation and use. O'Sullivan & Weir (2002) builds on Messick's ideas while keeping the UK tradition of connections to test development in mind. Weir's *socio-cognitive approach to test development and validation* clearly tries to bridge the divide between the UK and the US and explicitly incorporates Messick's conceptualisations. O'Sullivan & Weir (2011) and O'Sullivan (2011, 2014, 2016) have focused on how Weir's early conceptual frameworks might be more comprehensively described by suggesting an underlying socio-cognitive model of test development and validation in which the context of development and use figure largely in the conceptualisation of the underlying construct of focus.

Kane's (2006) argument outlines a series of claims that begin with performance quantification. Kane's argument-based validity approach pays little attention to the complex design and development issues that also impact the quality of a testing programme. Mislevy, on the other hand, has focused exactly on these design and development operations in a testing programme. Using the mantra of *impact by design*, Mislevy's ECD elaborates models inherent in the test development and administration phases of a testing programme. Validity as a matter of design represents a growing interest in educational measurement and embraces the longstanding tradition in the UK. It can, therefore, be said that of the approaches suggested in the literature from the US, that of Mislevy most closely reflects the work of Weir and O'Sullivan – though it should be stressed that there are still major differences, for example in the concept of test taker model. While Weir and O'Sullivan see this as attending to individual characteristics of the individual (physical, psychological and experiential) as well as to theoretical models related to the construct-of-focus (cognitive and social), Mislevy appears to suggest a more data-driven test taker profile. On a broader level, the socio-cognitive approach to development offers users the detail missing from Mislevy's evidence-centred design, which 'as a theoretical framework, needs greater definition and clarity as a model for practical assessment design' (Hain & Piper, 2013). Of course, the greatest point of difference between the UK approach, as represented in the work of Weir and O'Sullivan, and that of their US-based colleagues is that the former takes on a primarily participant-based approach, while the latter is more measurement-focused.

Approaches to validity such as Embretson's UVS and Bachman & Palmer's AUA seek to provide an inclusive system of evidence. Both UVS and AUA speak to the accumulation of evidence, which closely follows test design, development and administration operations, as well as performance and score analysis. In addition, both systems speak to issues of consequences. A major difference between Embretson's UVS and Bachman & Palmer's AUA is the positioning of consequences. Whereas UVS's impact category trails all other categories in the model, AUA's consequences are the starting point in assessment development. Also distinctive in AUA is its explicit attention to stakeholder groups. As already pointed out, Bachman & Palmer's *Table 8.1: Assessment Use Argument Claims, warrants and rebuttal* presents several statements that bring attention to clarity and suitability of communication with stakeholders to the fore. AUA emphasises not only the need to attend to stakeholders but also emphasises tailoring communication to reach stakeholders. In this way, the AUA approach offers important guidance to developers. A technical, rigid argument structure or indeed delivery channel (i.e., a written technical report) is highly unlikely to accommodate the needs of different stakeholder groups. The argument specifics as well as the delivery format need to explicitly have a user group(s) in mind.

Given the centrality of Kane's thinking in the current scholarship of validity and validation in the US, we have chosen to use his *Figure 2.2 Measurement Procedure and Interpretive Argument for Trait Interpretations*, to help pull in various argument threads highlighted throughout the monograph (see Figure 2 in Chapter 3 of this monograph). Though Kane has chosen to focus his ABV on the measurement part of the operations, i.e., the inferences that start with test takers' performance, we contend that his figure is rich in its representation of various operations/phases of a testing system. Kane's figure highlights on the left side, for example, variables that pertain to test design. The left side of the figure can be elaborated to articulate evidence that speaks to test design and development. The *Standards*' five sources of evidence can also be easily incorporated and plugged into various parts of the figure. Finally, the chain of evidence that starts at the design stage and moves to development, delivery, score analysis, interpretation and decisions, can loop and feed back to design and policy features. The figure becomes quite complex once these different arguments are included. However, this is, we argue, a better representation of the quality evidence that testing programmes typically require.

Within testing programmes, evidence of quality does not commence with data, nor is it the purview of psychometricians. It is part and parcel of every aspect of a testing programme. A key aspect of this expanded view of validity is a consideration of how to allocate responsibility for the various evidence pieces/arguments to the appropriate professionals involved in a testing system. Also fundamental is to employ a team across departments to pull the various arguments together. What we suggest is not an easy task but a more realistic representation of the type of validity work needed.

Figure 11, which is based on Chalhoub-Deville's (2012–present) course materials, displays a gestalt model of validity arguments. The proposed validity figure is a functional, integrative unit that incorporates major

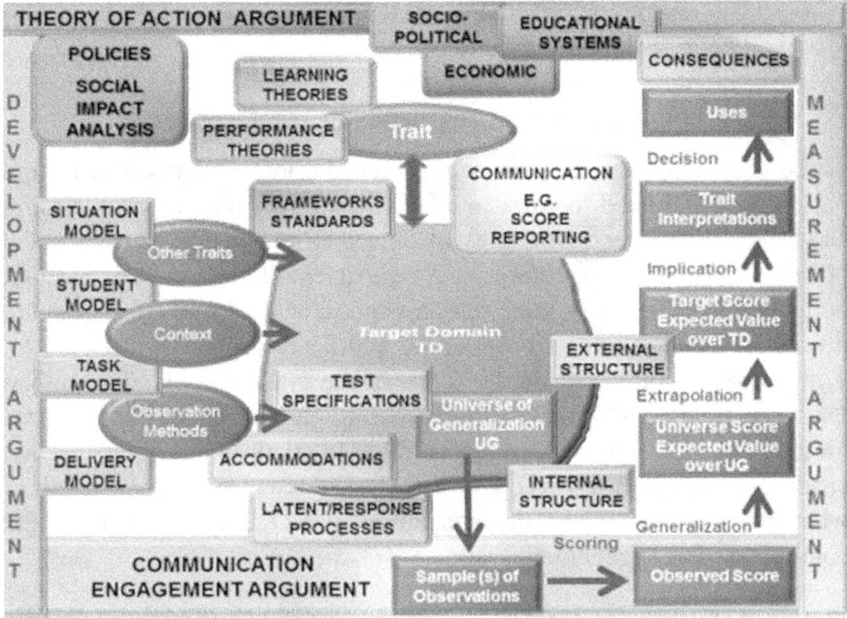

Figure 11: Validation model as integrated arguments (Chalhoub-Deville, 2012–present course materials)

ideas discussed throughout the monograph. It combines traditional notions such as the *Standards* (AERA, APA & NCME, 2014) sources of evidence and Kane's (2006, 2013) IUA, labelled as the measurement argument. As suggested by Bachman & Palmer (2010) and Embretson (2008), the figure comprises assessment development, specifically Mislevy's (2007) design models. While this representation is in conflict with notions that validity be scaled back to primarily issues of design and development, as suggested by Lissitz & Samuelsen (2007a, b), it does accommodate more attention to issues of test development. This is exemplified in Lissitz & Samuelsen's (2007b: 482) statement: 'we are attempting to move away from a unitary theory focused on construct validity and to reorient educators to the importance of content validity and the general problem of test development'. This encompassing validity figure fills the major gaps in Kane's IUA argument especially at the design and development stage.

Figure 11 references a validity model with an integrated system of arguments. We highlight here four such key arguments. The arguments are not specified in any particular order.

- The test development argument
- The measurement argument
- The theory of action argument
- The communication engagement argument

These arguments can be said to represent various aspects of a testing programme and need to work in concert to deliver quality products and services. Other aspects of quality also need to be considered such as the business side of the operation and what it entails in terms of pricing, budgets, securing test administration venues, sales force, etc. These are important facets of a test programme and need also to be attended to. This, however, falls outside the scope of the present book. We contend that a practical orientation to validity research, which is increasingly promoted in the published literature, is likely to result in a scholarship that encompasses such business operations. Below we provide some detail of what the test development, the measurement, the theory of action and the communication engagement arguments entail.

The test development argument

The test development argument connects the trait to theories and studies that elaborate a construct of interest. Validity research cannot start with documentation at, what Kane calls, the *Target Domain* and assume that appropriate connections to the construct of interest exist. An operational model or a target domain cannot be *assumed* to represent a given construct of interest. The target domain is typically the realm of the ubiquitous hierarchical frameworks or standards, e.g., Common Core State Standards, the Common European Framework of Reference and the American Council on the Teaching of Foreign Languages Proficiency Guidelines. Criticism of such standards and frameworks is well documented. Of concern to the present discussion is their tenuous depictions of learning and growth profiles as well as their generic representation of real-life performance. A persistent concern with such standards is their lack of theoretical and empirical support to be able to prescribe what students should know and do, and concomitantly be tested on, as they progress in their language proficiency across grade levels (Chalhoub-Deville and Deville, 2006, 2008).

Documentation based on theoretical arguments, latent processes analyses, test specifications, potential accommodations are critical categories of the test development argument. Information provided earlier with regard to ECD and the various models included: the situation model, the student model, the task model, the evidence model and the delivery model are also pertinent components that need to be documented in test development arguments. The published literature is rich with documentation of test development research and practices (e.g., iBT TOEFL monographs and book publications). It is critical to accord this research equal status with the measurement argument. The test development argument, we caution, is necessary but not sufficient documentation of a test quality. Validity evidence has to incorporate both the test development and the measurement arguments, while also including an element in which the ongoing performance of a test is critically evaluated.

The measurement argument

Kane's familiar IA argument has been renamed, following a suggestion made by Bennett, Kane & Bridgeman (2011) and Sabatini, Bennett & Deane (2011), as the measurement argument. This is an appropriate depiction given the nature of the inferences targeted in this argument. Hence, we will use that label to refer to that sequence of inferences. As detailed earlier in the monograph, this argument entails evidence to support inferences such as scoring, generalisation, extrapolation, implication and decision/utilisation. Measurement operations, such as scaling, linking and equating, standard setting, etc. are part of the measurement argument. This argument has been discussed widely in the published literature and reviewed in earlier parts of the monograph. The measurement argument has been accorded premier if not exclusive status in terms of validity documentation. While critical, a measurement argument provides an incomplete picture of the quality of a testing programme. Much work and cost is expended before a testing programme is live and the evidence amassed at the development stage is of primary importance to various stakeholder groups. It is part of the narrative shared to convince test users of the quality of a testing programme, its products as well as the outcomes – scores interpretation and use.

The theory of action argument

In line with Bachman & Palmer's (2010) AUA, we need to delineate intended consequences. The theory of action argument is placed at the top of Figure 11 to articulate that a plan needs to be put in place at the outset to indicate what exactly we would like to achieve with our testing programme, i.e., planned outcomes or consequences. The plan includes an articulation of the systems that will help us achieve intended outcomes. A theory of action argument considers the context for the testing system, including social and political conditions, major stakeholders driving as well as impacted by the desired change, intended outcomes, action plan to achieve desired consequences, assumptions that underlie the plan, and a contingency plan or mediation activities to address potential untended outcomes (Bennett, 2010; Sabatini et al., 2011; Chalhoub-Deville, 2016). The theory of action plan takes into account available resources and other practical constraints.

Consequences, integral to a theory of action plan, link the measurement and test development arguments. Responsibility for consequences will be allocated to various programmes/individuals within a test publishing organisation and related test-user groups, depending on professional expertise and negotiated roles and responsibilities. What is critical here is to detail inferences of consequences and to incorporate their research into a testing programme standard operating procedure. Consequences are critical inferences to consider also at the design stage of a testing system, as argued by Bachman & Palmer (2010). Inferences of consequences should be made explicit at the outset to guide development efforts and position a testing system to better achieve those intended inferences of consequences. Consequences can be articulated in terms of near-term, mid-term and long-term claims. Research is undertaken by test developers in conjunction with relevant stakeholders to document actual realisation of stated consequence claims.

A theory of action at the outset can serve a formative function. Later when used to appraise claims, a theory of action can play an evaluative role. It is typical that once a testing programme is operational, its scope of use is broadened. A theory of action, at the outset, has to build into its plans investigations to address unintended practices, test score interpretations, decisions and uses. While test publishers actively pursue *unwanted* practices, e.g., cheating cases, arguably such efforts are not expended when unintended interpretations and uses are lucrative to an organisation even when these practices are not supported by the research undertaken. Critical appraisal of intended and unintended – especially negative – inferences need to be undertaken, and an evaluative theory of action can accommodate such plans.

The communication engagement argument

Communication is imperative for the development, administration, and use of a test. For example, within a testing publishing organisation, consequences have to be translated into a variety of claims for item development, platform delivery, psychometric analysis, marketing plan, etc. All have to work in concert to affect change envisioned and to address unintended processes and outcomes, which inevitably emerge. Issues of communication are also at the forefront in discussion of consequences. Attention to consequences necessitates considerations of relevant stakeholder groups. In his *Language Testing Forum* presentation of 2014, O'Sullivan contends the following:

> It is now clear to me that stakeholders offer test developers a key to understanding the way in which test consequence can be operationalised in development and validation models. By taking stakeholder groups into account at the conceptualisation stage of development we are essentially building consequence into the test design. This, in turn, enables an accurate prediction of the impact of decisions made on the basis of test performance, and creates a clearly considered a priori and a posteriori role for consequence within the development and validation model. Consequence can therefore be seen as a critical and operationalisable source of validation evidence.
>
> Involving stakeholder groups in this way has other consequences, this time for the developer. By acknowledging the importance and relevance of stakeholder groups to test development, we must also recognise the importance of communicating our validation arguments appropriately to them.

This quote by O'Sullivan articulates the need, at the design stage, to attend to stakeholders and communication. Moving beyond the confines of providing information to ourselves – professionals in the field, requires that we pay attention to how to communicate our technical information to various key stakeholder groups.

Communication is closely related to discussions of validity documentation where research information has to be shared with various stakeholders. Figure 11 advances communication engagement as the anchor to a validity model. Featuring communication in a validity framework conveys the critical notion that validity research needs to be appropriately shared with diverse stakeholders, and not only fellow measurement professionals. Chapelle (2012: 26) raises awareness about the need to pay attention to the diverse 'audience for validity arguments'. It is important to think of this audience as active participants in the testing programme. They need to be identified and surveyed when a testing programme is being developed. Communication plans, in consultation with stakeholders, need to be developed to provide meaningful, relevant and understandable information about the quality of the testing programme. The scope and type of evidence, the weight of that evidence and the presentation format are key pieces to investigate with stakeholders when designing communication plans.

To render technical information meaningful to those who will need to work with that information and to turn it into usable actions is ultimately the goal of a testing programme. Invariably, our documentation and publications speak to professional peers. Very little information is reported in the literature about communicating with other stakeholders. Also scarce are professional outlets where our measurement community interacts with other industry specialists or related professionals who are integral to the operations and uses of a testing programme. This is a fertile area for scholarly activities. Future research should consider questions such as:

- Who are salient stakeholders for a given testing programme?
- How to engage key stakeholders?
- At what points in the life of a testing programme are various stakeholder groups engaged?
- What are guiding principles in engaging different stakeholders?
- How to identify key objectives for stakeholder engagement plans?
- Which formats are appropriate for engaging stakeholders for different purposes?
- Should communication engagement plans have terms/time cycles?
- Who should create the communications and the communication plans to these stakeholder groups? Language test developers and academics are likely to be ill-equipped to respond appropriately to the needs and will clearly need the support of communication experts.

Communication engagement plans have to accommodate the backgrounds, expertise and interests of the stakeholders targeted. What we need are frameworks to guide engagement and communication plans and professional outlets that allow the publication of such information. This integrated argument approach to validity necessitates that the measurement and language testing communities create professional opportunities where testing systems could present illustrative case studies, localised examples, of their operations. In the next section, we revisit the socio-cognitive model. The intention with this *socio-cognitive model as integrated arguments* is to showcase how an established validation model can be rendered more explicit in terms of articulating and presenting the arguments that undergird its operations. What we present remains a sketch in need of development of actual systems, which is no small undertaking.

Revisiting the socio-cognitive model

In light of the proposed integrated model, it is useful to revisit O'Sullivan's socio-cognitive model of 2014 to highlight the four arguments presented in Figure 11. Figure 12 continues to situate the test taker as the critical link between the test and the context of use. The development and measurement arguments are attended to as part of the *Test Model* and the *Scoring Model*. The socio-cognitive model has always argued that the development model (which addresses the test taker model, the test model and the scoring model) and the measurement model must be fully integrated. It is only by integrating the two models that a truly efficient (in Wiseman's terms) test can emerge from the development process. Test tasks should meet the expectations of the development model and the measurement model, if they are to offer meaningful estimates of ability. In other words, we should be able to estimate the difficulty of a test task theoretically using a model of language progression and then demonstrate that the task indeed measures the intended ability at the predicted level of difficulty on our measurement model. This is not easy to deliver in practice, of course, as the example below demonstrates.

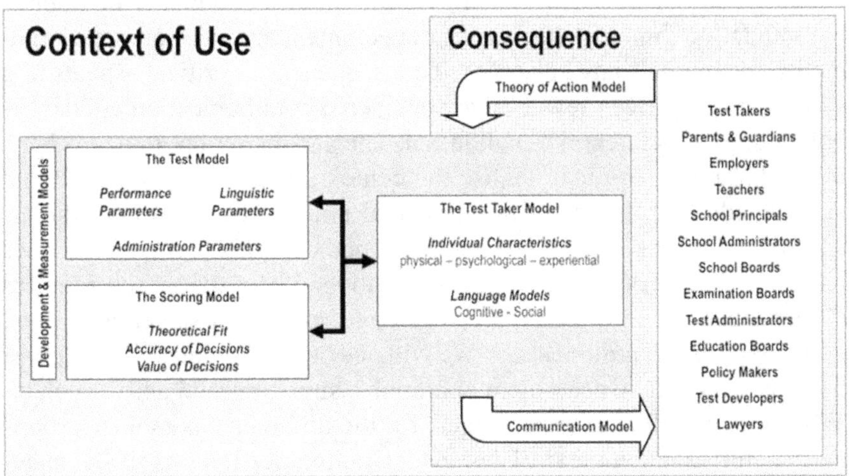

Figure 12: Socio-cognitive model as integrated arguments

We position consequences in Figure 12 as encompassing the theory of action, which drives the test development processes, similar to AUA suggestions. Consequences are also positioned to shape the *Communication Model* required to ensure that the needs and expectations of the stakeholders who comprise the context of use are addressed. The communication model showcases relevant stakeholder groups that the testing system needs to communicate with in various guises to promote appropriate interpretation of and adequate use of test scores. In the socio-cognitive model we present here, consequences are highlighted as the most salient element of a testing programme in a given context of use. It is these consequences which are then intended to drive various aspects of the internal testing operations as well as communication with individuals and groups who are interested in and/or affected by the testing programme.

Consequence has always been relevant to test use. Examples of this are to be found a millennium ago in the Chinese Imperial Examinations, where authorities constantly battled with test takers and their teachers who attempted to subvert the test by devising increasing complex and ingenious cheating systems – due no doubt to the consequence of failure to an individual and generations of his family in terms of social mobility, power and wealth. The point is that society has always been aware of the positive and negative consequences of competitive testing systems – test developers too have been aware of these consequences but have, until recently, ignored them when discussing the validity of their instruments, focusing only on the technical 'quality' of these instruments.

While predominant approaches to validity have undoubtedly broadened our validation thinking in terms of development and measurement arguments, few models have elaborated consequences as critical aspects of a validation plan. Even fewer have considered communication and stakeholder groups as integral to validation. The gap, in our opinion, has been in our failure to seriously realise the context of test use, specifically an understanding of the intended and actual impact of our testing systems and related scores. Consequences introduce complex and thorny issues into our testing operations. The evaluation of consequences requires an expanded scope of research, negotiated roles with stakeholders and more involved communication. We will need to devise, in addition to test development and measurement operations, structures and delivery channels, though with similar messages, for the different stakeholder groups that comprise the context of test use. Communication has to be stakeholder-centred. Our validity needs to comprise integrated arguments of test development, measurement, theory of action and communication engagement.

In conclusion, Edgeworth (1888: 461) distinguished between what he called 'the philosophy of examination' and 'the statistics of marks'. This distinction could be said to reflect the two different approaches which have informed language and other testing for over a century. Psychometrics have long reigned supreme in the US. On the other hand, commitment to quality test development has been the hallmark of the UK approach. Increasingly, however, the two traditions have been expanding their repertoires. UK professionals employ psychometrics as a standard part of their operations, and US researchers have been expanding the scholarship and practice of quality assurance to include test design and development. This combined attention in testing operations to measurement and test development arguments is to be viewed positively. In this volume, we have made a case that both test development and psychometrics or measurement are central to validity arguments. We have also discussed the need to integrate consequences and communication plans to quality assurance considerations.

CHAPTER 6

CONCLUSION: VALIDATION, LOCALISATION AND CASE STUDIES

In this book, we make the case to combine four key arguments to form the foundation for validity. The first two arguments have long been part of the language testing field: the measurement-focused and the test design and development arguments. Over-reliance on a measurement argument to uphold validity, we contend, is foolhardy because it directs attention to quality mostly after much of a testing programme has been put in place. Inadequate test development operations are hard, if not impossible, to remedy with psychometrics. To have a measurement argument as the primary foundation for a testing programme undermines the explanatory power of test scores, as Spolsky (1995) argued in his often quoted book, *Measured words*. The reverse conception of arguments is also a cause for concern. While critical attention to test development, represented traditionally as content-related evidence, strengthens a testing programme, it is not sufficient. The literature is rich with arguments against this practice. Messick (1989) and the *Standards* (1999, 2014) point to the shortfall of such evidence as the sole argument to support score interpretation and use. Technical information, including psychometric analyses of scores/outcomes (e.g., item banking, item, task and test difficulty estimation, scoring system development and score accuracy and consistency) are imperative to support quality assurance. Both test development and measurement provide evidence and lines of reasoning to formulate necessary arguments to support testing operations and outcomes, and as such both should be seen as critical to any validity argument made in support of a test.

Quality assurance of real-world testing operations compel us to argue for the need to expand our documentation to include, in addition to test development and the psychometric documentation, attention to consequences and communication. We made the case that especially with accountability testing, which is integrally connected to ambitious educational and societal goals, validity cannot afford to ignore research on consequences.

It is nonsensical for test developers to demarcate investigations of consequences in terms of construct-only violations and ignore the vast impact that testing programmes have on individuals, groups and larger societal structures. Validity needs to *convincingly engage with the wider scope of social consequences*. Engagement with consequences raises considerable challenges, including the need to investigate ambitious claims such as that particular exams yield information about test takers' *career readiness* (see Race to the Top or Every Student Succeeds accountability testing programmes in the US). The lack of expertise that professionals in the field typically have to engage with the consequence-related inferences entailed in such testing programmes is also a concern. The dearth of models to guide and verify the evaluation of consequences and the delineation of roles and responsibilities for research needed are also problematic.

We attempt to operationalise consequence by conceiving it as a theory of action that compels us to engage with those key stakeholder groups in the targeted test context. It is only when we engage meaningfully with these individual/groups that we can come to recognise and take into consideration in our development model a meaningful prediction of the consequences of test administration and an equally meaningful (to the stakeholders) approach to dealing with those consequences. Unpredicted consequences are, by their very nature, more problematic, though here reflection on the experiences of stakeholders of other testing initiatives can help the developer build contingencies into the development and administration processes. While the socio-cognitive model can be said to offer a positive starting point for operationalising consequence, it should be seen as just that, a starting point. The considerable challenges that attention-to-consequences present require serious scholarship with engagement from diverse disciplines and stakeholders. By developing a coherent theory-of-action, we are not only formulating the basis for how we deal with consequences. Within the socio-cognitive approach posited here, such a theory can actually help us to more accurately define the construct-in-context, resulting in tests that are more readily justified or validated.

The test development and measurement arguments in validity have traditionally been formulated to address an important segment of professionals, but they do not attend to other relevant stakeholder groups. Test development and measurement research tends to be inward-looking in terms of communication. It seeks to communicate vast amounts of information primarily to professionals working with a testing programme and researchers in the field. Other stakeholder groups, because they lack training in our discipline(s), are not capable of directly accessing such technical documentation. The technical documentation provided is exactly that – technical – and is of limited use to most individuals and groups. Schemes need to be developed that engage relevant stakeholder groups in interactions at various stages of our testing operations as well as testing outcomes and impact. This is another area where the measurement field and the language testing community have limited experience. Retooling and collaboration with other professionals who have relevant expertise in communication on technical matters are indispensable to create stakeholder engagement plans. To use educational accountability in the US as an example, ultimately, the goal of accountability testing is to support instruction in order to *move the needle* with regard to student college and career capabilities. Accumulated research that details quality in terms of development, psychometrics and consequences is of limited value if it does not involve meaningful communication with stakeholder groups such as test takers, teachers and related professionals that enables them to interpret and use test outcomes to shape learning, instruction, curricula and professional development to improve achievement.

In Chapter 5, we have proposed a pragmatically-oriented validity model, an *integrated argument-based approach to validation*, very much in keeping with Kane's IA/IUA, but moving beyond Kane's approach. What we present is a validation model with four integrated arguments: development, measurement, theory of action and communication engagement. The integrated argument-based approach to validation model offers a systematic approach to validity inquiry and documentation that can be flexibly fleshed out to accommodate different purposes and uses. Our main goal here is to advance what we believe to be a more realistic consideration of quality assurance that engages with real-world testing operations and relevant stakeholders. As we have seen in the present volume, the field has long-established traditions and scholarship with regard to the test development and measurement arguments. This is less the case with the consequences or theory of action and the communication engagement arguments where knowledge and research are relatively young to afford the kind of guidance needed moving forward. We call on professionals in our and related fields to explore and develop scholarship in these areas. We acknowledge that this will not be easy, as it will require us to engage with the difficult task of relating often quite technical information and concepts to audiences with little or no training in the area. It will also mean that we will have to concede at least some of our current power to control the messages that we deliver to people with expertise not in testing and assessment but in communication. In addition, we will have to accept that the modes of communication will have to change. The technical report may even be superseded by the tweet!

As repeatedly pointed out, the language testing field has been largely dominated by thinking and practices emanating from standardised testing programmes in the UK and the US. The future does not have – is not likely – to be that way. Ratcliffe (1983: 158) states that 'quite different notions of what constitutes validity have enjoyed the status of dominant paradigm at different times, in different historical contexts [and locales], and under different prevailing modes of thought and epistemology'. Important matters such as maturity in language testing literacy in varied regions of the world, expanded notions of quality control and assurance, technological advances and access capabilities, epistemological shifts in the social sciences, geopolitical changes around the globe, will inevitably shape the future of validity and validation. Changing global realities compel us to envision scholarly activities that embrace more localised notions of validity research. This echoes what Chalhoub-Deville (2003: 381) stated:

> I have argued in a previous publication (Chalhoub-Deville, 2001) that context is critical for test development as well as for test score validation. Then, as now, Anastasi's (1986: 484) well-known quote is fitting: 'when selecting or developing tests and when interpreting scores, consider context. I shall stop right there, because those are the words, more than any others, that I want to leave with you: *consider context*' (emphasis in original). My thinking in this area has evolved to where I now believe that context is paramount and thus advocate the need for a theory of context.

Localisation is about ensuring that testing systems are appropriate to the claims (as defined by the construct and content domain) and contexts of test use (as shaped by key stakeholders). The integrated approach to validity with its four principal arguments can serve as a framework to help develop a rationale and gather evidence to support claims sensitive to local norms, engage relevant, local stakeholders with regard to accepted quality assurance, and ultimately deliver tests appropriate to test takers.

In the field we rarely come across publications, beyond perhaps technical reports and such documentation, which detail research undertaken to develop and support various phases of a testing operation. The publication by Chapelle, Enright & Jamieson (2008), which describes the particulars with regard to validity investigations to support iBT TOEFL, is not a typical occurrence. The field needs more publications of this nature. Earlier in this volume we wrote: 'The *Standards* (2014) offer no guidance on what constitutes coherent validity research, how to marshal evidence and arguments to make a case for a particular interpretation and/or use, and what research might look like for differing testing programmes with different stakes (high-low).' We invite language testing professionals to consider case studies to enrich our scholarly activities in this area. Case studies can illustrate how evidence and arguments are pulled together in varied testing programmes to support the quality of assessments, scores, interpretations and decisions. Case studies afford us a mechanism to compile evidence into arguments to support – in a confirmationist or critical fashion – testing products and practices. They also allow us, if shared/published, to learn from each other.

With localised validity, it is imperative to accommodate the *likely* varied perspectives of stakeholders associated with a testing programme. Multi-perspective case studies can feed into the rationale/evidence being compiled and integrated into validity documentation. Multi-perspective, stakeholder-focused case studies can illustrate *what* and *how much* evidence is appropriate and adequate for diverse groups. Additionally, these studies can document how arguments are put together to speak to the background and interests of particular groups. Such multi-perspective case studies deserve to be shared and published because they can explicate validity theory in terms of operational work, reveal theory strengths and shortcomings, and inform validity scholarship. Moss (2003: 22) calls for such a repertoire of cases: '…not just those that illustrate how our guiding principles can be thoughtfully applied but, equally important, those that have not already been shaped by our principles so that we can learn about their limitations'. Case studies can help advance our validity theories and models. They represent a viable mechanism to converse about operational test development and research undertaken in a variety of environments with diverse stakeholders around the globe. Case studies are worth exploring and developing, moving forward.

We call on language testing researchers and professionals to engage in localised research and validation. For validation to be meaningful, it must sit as part of a whole range of connected activities that focus on the test itself, on its administration, its likely consequences and how it is perceived. To illustrate we describe the approach taken by the British Council's Assessment Research Group (ARG). This group, whose research supports British Council tests such as Aptis and the co-owned (with Cambridge Assessment English and IDP Australia) IELTS, has developed a programme comprising multiple elements:

Research Matrix Based on the socio-cognitive model as presented by O'Sullivan (2014, 2016) and designed to identify and adequately explore aspects of development, delivery and monitoring & evaluation.

Internal Research Undertaken by ARG members to assemble evidence of how well the test content reflects the language and measurement models that underpin the test. These studies are expected to contribute systematically to the Research Matrix and are primarily published online as a series of Technical Reports.

External Research The Assessment Research Awards and Grants (ARAGs) offer funding to researchers primarily in areas of immediate or longer-term importance to the test/tests – as identified in the Research Matrix. ARAGs reports are published online in complete form on the Aptis Research website, where short (1- to 2-page) non-technical summaries can also be accessed. These summaries are targeted at key stakeholders such as teachers and parents, to help them to develop a more complete understanding and appreciation of the testing process.

Collaborative Research This is where ARG members work with colleagues to undertake joint research projects to support Aptis or IELTS. An example of this is the work undertaken by the ARG, Cambridge Assessment English and the Centre for Research in English Language Learning and Assessment (CRELLA) at the University of

Bedfordshire in the UK. This work (see Berry et al., 2018) explored the appropriateness of the online 'real-time' delivery of spoken interviews involving human examiners and candidates. The research has had a positive impact on the decision of the IELTS partners to begin work on the administration of speaking tests in this way. Another example is the work undertaken with MetaMetrix in the US, linking their Lexile measure to the Aptis reading paper.

Case Studies

These are also written for non-technical stakeholder audience. These differ from the ARAGs studies as they typically document cases in which Aptis test variants are used (e.g., in government or corporate contexts). They are designed to demonstrate best practice across the world, highlighting the appropriate uses of the tests as well as establishing how decisions to use or not to use the tests are made. An example of such a case study is included here as an Appendix. See also the Aptis case studies online at: https://www.britishcouncil.org/exam/aptis/assessment/case-study

Assessment Literacy

Communication with stakeholders – the How Language Assessment Works (HowLAW) project – has been running for over five years. In that time, project outputs have included:

i. A MOOC (Massive Open Online Course) which focuses on practical aspects of test development – aimed at teachers.

ii. A Glossary of language testing terminology – written mainly for teachers by teachers. **A–Z Glossary of Second Language Assessment**: https://www.britishcouncil.org/z-second-language-assessment

iii. Twelve animated videos focusing on non-technical explanations of key concepts in language testing, from the theoretical (Validity) to the practical (Assessing Writing).

iv. Half of these videos come with worksheets for interested parties (primarily teachers or trainers) to use. These six animations also come with full workshop notes and guidance. These have been delivered by ARG members in a number of countries around the world. **Animated Assessment Videos**: https://www.britishcouncil.org/exam/aptis/research/assessment-literacy

Webinars on aspects of assessment for British Council staff (test administration and teaching) and increasingly for external teacher groups.

In summary, validity documentation starts at the design level of a testing programme and culminates with the formulation and sharing of arguments that accommodate relevant stakeholder groups. Test development and rigorous psychometric work are integral to validity arguments. Validity documentation necessitates that testing professionals also attend to the consequences – intended and realised – associated with their testing operations. Given that testing programmes increasingly entail higher stakes and wider implications, engagement with consequences – not only in terms of construct-focused investigations as endorsed in the *Standards* (1999, 2014) – is crucial. Detailing the network of consequence inferences entailed by policies/test purposes driving a testing programme deserves to be an explicit aspect of test development activities and measurement research. This is an ethical as well as a pragmatic imperative. A theory of action is an example of a structure that would help us delineate the network of consequence-related inferences, systematise our development and research activities, as well as position us to formulate the validity arguments. An *integrated argument-based approach to validation* also compels that we consider the extent to which operations are connected with pertinent stakeholders. Testing and related professionals need to be in close dialogue with those groups they are constructing the argument *with and for* – beyond measurement and language testing professionals. A communication engagement argument underscores the importance of accommodating stakeholder issues in test design and development. It also emphasises the importance of rendering testing outcomes actionable by those stakeholders. We contend that, moving forward, the scholarship of validity would benefit if localised quality assurance documentation is shared broadly around the world.

Scholarly work is still necessary to detail appropriate criteria to evaluate the quality of the rationale and empirical evidence embedded in each of the four arguments that comprise the *integrated argument-based approach to validation*: development, measurement, theory of action and communication engagement. Similar thought should be given to how to bring all the arguments together to document the quality of a given testing programme. Pertinent questions include:

- What criteria should be employed to evaluate the quality of the arguments when assembled?
- How much weight should be accorded to each of the arguments pulled together?
- Do the criteria and weights vary by differing intended and potential negative consequences?
- Would the criteria and weights be modified when communicating with diverse stakeholders? Here we have to consider stakeholders as individuals, as groups and as larger systems.
- To what extent are the *Standards*, which have been built around a measurement-driven approach to test development and validation, in need of updating, not just in terms of content, as has been the case in the past? While we accept that this is a hugely contentious question, the argument that we have posited here would suggest that its basic structure (e.g., with separate chapters on validity and reliability) might well benefit from a serious reconceptualisation.

These are some questions that we hope the field will address.

Thinking around validity and validation over the past half century lie at the heart of this book. When Cronbach & Meehl (1955) argued for a more systematic approach, primarily based on a systematised understanding of test construct within the parameters of a broader understanding that validity was concerned with the wider issues of content and criterion, they made a clear statement that the then traditional approach was in need of change. Scholars such as Messick brought this focus on change to a new level when they argued for a unified concept of validity. However, both Cronbach & Meehl and Messick ultimately failed to identify a definitive way forward; the former falling foul to the lack of any strong validity models for educational attainment (thus undermining their call for a structuralist-based nomological network-based definition of construct) and the latter failing to adequately describe how his complex model might best be operationalised – in particular his approach to test consequence. Mislevy, Almond & Lukas (2003), with their conceptualisation of *validity by design*, linked validity and test development, an approach mirrored by O'Sullivan & Weir (2002) and Weir (2005) in the socio-cognitive approach. While Mislevy et al.'s model offered a valuable high-level overview of the development process, it lacked the fine detail that would have made it fully operationalisable, failed to deal with the consequence issue and failed to describe how the evidence collected by developers in relation to the various parameters might be presented as a validation argument. In the case of the early iterations of the socio-cognitive approach, the identification of a series of practical parameters of test construction together with their interaction was to prove particularly attractive to test developers, particularly in Europe. However, like Mislevy et al. (2003), it failed to adequately deal with the consequence issue (relegating it to the role of an *a posteriori* activity in the validation process) and the validation argument construction issue. Kane and Bachman & Palmer adopted a Toulmin-based argument design as the basis of their approaches. While both offer feasible argument structures (see, for example, Chappell et al., 2008), they fail to respond adequately to the question of what the actual contents of the argument might be. In addition, they both reflect the contemporary reliance on a measurement-driven approach to validity, while focusing on an expert audience.

Language testing theories have helped us to understand our area more and more thoroughly over the recent six decades. However, the failure of our theories to adequately reflect the needs of key stakeholders in terms of operationalisability (for test developers), comprehensibility of validation arguments (for most stakeholders) and comprehensiveness (for test developers, for standards developers, for learning systems professionals) needs to be addressed. We hope that this book marks a first step in this process.

REFERENCES

Abad Florescano, A., O'Sullivan, B., Sanchez Chavez, C., Ryan, D. E., Zamora Lara, E., Santana Martinez, L. A., Gonzalez Macias, M. I., Maxwell Hart, M., Grounds, P. E., Reidy Ryan, P., Dunne, R. A. & Romero Barradas, T. de E. (2011). Developing affordable 'local' tests: The EXAVER project. In B. O'Sullivan (Ed.), *Language testing: Theory & practice* (pp. 228–243). Oxford: Palgrave.

Abbott, G. and Wingard, P. (1981). *The teaching of English as an international language*. London: Collins.

Alderson, J. C. (1979). The cloze procedure and proficiency in English as a foreign language. *TESOL Quarterly*, 13(2), 219–27. https://doi.org/10.2307/3586211

Alderson, J. C. (1988). New procedures for validating proficiency tests of ESP? *Language Testing*, 5(2), 220–232. https://doi.org/10.1177/026553228800500207

Alderson, J. C. (2000a). Testing in EAP: Progress? Achievement? Proficiency? In G. Blue, J. Milton & J. Saville (Eds.), *Assessing English for academic purposes* (pp. 21–47). Oxford: Peter Lang.

Alderson. J. C. (2000b). *Assessing reading*. Cambridge: Cambridge University Press.

Alderson, J. C., Clapham, C. & Wall, D. (1995). *Language test construction and evaluation*. Cambridge: Cambridge University Press.

Alderson, J. C. & Hamp-Lyons, L. (1996). TOEFL preparation courses: A study of washback. *Language Testing*, 13(3), 280–297. https://doi.org/10.1177/026553229601300304

Alderson, J. C. & Urquhart, A. H. (1985). This test is unfair: I'm not an economist. In P. Hauptman, G. Leblanc & M. Wesche (Eds.), *Second language performance testing* (pp. 25–43). Ottawa: University of Ottawa Press.

American Council on the Teaching of Foreign Languages. (1982). *ACTFL proficiency guidelines*. Yonkers, NY: ACTFL.

American Council on the Teaching of Foreign Languages. (1986). *ACTFL proficiency guidelines*. Yonkers, NY: ACTFL.

American Council on the Teaching of Foreign Languages. (2012). *ACTFL proficiency guidelines*. Yonkers, NY: ACTFL.

American Educational Research Association and National Council on Measurement Used in Education. (1955). *Technical recommendations for achievement tests*. Washington, DC: National Council on Measurement Used in Education.

American Educational Research Association, American Psychological Association and National Council on Measurement in Education (1985). *Standards for educational and psychological testing*. Washington, DC: American Psychological Association.

American Educational Research Association, American Psychological Association and National Council on Measurement in Education. (1999). *Standards for educational and psychological testing*. Washington, DC: American Psychological Association.

American Educational Research Association, American Psychological Association and National Council on Measurement in Education. (2014). *Standards for educational and psychological testing*. Washington, DC: American Educational Research Association.

American Psychological Association, Committee on Test Standards. (1952). Technical recommendations for psychological tests and diagnostic techniques: A preliminary proposal. *American Psychologist*, 7, 461–465. https://doi.org/10.1037/h0056631

American Psychological Association. (1954). *Technical recommendations for psychological tests and diagnostic techniques*. Washington, DC: American Psychological Association.

American Psychological Association, American Educational Research Association and National Council on Measurement in Education. (1966). *Standards for educational and psychological tests and manuals*. Washington, DC: American Psychological Association.

American Psychological Association, American Educational Research Association and National Council on Measurement in Education. (1974). *Standards for educational and psychological tests*. Washington, DC: American Psychological Association.

Anastasi, A. (1986). Evolving concepts of test validation. *Annual Review of Psychology*, 37, 1–15.

AQA. (2017). Home Page. Retrieved on July 6, 2017 from: http://www.aqa.org.uk/

Aryadoust, S. V. (2009). Mapping Rasch-based measurement onto the argument-based validity framework. *Rasch Measurement Transactions*, 23, 1192–1193.

Aryadoust, S. V. (2013). *Building a validity argument for a listening test of academic proficiency.* Newcastle: Cambridge Scholars Publishing.

Bachman, L. F. (1990). *Fundamental considerations in language testing.* Oxford: Oxford University Press.

Bachman, L. F. (2005). Building and supporting a case for test use. *Language Assessment Quarterly*, 2, 1–34. https://doi.org/10.1207/s15434311laq0201_1

Bachman, L. F., Davidson, F., Ryan, F. & Choi, I.-C. (1995). *An investigation into the comparability of two tests of English as a foreign language*. Cambridge: Cambridge University Press.

Bachman, L. F. & Palmer, A. S. (1996). *Language testing in practice: Designing and developing useful language tests*. Oxford: Oxford University Press.

Bachman, L. F. & Palmer, A. S. (2010). *Language assessment in practice*. Oxford: Oxford University Press.

Baumann, C., Dursun, A., Swinehart, N. & McCormick, J. (2017). Embarking on developing a meaningful measure of graduate-level L2 reading comprehension: The role of primary stakeholders' understanding of the construct. Paper presented at the *Language Testing Research Colloquium*, Bogota.

Bennett, R. E. (2010). Cognitively based assessment of, for, and as learning: A preliminary theory of action for summative and formative assessment. *Measurement: Interdisciplinary Research and Perspectives*, 8, 70–91. https://doi.org/10.1080/15366367.2010.508686

Bennett, R. E., Kane, M. T. & Bridgeman, B. (2011). Theory of action and validity argument in the context of through-course summative assessment. Paper presented at *Invitational Research Symposium on Through Course Summative Assessment*, Atlanta, GA. Retrieved on July 6, 2017 from: http://www.k12center.org/rsc/pdf/TCSA_Symposium_Final_Paper_Bennett_Kane_Bridgeman.pdf

Berry, V. (2007). *Personality differences and oral test performance*. Frankfurt: Peter Lang.

Berry, V., Nakatsuhara, F., Inoue, C. & Galaczi, E. (2018). Exploring the use of video-conferencing technology to deliver the IELTS Speaking Test: Phase 3 technical trial. *IELTS Partnership Research Papers*, 2018(1), https://www.ielts.org/-/media/research-reports/ielts-research-partner-paper-4.ashx

Berry, V., O'Sullivan, B. & Rugea, S. (2012). Identifying the appropriate IELTS score levels for IMG applicants to the GMC register. London: University of Roehampton/The General Medical Council, http://www.gmc-uk.org/Identifying_the_appropriate_IELTS_score_levels_for_IMG_applicants_to_the_GMC_register.pdf_55197989.pdf

Binet, A. & Simon, T. (1916 [1905]). *The development of intelligence in children: The Binet-Simon scale*. Publications of the Training School at Vineland New Jersey Department of Research No. 11. E. S. Kite (Trans.). Baltimore: Williams & Wilkins. https://doi.org/10.1037/11069-000

Bingham, W. V. (1937). *Aptitudes and aptitude testing*. New York: Harper.

Bloomfield, L. (1926). A set of postulates for the science of language. *Language*, 2, 153–164. https://doi.org/10.2307/408741

Bloomfield, L. (1933). *Language*. New York: Henry Holt.

Borsboom, D., Mellenbergh, G. J. & Van Heerden, G. 2004. The concept of validity. *Psychological Review*, 111, 1061–1071. https://doi.org/10.1037/0033-295X.111.4.1061

Brantmeier, C. (2003). Does gender make a difference? Passage content and comprehension in second language reading. *Reading in a Foreign Language*, 15(1), 1–27.

Brennan, R. L. (2006). Perspectives on the evolution and future of educational measurement. In R. L. Brennan (Ed.), *Educational measurement*, 4th ed. (pp. 1–16). Westport, CT: Praeger.

British Council. (2017). *Evaluating speaking: the IELTS speaking test*. Retrieved on July 5, 2017 from: https://www.teachingenglish.org.uk/article/evaluating-speaking-ielts-speaking-test

Brunfaut, T. (2016). *Looking into Reading II: A follow-up study on test-takers' cognitive processes while completing Aptis B1 reading tasks*. British Council Validation Series (VS/2016/001). London: British Council. Retrieved on July 26, 2018 from: https://www.britishcouncil.org/sites/default/files/brunfaut_final_with_hyperlinks_3.pdf

Brunfaut, T. & McCray, G. (2015). *Looking into test-takers' cognitive processes while completing reading tasks; A mixed-method eye-tracking and stimulated recall study*. ARAGs Research Reports Online (ARG/2015/001). London: British Council. Retrieved on July 26, 2018 from: https://www.britishcouncil.org/sites/default/files/brunfaut_and_mccray_report_final_0.pdf

Buck, G. (2001). *Assessing listening*. Cambridge: Cambridge University Press. https://doi.org/10.1017/CBO9780511732959

Bui, H. Y. G. (2014). Task readiness: Theoretical framework and empirical evidence from topic familiarity, strategic planning, and proficiency levels. In P. Skehan (Ed.), *Processing perspectives on task performance* (pp. 63–94). Amsterdam: John Benjamins. https://doi.org/10.1075/tblt.5.03gav

Caccamise, D., Friend, A., Littrell-Baez, M. K. & Kintsch, E. (2015). Constructivist theory as a framework for instruction and assessment of reading comprehension. In S. R. Parris & K. Headley (Eds.), *Comprehension instruction: Research-based best practices*, 3rd ed. New York: NY: Guilford.

Campbell, D. T. & Fiske, D. W. (1959). Convergent and discriminant validation by the multitrait-multimethod matrix. *Psychological Bulletin*, March 1959, 81–105. https://doi.org/10.1037/h0046016

Canale, M. & Swain, M. (1980). Theoretical bases of communicative approaches to second language teaching and testing. *Applied Linguistics*, 1, 1–47. https://doi.org/10.1093/applin/I.1.1

Chalhoub-Deville, M. (1997). Theoretical models, assessment frameworks, and test construction. *Language Testing*, 14, 3–22. https://doi.org/10.1177/026553229701400102

Chalhoub-Deville, M. (2001). Task-based assessment: Characteristics and validity evidence. In P. Skehan, M. Swain & M. Bygate (Eds.), *Applied language studies: Task based research* (pp. 210–228). New York: Longman.

Chalhoub-Deville, M. (2003). Second language interaction: Current perspectives and future trends. *Language Testing*, 20, 369–383. https://doi.org/10.1191/0265532203lt264oa

Chalhoub-Deville, M. (2009a). The intersection of test impact, validation, and educational reform policy. *Annual Review of Applied Linguistics*, 29, 118–131. https://doi.org/10.1017/S0267190509090102

Chalhoub-Deville, M. (2009b). Content validity considerations in language testing contexts. In R. Lissitz (Ed.), *The concept of validity* (pp. 241–263). Charlotte, NC: Information Age Publishing.

Chalhoub-Deville, M. (2009c). Standards-based assessment in the U.S.: Social and educational impact. In L. Taylor & C. J. Weir (Eds.), *Language testing matters: Investigating the wider social and educational impact of assessment* (pp. 281–300). Studies in Language Testing 31. Cambridge: Cambridge University Press and Cambridge ESOL.

Chalhoub-Deville, M. (2012–present). *Educational Research Methodology 600: Validity and Validation*, course materials. Greensboro, NC: University of North Carolina at Greensboro.

Chalhoub-Deville, M. (2016). Validity theory: Reform policies, accountability testing, and consequences. *Language Testing*, 453–472. Appeared online in 2015. https://doi.org/10.1177/0265532215593312

Chalhoub-Deville, M., & Deville, C. (2006). Old, borrowed, and new thoughts in second language testing. In R. L. Brennan (Ed.), *Educational measurement*, 4th ed. (pp. 517–530). Westport, CT: American Council on Education/Praeger.

Chalhoub-Deville, M. & Deville, C. (2008). National standardised English language assessments. In B. Spolsky and F. Hults (Eds.), *Handbook of educational linguistics* (pp. 510–522). Oxford, UK: Blackwell Publishers. https://doi.org/10.1002/9780470694138.ch36

Chapelle, C. (1999). Validity in language assessment. *Annual Review of Applied Linguistics*, 19, 254–272. https://doi.org/10.1017/S0267190599190135

Chapelle, C. (2012). Validity argument for language assessment: The framework is simple… *Language Testing*, 29, 19–27. https://doi.org/10.1177/0265532211417211

Chapelle, C., Enright, M. & Jamieson, J. (Eds.). (2008). *Building a validity argument for TOEFL*. New York: Routledge.

Chapelle, C., Enright, M. & Jamieson, J. (2010). Does an argument-based approach to validity make a difference? *Educational Measurement: Issues and Practice*, 29, 3–13. https://doi.org/10.1111/j.1745-3992.2009.00165.x

Cheng, L. (2008). Washback, impact and consequences. In E. Shohamy & N. H. Horberger (Eds.), *Encyclopedia of language and education, Vol. 7: Language testing and assessment*, 2nd ed. (pp. 349–364). Dordrecht, The Netherlands: Springer.

Cheng, L. & Sun, Y. (2015). Interpreting the impact of the Ontario Secondary School Literacy Test on second language students within an argument-based validation framework. *Language Assessment Quarterly*, 12, 50–66. https://doi.org/10.1080/15434303.2014.981334

Cizek, G. J. (April 2011). Reconceptualizing validity and the place of consequences. Paper presented at the *Annual Meeting of the National Council on Measurement in Education*, New Orleans, LA.

Clapham, C. (1996). *The development of IELTS: A study of the effect of background knowledge on reading comprehension*. Cambridge: Cambridge University Press.

Clark, J. L. D. (1977). *The performance of native speakers of English on the Test of English as a Foreign Language*. TOEFL Research Report No. RR-01. Retrieved on July 6, 2017 from: https://www.ets.org/Media/Research/pdf/TOEFL-RR-01.pdf

Committee to enquire into the position of modern languages in the educational system of Great Britain (Committee GB). (1918). *Report of the Committee appointed by the Prime Minister to enquire into the position of modern languages in the educational system of Great Britain*. London: His Majesty's Stationery Office.

Council of Europe. (2001). *Common European Framework of Reference for Languages: Learning, teaching, and assessment*. Cambridge: Cambridge University Press.

Courtis, S. A. (1914). Standard tests in English. *The Elementary School Teacher*, 14(8), 374–392. https://doi.org/10.1086/454342

Criper, C. & Davies, A. (1988). *Research Report 1 (i). ELTS Validation Project Report*. Cambridge: British Council/UCLES.

Cronbach, L. J. (1971). Test validation. In R. L. Thorndike (Ed.), *Educational measurement*, 2nd ed. (pp. 443–507). Washington, DC: American Council on Education.

Cronbach, L. J. (1980). Validity on parole: How can we go straight. *New Directions for Testing and Measurement*, 5, 99–108.

Cronbach, L. J. (1988). Five perspectives on validity argument. In H. Wainer & H. I. Braun (Eds.), *Test validity* (pp. 3–18). Hillsdale, NJ: Lawrence Erlbaum Associates.

Cronbach, L. J. (1989). Construct validity after thirty years. In R. L. Linn (Ed.), *Intelligence: Measurement, theory, and public policy: Proceedings of a symposium in honor of Lloyd G. Humphreys* (pp. 147–171). Champaign, IL: University of Illinois Press.

Cronbach, L. J. & Meehl, P. E. (1955). Construct validity in psychological tests. *Psychological Bulletin*, 52, 281–230. https://doi.org/10.1037/h0040957

Cureton, E. E. (1951). Validity. In E. F. Lindquist (Ed.), *Educational measurement* (pp. 621–694). Washington, DC: American Council on Education.

Davidson, F. and Lynch, B. (2002). *Testcraft: A teacher's guide to writing and using language test specifications.* New Haven, CT: Yale University Press.

Davies, A. (1965). *Proficiency in English as a second language*. Unpublished PhD dissertation, University of Edinburgh.

Davies, A. (1990). *Principles of language testing.* Oxford: Blackwell.

Davies, A. (2008). Ethics, professionalism, rights and codes. In E. Shohamy & N. H. Hornberger (Eds.), *Language testing and assessment, Volume 7 of Encyclopedia* of *language and education*, 2nd ed. (pp. 429–443). Dordrecht, The Netherlands: Springer.

Douglas, D. (2000). *Assessing English for Specific Purposes*. Cambridge: Cambridge University Press.

Dunlea, J. (2016). *Validating a set of Japanese EFL proficiency tests: Demonstrating locally designed tests meet international standards*. Unpublished PhD dissertation, Centre for Research in English Language Learning and Assessment, University of Bedfordshire, UK.

Ebel, R. L. (1956). Obtaining and reporting evidence on content validity. *Educational and Psychological Measurement*, 16(3), 269–282. https://doi.org/10.1177/001316445601600301

Ebel, R. L. & Frisbie, D. A. (1991). *Essentials of educational measurement*, 5th ed. Englewood Cliffs, NJ: Prentice-Hall.

Edgeworth, F. Y. (1888). The statistics of examinations. *Journal of the Royal Statistical Society*, 51, 599–635.

Edgeworth, F. Y. (1890). The element of chance in competitive examinations. *Journal of the Royal Statistical Society*, 51, 460–475 and 644–663.

Elder, C., Iwashita, N. & McNamara, T. (2002). Estimating the difficulty of oral proficiency tasks: What does the test-taker have to offer? *Language Testing*, 19(4), 347–368. https://doi.org/10.1191/0265532202lt235oa

Embretson, S. E. (1983). Construct validity: Construct representation versus nomothetic span. *Psychological Bulletin*, 93, 179–197. https://doi.org/10.1037/0033-2909.93.1.179

Embretson, S. E. (2007). Construct validity: A universal validity system or just another test evaluation procedure? *Educational Researcher*, 36, 449–455. https://doi.org/10.3102/0013189X07311600

Embretson, S. E. (2008). Construct validity: A universal validity system. Paper presented at the *Maryland Assessment Research Center for Education Success (MARCES) 9th Annual Conference: The Concept of Validity: Revisions, New Directions and Applications*, University of Maryland, College Park. https://marces.org/conference/validity/8Susan%20Embretson.ppt

Field, J. (2014). *Aptis test of listening: Final report on revision project with recommendations*. Internal Report, British Council.

Field, J. (2019). *Rethinking the second language listening test: From theory into practice*. Sheffield: Equinox.

Foster, P. and Skehan, P. (1996). The influence of planning and task type on second language performance. *Studies in Second Language Acquisition*, 18, 299–323. https://doi.org/10.1017/S0272263100015047

Foster, P. and Skehan, P. (1999). The influence of source of planning and focus of planning on task-based performance. *Language Teaching Research*, 3, 215–247. https://doi.org/10.1177/136216889900300303

Fries, C. (1945). *Teaching and learning English as a foreign language*. Michigan: Michigan University Press.

Fulcher, G. (1999). Assessment in English for academic purposes: Putting content validity in its place. *Applied Linguistics*, 20(2), 221–236. https://doi.org/10.1093/applin/20.2.221

Fulcher, G. (2014). Language testing and philosophy. In Kunnan, A. J. (Ed.), *The companion to language assessment* (pp. 1431–1451). London: Wiley-Blackwell. https://doi.org/10.1002/9781118411360.wbcla032

Fulcher, G. (2015). *Re-examining language testing: A philosophical and social inquiry*. London and New York: Routledge. https://doi.org/10.4324/9781315695518

Fulcher, G. & Davidson, F. (2007). *Language testing and assessment: An advanced resource book*. New York: Routledge. https://doi.org/10.4324/9780203449066

Galton, F. (1879). Psychometric experiments. *Brain*, 2(2), 149–162. https://doi.org/10.1093/brain/2.2.149

Geranpayeh, A. & Taylor, L. (Eds.). (2013). *Examining listening: Research and practice in assessing second language listening*. Cambridge: Cambridge University Press.

Guilford, J. P. (1946). New standards for test evaluation. *Educational and Psychological Measurement*, 6, 427–439. https://doi.org/10.1177/001316444600600401

Haake, M., Hansson, K., Gulz, A., Schötz, S. & Sahlén, B. (2014). The slower the better? Does the speaker's speech rate influence children's performance on a language comprehension test? *International Journal of Speech Language Pathology*, 16(2), 181–190. https://doi.org/10.3109/17549507.2013.845690

Hain, B. & Piper, C. (2013). PARCC as a case study in understanding the design of large-scale assessment in the era of CCSS. Paper presented at the *Annual Maryland Assessment Conference*, College Park, PA.

Hamp-Lyons, L. (1987). *Testing second language writing in academic settings*. Unpublished PhD dissertation, University of Edinburgh.

Hamp-Lyons, L. & Henning, G. (1991). Communicative writing profiles: An investigation of the transferability of a multiple-trait scoring instrument across ESL writing assessment contexts. *Language Learning*, 41(3), 337–373. https://doi.org/10.1111/j.1467-1770.1991.tb00610.x

Hamp-Lyons, L. & Mathias, S. P. (1994). Examining expert judgments of task difficulty on essay tests. *Journal of Second Language Writing*. 3(1), 49–68. https://doi.org/10.1016/1060-3743(94)90005-1

Harding, L. (2011). *Accent and listening assessment: A validation study of the use of speakers with L2 accents on an academic English listening test*. Frankfurt: Peter Lang.

Hasselgreen, A. & Caudwell, G. (2016). *Assessing the language of young learners*. Sheffield: Equinox.

Hidi, S. (2001). Interest, reading and learning: Theoretical and practical considerations. *Educational Psychology Review*, 13, 191–209. https://doi.org/10.1023/A:1016667621114

Hidi, S. & McLaren, J. (1991). Motivational factors and writing: The role of topic interestingness. *European Journal of Psychology of Education*, 6, 187–197. https://doi.org/10.1007/BF03191937

Hillegas, M. B. (1912). *A scale for the measurement of quality in English composition by young people*. New York: Teachers College

Hoffman, B. (1962). *The tyranny of testing*. New York: Crowell Collier Press.

Howatt, A. P. R. & Widdowson, H. G. (1984). *A history of English language teaching*. Oxford: Oxford University Press.

Hughes, A. (1989). *Language testing for teachers*. Cambridge: Cambridge University Press.

Hymes, D. H. (1972). On communicative competence. In J. B. Pride and J. Holmes (Eds.), *Sociolinguistics. selected readings* (pp. 269–293). Harmondsworth: Penguin.

Jenkins, J. G. (1946). Validity for what? *Journal of Consulting Psychology*, 10, 93–98. https://doi.org/10.1037/h0059212

Jespersen, O. (1904). *How to teach a foreign language*. London: G. Allen & Unwin.

Johanningmeier, E. V. & Richardson, T. (Eds.). (2008). *Educational research, the national agenda, and educational reform: A history*. Charlotte, NC: Information Age Publishing.

Kane, M. T. (1992). An argument-based approach to validity. *Psychological Bulletin*, 112, 527. https://doi.org/10.1037/0033-2909.112.3.527

Kane, M. T. (2001). Current concerns in validity theory. *Journal of Educational Measurement*, 38, 319–342. https://doi.org/10.1111/j.1745-3984.2001.tb01130.x

Kane, M. T. (2002). Validating high-stakes testing programs. *Educational Measurement: Issues and Practice*, 21, 31–41. https://doi.org/10.1111/j.1745-3992.2002.tb00083.x

Kane, M. T. (2006). Validation. In R. Brennan (Ed.), *Educational measurement*, 4th ed. (pp. 17–64). Westport, CT: American Council on Education and Praeger.

Kane, M. T. (2010). Validity, fairness, and testing. Paper presented at the invitational conference *Educational assessment, accountability, and equity: Conversations on validity around the World*, Columbia University, New York. https://www.ets.org/c/18486/pdf/19633_ets_tc_validityconference_Kane%202012_03_28.pdf

Kane, M. T. (2012a). All validity is construct validity. Or is it? *Measurement: Interdisciplinary Research and Perspectives*, 10, 66–70. https://doi.org/10.1080/15366367.2012.681977

Kane, M. T. (2012b). Validating score interpretations and uses. *Language Testing*, 29, 3–17. https://doi.org/10.1177/0265532211417210

Kane, M. T. (2013). Validating the interpretations and uses of test scores. *Journal of Educational Measurement*, 50, 1–73. https://doi.org/10.1111/jedm.12000

Kane, M. T., Crooks, T. & Cohen A. (1999). Validating measures of performance. *Educational Measurement: Issues and Practice*, 18, 5–17. https://doi.org/10.1111/j.1745-3992.1999.tb00010.x

Kelley, T. L. (1927). *Interpretation of educational measurement*. Yonkers-on-Hudson, NY: World Book Co.

Kelly, F. J. (1916). The Kansas silent reading tests. *The Journal of Educational Psychology*, 7(2). 63–80. https://doi.org/10.1037/h0073542

Khalifa, H. & Weir, C. J. (2009). *Examining reading: Research and practice in assessing second language reading*. Cambridge: Cambridge University Press.

Knoch, U., Fairbairn, J. & Huisman, A. (2015). *Effectiveness of training Aptis raters online*. Aptis Validation Report VS/2015/001. Retrieved on July 5, 2017 from: https://www.britishcouncil.org/exam/aptis/research/publications/evaluation-effectiveness-training-aptis-raters.

Kunnan, A. (2000). Test fairness. In M. Milanovic & C. Weir (Eds.), *European language testing in a global context* (pp. 27–48). Cambridge: Cambridge University Press.

Kunnan, A. (2018). *Evaluating language assessments*. New York: Routledge. https://doi.org/10.4324/9780203803554

Lane, S. (2014). Validity evidence based on testing consequences. *Psicothema*, 26, 127–135.

Levelt, W. (1989). *Speaking: From intention to articulation*. Boston: MIT Press.

Linn, R. L. (Ed.). (1989). *Educational measurement*, 3rd ed. New York: American Council on Education & Macmillan.

Lissitz, R. (Ed.) (2009). *The concept of validity*. Charlotte, NC: Information Age Publishing.

Lissitz, R. W., Hou, X. & Cadman Slater, S. (2014). The contribution of constructed response items to large scale assessment: Measuring and understanding their impact. *Journal of Applied Testing Technology*. Retrieved on July 5, 2017 from: http://www.jattjournal.com/index.php/atp/article/view/48366.

Lissitz, R. W. & Samuelsen, K. (2007a). A suggested change in terminology and emphasis regarding validity and education. *Educational Researcher*, 36, 437–448. https://doi.org/10.3102/0013189X07311286

Lissitz, R. W. & Samuelsen, K. (2007b). Further clarification regarding validity and education. *Educational Researcher*, 36, 482–484. https://doi.org/10.3102/0013189X07311612

Loevinger, J. (1957). Objective tests as instruments of psychological theory. *Psychological Reports*, 3, 635–694. https://doi.org/10.2466/pr0.1957.3.3.635

Lumley, T. & O'Sullivan, B. (2002). The effect of test-taker gender, audience and topic on task performance in tape-mediated assessment of speaking. *Language Testing*, 22(4), 415–437. https://doi.org/10.1191/0265532205lt303oa

Luoma, S. (2004). *Assessing speaking*. Cambridge: Cambridge University Press. https://doi.org/10.1017/CBO9780511733017

Lynch, B. (2001). Rethinking assessment from a critical perspective. *Language Testing*, 18, 351–372. https://doi.org/10.1191/026553201682430085

Martyniuk, W. (Ed.). (2011). *Aligning tests with the CEFR: Reflections on using the Council of Europe's draft manual*. Cambridge: Cambridge University Press.

McCann, T. M. (1989). Student argumentative writing knowledge and ability at three grade levels. *Research in the Teaching of English*, 23(1), 62–76.

McNamara, T. (2006). Validity in language testing: The challenge of Sam Messick's legacy. *Language Assessment Quarterly*, 3, 31–51. https://doi.org/10.1207/s15434311laq0301_3

McNamara, T. (2008). The social-political and power dimensions of tests. In E. Shohamy, and N. H. Honberger (Eds.), *Language testing and assessment, Volume 7 of Encyclopedia of language and education*, 2nd ed. (pp. 415–427). Dordrecht, The Netherlands: Springer.

McNamara, T. & Roever, C. (2006). *Language testing: The social dimension*. Oxford: Blackwell.

Meehl, P. & Challman, R. C. (1954). Technical recommendations for psychological tests and diagnostic techniques. *Psychological Bulletin Supplement*, 51(2), Part 2, 1–38. https://doi.org/10.1037/h0053479

Mehrens, W. A. (1997). The consequences of consequential validity. *Educational Measurement: Issues and Practice*, 16(2), 16–18. https://doi.org/10.1111/j.1745-3992.1997.tb00588.x

Messick, S. (1989). Validity. In R. L. Linn (Ed.), *Educational measurement*, 3rd ed. (pp. 13–103). New York: American Council on Education & Macmillan.

Messick, S. (1995). Validity of psychological assessment: Validation of inferences from persons' responses and performances as scientific inquiry into score meaning. *American Psychologist*, 50, 741–749. https://doi.org/10.1037/0003-066X.50.9.741

Mislevy, R. J. (2007). Validity by design. *Educational Researcher*, 36, 463–469. https://doi.org/10.3102/0013189X07311660

Mislevy, R. J. (2018). *Sociocognitive foundations of educational measurement.* New York: Routledge. https://doi.org/10.4324/9781315871691

Mislevy, R. J., Almond, R. & Lukas, J. (July 2003). *A brief introduction to evidence-centered design.* Princeton, NJ, ETS Research Report No. RR-03-16. https://doi.org/10.1002/j.2333-8504.2003.tb01908.x

Mislevy, R. J., & Haertel, G. D. (2006). Implications of evidence-centered design for educational testing. *Educational Measurement: Issues and Practice*, 25, 6–20. https://doi.org/10.1111/j.1745-3992.2006.00075.x

Mislevy, R. J., Steinberg, L. S. & Almond, R. G. (2003). On the structure of educational assessments. *Measurement: Interdisciplinary Research and Perspectives*, 7, 3–67.

Moss, P. A. (2003). Reconceptualizing validity for classroom assessment. *Educational Measurement: Issues and Practice*, 22, 13–25. https://doi.org/10.1111/j.1745-3992.2003.tb00140.x

Moss, P. A. (2016). Shifting the focus of validity for test use. *Assessment in Education: Principles, Policy & Practice*, 23, 236–251. https://doi.org/10.1080/0969594X.2015.1072085

Moss, P. A., Pullin, D. C., Gee, J. P., Haertel, E. H. & Young, L. J. (2008). *Assessment, equity, and opportunity to learn.* New York, NY: Cambridge University Press. https://doi.org/10.1017/CBO9780511802157

Munby, J. L. (1978). *Communicative syllabus design.* Cambridge: Cambridge University Press.

Newton, P. (2013). *The importance of ideas: The semantics of validity.* Invited presentation at *Cambridge English Assessment*, Cambridge, UK, September 23, 2013. Slides retrieved on July 27, 2018 from: http://www.cambridgeassessment.org.uk/images/the-importance-of-ideas-paul-newton-presentation.pdf

Newton, P. E. & Shaw, S. D. (2014). *Validity in educational and psychological assessment*. London: Sage. https://doi.org/10.4135/9781446288856

Nichols, P. D. & Williams, N. (2009). Consequences of test score use as validity evidence: Roles and responsibilities. *Educational Measurement: Issues and Practice*, 28, 3–9. https://doi.org/10.1111/j.1745-3992.2009.01132.x

O'Loughlin, K. (2002). The impact of gender in oral proficiency testing. *Language Testing*, 19(2), 169–192. https://doi.org/10.1191/0265532202lt226oa

O'Sullivan, B. (2000a). *Towards a model of performance in oral language tests*. Unpublished PhD dissertation, University of Reading, UK.

O'Sullivan, B. (2000b). Exploring gender and oral proficiency interview performance. *System*, 28(3), 373–386. https://doi.org/10.1016/S0346-251X(00)00018-X

O'Sullivan, B. (2002). Learner acquaintanceship and oral proficiency test pair-task performance. *Language Testing*, 19(3), 277–295. https://doi.org/10.1191/0265532202lt205oa

O'Sullivan, B. (2005). *Levels specification project report*. Internal report, Zayed University, United Arab Emirates.

O'Sullivan, B. (March 2006). *Daring to lead or failing to follow: 40 years of language testing*. Plenary Address, *TESOL International Conference*, Tampa Florida.

O'Sullivan, B. (2008). *Modelling performance in tests of spoken language*. Frankfurt: Peter Lang.

O'Sullivan, B. (2011). Theories and practices in language testing. In P. Powell-Davies (Ed.), *New directions: Assessment and evaluation – A collection of papers* (pp. 15–24). London/East Asia: British Council. Retrieved on July 27, 2018 from: https://www.teachingenglish.org.uk/sites/teacheng/files/download-accessenglish-publications-ebe-proceedings-2012.pdf

O'Sullivan, B. (2014). *Stakeholders and consequence in test development and validation*. Plenary Address at the *Language Testing Forum*, University of Southampton, November.

O'Sullivan, B. (2016). Validity: What is it and who is it for? In Yiu-nam Leung (Ed.), *Epoch making in English teaching and learning: Evolution, innovation, and revolution*. Taipei: Crane Publishing Company Ltd.

O'Sullivan, B. (2019). Foreword: Localisation. In C. J. Weir & J. Wu (Eds.), *Language testing in East Asia* (pp. 1–25). New York: Routledge.

O'Sullivan, B. & Dunlea, J. (2015). *Aptis General technical manual, 1.0*. London: British Council. Retrieved on April 14, 2020 from: https://www.britishcouncil.org/sites/default/files/aptis_general_technical_manual_v-1.0.pdf

O'Sullivan, B. & Weir, C. J. (2002). *Research issues in testing spoken language*. Report for the University of Cambridge Local Examinations Syndicate. London: University of Surrey, Roehampton.

O'Sullivan, B. & Weir, C. (2011). Language testing and validation. In B. O'Sullivan (Ed.), *Language testing: Theory & practice* (pp. 13–32). Oxford: Palgrave.

Ofqual. (2017). *Accredited qualifications*. Retrieved on July 6, 2017 from: http://www.accreditedqualifications.org.uk/office-of-qualifications-and-examinations-regulation-ofqual.html

Ortega, L. (1999). Planning and focus on form in L2 oral performance. *Studies in Second Language Acquisition*, 20, 109–148. https://doi.org/10.1017/S0272263199001047

Palmer, H. E. (1921). *The oral method of teaching languages*. Cambridge: Heffers.

Palmquist, M. (1994–2012). Understanding writing situations. Writing@CSU. Colorado State University. Retrieved on July 27, 2018 from: https://writing.colostate.edu/guides/guide.cfm?guideid=3.

Passy, P. (1899). *De la méthode directe dans l'enseignment des langues vivante*. Paris: Colin.

Pearson, K. (1900). On the criterion that a given system of deviations from the probable in the case of a correlated system of variables is such that it can be reasonably supposed to have arisen from random sampling. *Philosophical Magazine*, Series 5.50(302), 157–175. Retrieved on July 27, 2018 from: http://www.economics.soton.ac.uk/staff/aldrich/1900.pdf https://doi.org/10.1080/14786440009463897

Pearson, K. (1939). Student. *Annals of Eugenics*, 9, 1–9. https://doi.org/10.1111/j.1469-1809.1939.tb02192.x

Pitoniak, M. J., Sireci, S. G. & Luecht, R. M. (2002). A multitrait-multimethod validity investigation of scores from a professional licensure examination. *Educational and Psychological Measurement*, 62(3), 498–516. https://doi.org/10.1177/0016440206200300

Pittman, G. (1963). *Teaching Situational English*. London: Evans.

Popham, W. J. (1997). Consequential validity: Right concern – wrong concept. *Educational Measurement: Issues and Practice*, 16(2), 9–13.

https://doi.org/10.1111/j.1745-3992.1997.tb00586.x

Porter, D. (1991a). Affective factors in language testing. In J.C. Alderson & B. North (Eds.), *Language testing in the 1990s* (pp. 32–40). London: Macmillan (Modern English Publications in association with The British Council).

Porter, D. (1991b). Affective factors in the assessment of oral interaction: gender and status. In S. Arnivan (Ed.), *Current developments in language testing* (pp. 92–102). Singapore: SEAMEO Regional Language Centre. Anthology Series 25.

Porter, D. & O'Sullivan, B. (1999). The effect of audience age on measured written performance. *System*, 27, 65–77. https://doi.org/10.1016/S0346-251X(98)00050-5

Prat, C. S. (2011). The brain basis of individual differences in language comprehension abilities. *Language and Linguistics Compass*, 5, 635–649. https://doi.org/10.1111/j.1749-818X.2011.00303.x

Pressey, S. L. (1920). Suggestions looking toward a fundamental revision of current statistical procedure, as applied to tests. *Psychological Review*, 27(6), 466–472. https://doi.org/10.1037/h0075018

Prokosch, E. (1922). Reading knowledge by self-instruction. *Modern Language Journal*, 6(8), 446–452.

QALSPELL. (2004). *Quality assurance in language for specific purposes, Estonia Latvia, and Lithuania*. Council of Europe Leonardo da Vinci funded project.

Ratcliffe, J. W. (1983). Notions of validity in qualitative research methodology. *Knowledge: Creation, Diffusion, Utilization*, 5, 147–167. https://doi.org/10.1177/107554708300500201

Read, J. (2000). *Assessing vocabulary*. Cambridge: Cambridge University Press. https://doi.org/10.1017/CBO9780511732942

Read, J. (2015). The DELNA programme at the University of Auckland. In J. Read (Ed.), *Assessing English proficiency for university study* (pp. 47–69). London: Palgrave Macmillan. https://doi.org/10.1057/9781137315694_3

Rethinasamy, S. (2006). *The effects on rating performance of different training interventions*. Unpublished PhD dissertation, Roehampton University, London, UK.

Roach, J. O. (1945). *Some problems of oral examinations in modern languages: An experimental approach based on the Cambridge Examinations in English for foreign students*. UCLES report circulated to Oral Examiners and Local Examiners.

Robinson, P. (2011). Second language task complexity, the cognition hypothesis, language learning and performance. In P. Robinson (Ed.), *Second language task complexity: Researching the cognition hypothesis of language Learning and Performance* (pp. 3–38). Amsterdam: John Benjamins. https://doi.org/10.1075/tblt.2.05ch1

Rulon, P. J. (1946). On the validity of educational tests. *Harvard Educational Review*, 16, 290–296.

Sabatini, J. P., Bennett, R. & Deane, P. (2011). *Four years of cognitively based assessment of, for, and as learning (CBAL): Learning about through-course assessment (TCA).* Princeton, NJ: Educational Testing Service.

Savignon, S. (1972). *Communicative competence: An experiment in foreign language teaching.* Philadelphia: Center for Curriculum Development.

Savignon, S. (1983). *Communicative competence: Theory and classroom practice.* Reading, MA: Addison-Wesley.

Schwabe, F., von Davier, A. and Chalhoub-Deville, M. (2016). Language and culture in testing. In F. T. L. Leong, D. Bartram, F. M. Cheung, K. F. Geisinger & D. Iliescu (Eds.), *The ITC international handbook of testing and assessment* (pp. 300–317). New York: Oxford University Press. https://doi.org/10.1093/med:psych/9780199356942.003.0021

Selvaruby, P. (2006). *Validating a national test of physics*. Unpublished PhD dissertation, Roehampton University, School of Education, London, UK.

Selvaruby, P., O'Sullivan, B. & Watts, M. (2008). School-based assessment in Sri Lanka: Ensuring valid processes for assessment-for-learning in physics. In R. Coll & N. Taylor (Eds.), *Education in context: An international perspective of the influence of context on science curriculum development, implementation and the student-experienced curriculum* (pp. 131–144). Rotterdam: Sense Publishers. https://doi.org/10.1163/9789087902490_012

Shaw, S. & Weir, C. J. (2007). *Examining writing: Research and practice in assessing second language writing.* Cambridge: Cambridge University Press.

Shepard, L. A. (1993). Evaluating test validity. *Review of Research in Education*, 19, 405–450. https://doi.org/10.2307/1167347

Shohamy, E. (2001). *The power of tests: A critical perspective on the uses of language tests*. London: Pearson.

Shohamy, E. (2007). Language tests as language policy tools. *Assessment in Education: Principles, Policy & Practice*, 14, 117–130.

https://doi.org/10.1080/09695940701272948

Sireci, S. G. (2007). On validity theory and test validation. *Educational Researcher*, 36, 477–481. https://doi.org/10.3102/0013189X07311609

Sireci, S. G. (2009). Packing and upacking sources of validity evidence: History repeats itself again. In R. Lissitz (Ed.), *The concept of validity: Revisions, new directions and applications* (pp. 19–37). Charlotte, NC: Information Age Publishing Inc.

Sireci, S. G. (2013). Agreeing on validity arguments. *Journal of Educational Measurement*, 50, 99–104. https://doi.org/10.1111/jedm.12005

Skehan, P. (1996). A framework for the implementation of task based instruction. *Applied Linguistics*, 17, 38–62. https://doi.org/10.1093/applin/17.1.38

Skehan, P. (1998). *A cognitive approach to language learning*. Oxford: Oxford University Press. https://doi.org/10.1177/003368829802900209

Skehan, P. (2009). Modelling second language performance: Integrating complexity, accuracy, fluency and lexis. *Applied Linguistics*, 30, 510–532. https://doi.org/10.1093/applin/amp047

Skehan, P. & Foster, P. (1997). Task type and task processing conditions as influences on foreign language performance. *Language Teaching Research*, 1, 185–211. https://doi.org/10.1177/136216889700100302

Skehan, P. & Foster, P. (1999). The influence of task structure and processing conditions on narrative retellings. *Language Learning*, 49, 93–120. https://doi.org/10.1111/1467-9922.00071

Skehan, P. & Shum, S. (2014). Structure and processing condition in video-based narrative retelling. In P. Skehan (Ed.), *Processing perspectives on task performance* (pp. 187–210). Amsterdam: John Benjamins. https://doi.org/10.1075/tblt.5.07ske

Spolsky, B. (1995). *Measured words: The development of objective language testing*. Oxford: Oxford University Press.

Strauss, M. & Smith, G. (2009). Construct validity: Advances in theory and methodology. *Annual Review Clinical Psychology*, 27, 1–25. https://doi.org/10.1146/annurev.clinpsy.032408.153639

Student. (1908). The probable error of a mean. *Biometrika*, 6, 1–25. https://doi.org/10.2307/2331554

Sweet, H. (1899). *The practical study of languages*. London: Dent.

Taylor, D., O'Sullivan, B. and Quilter, N. (2009). *Advanced international ophthalmology examination proposal*. London: International Council of Ophthalmology.

Taylor, L. (Ed.). (2011). *Examining speaking: Research and practice in assessing second language speaking*. Cambridge: Cambridge University Press.

Thorndike, E. L. (1913). *An introduction to the theory of mental and social measurements*. New York: Teachers College, Columbia University. https://doi.org/10.1037/10866-000

Thurstone, L. L. (1932). *The reliability and validity of tests*. Ann Arbor, Michigan: Edwards Brothers.

Thyne, J. M. (1974). *Principles of examining*. London: University of London Press.

Torres Pereira de Eça, M. T. (2005). Using portfolios for external assessment: An experiment in Portugal. *International Journal of Art & Design Education*, 24, 209–218. https://doi.org/10.1111/j.1476-8070.2005.00441.x

Urquhart, A. H. & Weir, C. J. (1998). *Reading in a second language: Process, product and practice*. Harlow, UK: Longman.

U.S. Department of Education. (April 28, 2004). Standards and Assessments Peer Review Guidance: Information and examples for meeting requirements of the No Child Left Behind Act of 2001. Washington, DC 20202: Office of Elementary and Secondary Education. https://files.eric.ed.gov/fulltext/ED483111.pdf

Van Ek, J. (1975). *Systems development in adult language learning: The threshold level*. Strasbourg: Council of Europe.

Vernon, P.E. (1958). *Educational testing and test-form factors*. ETS Research Report Series, 1958(1). Princeton, NJ: ETS. https://doi.org/10.1002/j.2333-8504.1958.tb00079.x

Viëtor, W. (1882). *Der Sprachunterricht muss umkehren! Ein Beitrag zur Überburdüngsfrage (Language teaching must turn around! A contribution to the overloading question)*. Heilbronn: Henninger.

Wall, D. & Alderson, J. C. (1993). Examining washback: The Sri Lankan impact study. *Language Testing*, 10(1), 41–69. https://doi.org/10.1177/026553229301000103

Weideman, A. (2012). Validation and validity beyond Messick. *Per Linguam*, 28(2), 1–14. https://doi.org/10.5785/28-2-526

Weir, C. J. (1983). *Identifying the language problems of the overseas students in tertiary education in the United Kingdom*. Unpublished PhD dissertation, University of London.

Weir, C. J. (1988). *Communicative language testing with special reference to English as a foreign language*. Exeter: A. Wheaton & Co. Ltd.

Weir, C. J. (1990). *Communicative language testing*. Englewood Cliffs, NJ: Prentice Hall.

Weir, C. J. (1993). *Understanding and developing language tests*. London: Prentice Hall.

Weir, C. J. (2003). A survey of the history of the Certificate of Proficiency in English (CPE) in the twentieth century. In C. J. Weir and M. Milanovic (Eds.), *Continuity and innovation: The history of the CPE 1913–2002, Studies in Language Testing 15* (pp. 1–56). Cambridge: Cambridge University Press.

Weir, C. J. (2005). *Language testing and validation: An evidence-based approach*. Basingstoke: Palgrave Macmillan. Macmillan.

Weir, C. J. (2013). An overview of the influences on English language testing in the United Kingdom 1913–2012. In C.J. Weir, I. Vidakovic & E. Galaczi, *Measured constructs: A history of Cambridge English language examinations 1913–2012* (pp. 1–102). *Studies in Language Testing* 37. Cambridge: Cambridge University Press.

Weir, C. J. & O'Sullivan, B. (2017). *Assessing English on the global stage: The British Council and English language testing 1941–2016*. Sheffield: Equinox.

Weir, C. J., Vidakovic, I. & Galaczi, E. D. (2013). *Measured constructs: A history of the constructs underlying Cambridge English language (ESOL) examinations 1913–2012. Studies in Language Testing* 37. Cambridge: Cambridge University Press.

West, R. (1994). *Needs analysis in language teaching*. Cambridge: Cambridge University Press.

Widdowson, H. G. (1978). *Teaching language as communication*. Oxford: Oxford University Press.

Widdowson, H. G. (1983). *Learning purpose and language use*. Oxford: Oxford University Press.

Wigglesworth, G. (1997). An investigation of planning time and proficiency level on oral test discourse. *Language Testing*, 14, 85–106. https://doi.org/10.1177/026553229701400105

Wilkins, D. A. (1976). *Notional syllabuses*. London: Oxford University Press.

Wiseman, S. (1961). The efficiency of examinations. In S. Wiseman (Ed.), *Examinations and English education* (pp. 133–164). Manchester: Manchester University Press.

Xu, F. (2011). The priority of listening comprehension over speaking in the language acquisition process. *International Education Studies*, 4(1), 161–165. https://doi.org/10.5539/ies.v4n1p161

Zhang, Y. & Elder, C. (2011). Judgements of oral proficiency by non-native and native English speaking teacher raters: Competing or complementary constructs? *Language Testing*, 28(1), 31–50. https://doi.org/10.1177/0265532209360671

APPENDIX

CASE STUDY

Localisation in action – the BCT-S project

Barry O'Sullivan, British Council Assessment Research Group

Jamie Dunlea, British Council Assessment Research Group

Judith Fairbairn, British Council Global Assessment

Masashi Negishi, Tokyo University of Foreign Studies

Yujia Zhou, Tokyo University of Foreign Studies

Overview

This appendix provides a brief overview of a collaborative development project which applied the principles of localisation described in Chapters 3 and 6 in this volume in the development of a speaking test for university entrance purposes in Japan. The following description is intended as a short narrative overview, and not a detailed technical description or comprehensive validity argument for the test. Further, this brief discussion is from the perspective of the international partners in this project, describing from that perspective how some of the principles of localisation described from a theoretical perspective in this volume, and for example in O'Sullivan & Dunlea (2015), were applied in practice, including the crucial element of working with a local partner to achieve the project goals. For a detailed discussion of the theoretical basis for the development and the evidence collected during the project, see Zhou et al. (2018a, b).

The development of the test was framed within the validation principles of the socio-cognitive model of test development and validation (see Chapters 3 and 4 in this volume for a discussion of the development of the model and recent adaptions). At the outset of the project, the Assessment Research Group and Global Assessment teams at the British Council, based in the UK, had already developed experience applying this model to test development with the Aptis test system. Table A1, from O'Sullivan & Dunlea (2015), presents an outline of the different levels of adaptation which were defined early in the Aptis test system to provide a model which could guide both theoretical concerns for the development and localisation of new variants within the system, and importantly also help predict the logistical and resource demands to be expected at each level.

The UK teams thus had experience of adapting the original design of Aptis for different degrees of change requiring different degrees of effort and evidence. In addition, two major test comparability projects had been undertaken in which the appropriacy, or what O'Sullivan (2016: 155) refers to as the fitness for purpose, of the existing Aptis General four-skills test for use with university students in the EFL higher-education contexts of Taiwan (Wu et al., 2016) and Vietnam (Dunlea et al., 2018) was examined. In both these cases, extensive evidence was gathered to investigate the fit of the tests with a specific target group and context of use.

This project employed a mix of these approaches, with the research teams from both the international and local partners first reviewing the test to determine the level of localisation required to provide a sufficient fit for the context and purpose of use. As described below, this was determined to sit within a Level 2 localisation in relation to Table A1. While this level does not represent a drastic change to the underlying design of the original test, a research programme to gather a range of quantitative and qualitative evidence to confirm the fit of the test localised in this way to the context was designed and carried out by the local research team with support from the international partner (Zhou et al., 2018a, b).

Context of use

Sasaki (2008) provides a thorough overview of the history of EFL testing in Japan through the 20th and early years of the 21st centuries, and notes that university entrance exams have consistently been seen as an impediment to reform of the teaching and learning carried out in secondary school. In particular, a number of initiatives by the Ministry of Education, Culture, Science and Technology (MEXT) from the early 2000s, such as the *Action Plan for Cultivating Japanese with English Abilities* (2003), have encouraged the use of external, including international, proficiency tests in the university entrance process to promote the assessment of productive skills (O'Sullivan & Dunlea, 2015).

Level 0	Aptis General (or other existing variant) in a full, four-skills package.	User selects a four-skills package of any Aptis (General or variant) available for use.
Level 1	Options for localisation are limited to selection from a fixed range of pre-existing features, such as delivery mode and/or components.	User is able to select the skills to be tested and/or the mode of delivery that is appropriate. For example, the Reading package (Core component + Reading component) of Aptis General, taken as a pen-and-paper administration.
Level 2	Contextual localisation: lexical, topical modification.	Development of specifications for generating items using existing task formats but with topics, vocabulary, etc. relevant for specific domains (e.g. Aptis for Teachers).
Level 3	Structural reassembly: changing the number of items, proficiency levels targeted, etc., while utilising existing item-bank content.	Developing a test of reading targeted at a specific level, e.g. B1, using existing task types and items of known difficulty calibrated to the Aptis reading scale.
Level 4	Partial re-definition of target construct from existing variants. Will involve developing different task types to elicit different aspects of performance.	Developing new task types that are more relevant for a specific population of test-takers, while remaining within the overall framework of the Aptis test system (e.g. Aptis for Teens).
Level 5	The construct and/or other aspects of the test system are changed to such an extent that the test will no longer be a variant within the system.	For example, developing a matriculation test for uses within a formal secondary educational context, developing a certification test available to individuals rather than organisations, etc.

Table A1: Levels of localisation in the Aptis test system (O'Sullivan and Dunlea, 2015: 8)

Recently the focus of these reform efforts has resulted in a direct focus on the *National Center Test for University Admissions* (大学入試センター試験 *Daigaku Nyūshi Sentā Shiken*) to ensure that productive skills are included in entrance exams. The *Center Test* (as it is commonly referred to) is a multi-subject standardised test used for admission to higher education in Japan. The test is administered by the National Center for University Entrance Examinations at approximately 700 locations across the country. All public and many private institutions use the test as part of their admissions policy. The test comprises papers on Science, Mathematics, History, Geography & Civics, Japanese Literature and Foreign Language (Watanabe, 2013). As Sasaki (2008), notes, while English is not compulsory it is by far the most commonly taken foreign language exam. In fact, in 2019, of students taking the foreign language paper, 537,663 took English with the next largest number of test takers being 665 for Chinese (National Center for University Entrance Exams, n.d). Since the test forms such a crucial part of higher education admissions, it is extremely high-stakes for those students who sit it every year.

The English Language paper of the *Center Test* is focused on reading comprehension and listening, though there has always been a significant additional emphasis on aspects of language knowledge such as grammar and vocabulary. Speaking has long been represented in the test through a set of items which purport to assess knowledge of pronunciation (Watanabe, 2013). These items ask candidates to identify in a multiple-choice format the location of the stress point for a series of multi-syllable words. The format remains popular with test developers despite Buck's (1988) demonstration that the item consistently failed to predict students' ability to actually pronounce the words tested, even when they accurately identified the stress location.

In 2006, a listening test was included and has remained part of the test since then. However, in recent years, the *Center Test* has been criticised for its negative washback, which many in Japan see as a failure to promote interest among students in English for communication, a situation that the current government believe is hurting Japan's economic recovery (see Aspinall, 2012).

The MEXT, which has oversight of the *Centre Test*, originally indicated that it was considering removing the English section from the test, but later decided that between 2020 and 2023 it would allow universities to admit candidates based on their performance on a new *Centre Test* English section, which would assess all four skills. Alternatively, candidates who demonstrated their English Proficiency on the TOEFL could be exempted. After much discussion, a list of eight appropriate external tests was approved (Anon, 2018):

Local

- Test of English for International Communication (TOEIC)
- Global Test of English Communication (GTEC)
- Test of English for Academic Purposes (TEAP)
- Test of English for Academic Purposes Computer Based Test (TEAP CBT),
- Eiken, (Test in Practical English Proficiency)

International

- Cambridge English Main Suite (KET, PET, FCE, CAE, CPE)
- Test of English as a Foreign Language (TOEFL)
- International English Language Testing System (IELTS)

By forcing candidates to demonstrate a degree of mastery of all four skills, MEXT hoped to influence the way in which language is taught in Japanese schools and universities, and further the reforms it had proposed for more than two decades.

As might be expected, there has been considerable debate around this topic (summarised by Brasor, 2018). The additional cost of an external test (over ¥30,000 in the case of the international tests) on top of the cost of the *Center Test* (¥18,000) is seen by many as an unacceptable burden on Japanese families – particularly given the fact that only the scores for the productive skills will be required. In addition, Brasor (2018) reports on articles in the Japanese media in which reporters who sat for different tests highlighted the very different nature and focus of these tests. Masahiko Abe, a professor at the University of Tokyo, for example has argued that the change in policy will only benefit the testing companies and will have no meaningful impact on English language teaching or learning (Abe, 2018).

While the changes to the *Center Test* will have the greatest impact on public universities, MEXT has indicated a series of changes to the regulations governing admission to private higher education institutions. Among these changes (well summarised by McCrostie, 2017), is an expectation that where entrance examinations are held all four skills should be included in the English section. Currently, it is rare to find a written production paper in such a test and even more so for spoken production. Currently approximately 49% of almost 480,000 students who enter private institutions take such examinations; the rest enter either through a recommendation system or through Admissions Office examinations (described by McCrostie as essentially a form-filling exercise).

So, the issue for public and private higher education institutions is that they are expected to include both written and spoken production in their entrance tests in the very near future. However, the resources needed to manage this are often beyond the capacity of all but a very small number of institutions. The development of productive skills tests, particularly speaking, are resource-intensive and require the development of a comprehensive system of rater training, etc., in order to ensure fair and reliable results, a particular concern in the high-stakes context of university entrance. Speaking tests, particularly those administered face-to-face, also require more space and time than is required for pen-and-paper tests, including listening, which can be administered to large numbers of students in one sitting.

The British Council / Tokyo University of Foreign Studies Project

It is against the background of this dynamic policy change, and the practical implications that it entails for both institutions and test takers, that the project to develop a speaking test for use by the Tokyo University of Foreign Studies in their second stage entrance procedures was undertaken. The visual representation of the socio-cognitive model in Figure 8 in this volume, in which the test system interacts in a cyclical way with important stakeholders, with impact in both directions, and in which test system and stakeholders are embedded within a wider social context, can immediately be seen to be relevant to this project. This visual representation clearly helps tease out the various factors beyond technical adequacy of the test instrument which the test development collaboration would need to keep in mind when approaching the project.

The project could be seen as going through four stages, each of which will be briefly described: stage one was an initial informal discussion and feasibility stage; stage two saw the project formally agreed and a project team formed with researchers from both international and local partners to evaluate the level of localisation required to ensure the Aptis speaking test could be used with adequate fit to the context and purpose of use; stage three involved quantitative and qualitative evidence collection, evaluation, and iterative adjustment of the test specifications; stage four saw the implementation of the live test.

Stage one

In 2015, Professor Masashi Negishi from Tokyo University of Foreign Studies (TUFS) and Professor Barry O'Sullivan from the British Council began a conversation at the Japanese Language Testing Association (JLTA) conference in Tokyo following O'Sullivan's paper on the operationalisation of localisation within the British Council's Aptis test system. They concluded at that time that it would be interesting to explore the possibility of working together to develop a locally appropriate test of spoken production that could be used as a *plug-in* by TUFS to enable them to include speaking in their entrance test.

The British Council had just published its Aptis technical manual (O'Sullivan & Dunlea, 2015), which included Table A1 above. Initially, no limit was placed on the possible level of localisation that would be required. However, the original Aptis principles of flexibility, affordability and accessibility were to be adhered to. The aim of this collaboration was to bring the best aspects of experience in the provision of international, large-scale speaking tests together with the understanding of the local context and needs of stakeholders, including students, parents and the administering institution which would be using the scores. Against those demands were also the need to be logistically feasible and cost-effective (for both developers and users). Would Aptis fit the bill?

During the first stage of the project, a class of undergraduates were asked to work independently in three teams to first take the Aptis speaking paper in its operational form. Having done this, they were tasked with first critiquing the paper from the perspective of its possible use as an element of the University entrance test. This done, they were asked to recommend changes to the structure (i.e., task design and ordering). Finally, they were tasked with putting together an alternative test proposal. This innovative approach, designed by Professor Negishi, was expected to give us a good idea of the appropriateness of the Aptis speaking test for use in this context, with university students from that context acting as key informants.

The three groups concluded that the format and structure of the test were appropriate, with all three groups reporting that their experience of taking the test was positive from this perspective. However, all agreed that the test needed to be more closely linked to their experiences. Their recommended alternatives focused on themes and situations familiar to Japanese high-school students, and two of the three test designs were of particular value, as they had attempted to link the contents to the high-school course of study (curriculum).

The success of this first stage of the project prompted TUFS and the British Council to pursue the project in a systematic way, with a Level 2 localisation of the Aptis speaking according to Table A1 above as the estimated development target. This target was then to be investigated, and the evidence collected to support or adjust it in the following stages. Table A2, adapted from Zhou et al. (2018b), gives an overview of the main development activities from stages two through four. This table focuses only on the main activities directly related to the test specification and data collection for test development. The actual project involved a range of other activities, with communication with stakeholders and administrative planning for registration, provision of test results, etc., all playing important roles, but which are beyond the scope of this brief overview.

Stage two

In 2017, a formal project group was set up. This team included a dedicated researcher appointed by TUFS to lead the local development and research agenda, the local British Council exams team based in Tokyo, and members of the Assessment Research Group and Global Assessment units of the British Council.

As can be seen, stage two involved close collaboration between the project members from both international and local partners to intensively review the specifications and consider what aspects would need to be adapted at a Level 2 localisation to ensure the test would fit the local context. The full test and detailed task specifications for the Aptis General speaking test which is used internationally and was the basis for test development are publicly available in O'Sullivan & Dunlea (2015), and these provided the starting point for localisation.

The Level 2 localisation focuses mostly on the contextual aspects of topics, situations, participants, and vocabulary items likely to be familiar/unfamiliar to the typical test takers, Japanese high school students taking university entrance exams in Japan. As such, a key part of this process was creating a consensus definition of the typical test taker characteristics that give the project team explicit criteria against which to evaluate the appropriateness of test content and whether such content could

		Stage two
Apr to Sep 2017	TUFS	Review the feasibility of localising Aptis speaking test to TUFS admission system (Qualitative, expert judgement)
Nov 2017	TUFS & British Council	Review test design, decide on level of localisation and test administration system suitable for entrance exams (Qualitative, expert judgement)
Dec 2017	TUFS & British Council	Signing ceremony
		Stage three
Jan 2018	TUFS	Mini-trial with TUFS students using existing Aptis speaking test (Quantitative score data, qualitative questionnaire and focus group data)
Mar 2018	TUFS & British Council	Finalise test tasks for pilot study, refine test specifications during workshops in UK (Qualitative, expert judgement)
Apr 2018	TUFS	Pilot study with TUFS students (Quantitative score data, qualitative questionnaire and focus group data)
Apr to Sep 2018	TUFS & British Council	Transcription of actual spoken performances and analysis of data (scoring, transcriptions, questionnaires)
Sep to Dec 2018	TUFS & British Council	Finalise test specifications and content for live administrations
		Stage four
Feb 2019	TUFS & British Council	Administration of live test for admissions purposes

Table A2: Overview of development activities, British Council / TUFS Project

be considered to have operationalised the localised test specifications appropriately.

At the same time, a key point of discussion between the content experts from the British Council and the TUFS researcher was identifying and maintaining those criterial aspects of the specifications related to functions and cognitive demand which would maintain the tasks at the targeted levels of difficulty intended, expressed in terms of the *Common*

European Framework of Reference (Council of Europe, 2001) proficiency levels in the original design. Aptis tasks are targeted at levels A1, A2, B1 and B2, and criterial features associated with these levels were kept in place.

Stage three

Once the project team had identified the key areas of the test specifications to be adapted, pilot tasks were developed to operationalise these specs and provide concrete examples for expert valuation of the appropriacy of the content. Stage three however was designed to go beyond this expert judgment phase of development and collect a range of quantitative and qualitative evidence to feed into the iterative revision of the test specifications, and provide the project team with the evidence to evaluate the initial claims and design assumptions they had made. Multi-Facet Rasch Measurement analysis of pilot test scores along with questionnaire and focus group data was collected from test takers during a pilot of the BCT-S. In addition, performances were transcribed and a detailed function analysis was carried out. Aptis speaking tests include a function list derived from O'Sullivan, Weir & Saville (2002) in the task specifications. In order to establish that the test tasks elicited the type of language in actual test performance as was predicted in the specifications, a function analysis was undertaken, based on the approach suggested by O'Sullivan et al. (2002) and adapted successfully by Nakatsuhara (2014).

Stage four

The test was successfully administered in February 2019 to the first cohort of candidates applying to enter a new faculty at TUFS to study in the Japanese academic year beginning April 2019. The use of the test will be expanded to other TUFS faculties in subsequent years.

Conclusion

The model of development described above has benefited from, and indeed has only been possible due to, the strong level of local expertise which the local development partner was able to bring to the project. The process of collaboration has been a truly interesting experience providing learning opportunities for all involved. Evidence collected in the course of validating the claims and design assumptions of the test for the specific context of use for which BCT-S is intended have also proven useful in the ongoing validation of Aptis itself. Nonetheless, this process, while the developers would posit has been initially successful, is not intended as a one-off event. Not only is the process of development iterative, as described above in Table A2, but ongoing validation will provide further learning opportunities, and likely require further adaption of both the BCT-S design and the test development model over time. In addition, the British Council and TUFS have offered the test to other universities for consideration as a successful model of localisation which can bring international standards of technical quality together with practical and cost-effective administration, and locally appropriate content for Japanese high-school students intending to study at a Japanese university.

References

Abe, M. (2018). A reform that will profit the English teaching and testing industry. *Nippon.com*, July 13. Retrieved on March 5, 2019 from: https://www.nippon.com/en/currents/d00413/the-ill-considered-reform-of-japanese-university-entrance-exams.html#

Anon (2018). 8 private English tests accepted for future university admission system. *The Mainichi Daily Online*, March 27. Retrieved on March 7, 2019 from: https://mainichi.jp/english/search?q=8+private+English+tests+accepted+for+future+university+admission+system

Aspinall, R. (2012). *International education policy in Japan in an age of globalisation and risk*. Leiden, Netherlands: Global Oriental.

Brasor, P. (2018). Testing times for students' English-language ability in Japan. *Japan Times Online*, November 3. Retrieved on March 5, 2019 from: https://www.japantimes.co.jp/news/2018/11/03/national/media-national/testing-times-students-english-language-ability-japan/#.XH6lZJNKh0s

Buck, G. (1988). Testing listening comprehension in Japanese university entrance examinations. *JALT Journal*, 10(1), 15–42.

Council of Europe. (2001). *Common European Framework of Reference for Languages: Learning, Teaching, and Assessment*. Cambridge: Cambridge University Press.

Dunlea, J., Spiby, R., Nguyen, T. N. Q., Nguyen, T. Q. Y., Nguyen, T. M. H., Nguyen, T. P. T., Thai, H.L.T. & Bui, T. S. (2018). *Aptis-VSTEP Comparability Study: Investigating the usage of two EFL tests in the context of higher education in Vietnam*. British Council Validation Series (VS/2018/001). London: British Council. Retrieved on July 8, 2020 from: https://www.britishcouncil.org/sites/default/files/aptis-vstep_study.pdf

McCrostie, J. (2017). Spoken English tests among entrance exam reforms Japan's students will face in 2020. *Japan Times*, Tokyo, July 5. Retrieved on March 5, 2019 from: https://www.japantimes.co.jp/community/2017/07/05/issues/spoken-english-tests-among-entrance-exam-reforms-japans-students-will-face-2020/

Nakatsuhara, F. (2014). *A research report on the development of the Test of English for Academic Purposes (TEAP) Speaking Test for Japanese university entrants – Study 1 & Study 2*. Retrieved from http://www.eiken.or.jp/teap/group/report.html

National Center for University Entrance Exams (n.d.). 受験者数・平均点の推移（本試験）平成30年度センター試験以降. Retrieved from https://www.dnc.ac.jp/center/suii/h30.html

O'Sullivan, B. (2016). Adapting tests to the local context. *New directions in language assessment, Special edition of the JASELE Journal*. Tokyo: Japan Society of English Language Education & the British Council, pp. 145–158.

O'Sullivan, B. & Dunlea, J. (2015). *Aptis General technical manual, Version 1.0*. Retrieved on March 19, 2019 from: https://www.britishcouncil.org/sites/default/files/aptis_general_technical_manual_v-1.0.pdf

O'Sullivan, B., Weir, C. & Saville, N. (2002). Using observation checklists to validate speaking-test tasks. *Language Testing*, 19(1), 33–56.

Sasaki, M. (2008). The 150-year history of English language assessment in English education in Japan. *Language Testing*, 25(1), 63–83.

Watanabe, Y. (2013). The National Centre test for university admissions: Test review. *Language Testing*, 30(4), 565–573.

Wu, R., Yeh, H., Dunlea, J. & Spiby, R. (2016). Aptis-GEPT comparison study: Looking at two tests from multiple perspectives using the socio-cognitive model. *British Council Validations Series* VS/2016/002. London: British Council.

Zhou, Y., Dunlea, J., Negishi, M. & Yoshitomi, A. (2018a). Localisation of an international speaking test for Japanese university admission. Paper presented at the *6th British Council New Directions in English Language Assessment Conference*, Kuala Lumpur, Malaysia.

Zhou, Y., Dunlea, J., Negishi, M. & Yoshitomi, A. (2018b). Collecting a priori validity evidence during the development of a computer-based speaking test for Japanese university admission purposes. Paper presented at the *1st JAAL (The Japan Association for Applied Linguistics) Conference*, Takachiho University, Tokyo.

INDEX

Authors

www.ingramcontent.com/pod-product-compliance
Lightning Source LLC
LaVergne TN
LVHW021126110826
R19582500001B/R195825PG844660LVX00004B/5

* 9 7 8 1 7 8 1 7 9 9 8 9 5 *